THE MINNESOTA ARCHAEOLOGIST

VOLUME 64   2005

Publications Committee

Managing Editor: Deborah Schoenholz
Editor: Kent Bakken
Proofreader: Anna Morrow

Executive Board of the Minnesota Archaeological Society

President: Rod Johnson
Vice President: Paul Mielke
Secretary: Deborah Schoenholz
Treasurer: Debbie Pommer
Directors: Jim Cummings, Chuck Diesen, Patricia Emerson,
Rhoda R. Gilman, Joe McFarlane, Ron Miles, Anna Morrow

The Minnesota Archaeologist is published annually by the Minnesota Archaeological Society. Subscription is by membership in the Society. For information on membership and on the Society's other activities, see the last page of this volume.

Copyright © 2006 by the Minnesota Archaeological Society. All rights reserved.

Requests to reprint should be addressed to Anna Morrow, 612-922-7006 or anmorrow@earthlink.net.

THE MINNESOTA ARCHAEOLOGIST

| VOLUME 64 | 2005 |

Contents

IN MEMORIAM

A Passing of Note: Kim Breakey
Jeremy Nienow..7

Kim Breakey and the Art of Can-Do
Jim Wilson..9

Tim Fiske: He Will Be Missed
Debbie Schoenholz..10

ARTICLES

Theodore H. Lewis (1856-1930): An Obituary
Fred A. Finney...11

Archaeological Investigations at the Waskish Site (21BL2), Past and Present
LeRoy Gonsior and David S. Radford...21

A Prairie Blackduck Site in Northwestern Minnesota
Michael G. Michlovic..49

Photospread: The Elliot Park Neighborhood Archaeology Project
Debbie Schoenholz, Pat Emerson, and Kent Bakken..85

Triangular Cross-Section Adzes from the Upper Mississippi River Valley: The Liska Cache
Robert "Ernie" Boszhardt..91

Animal Remains from the Midway Site (21BL37), Beltrami County, Minnesota
Jonathan D. Baker and James L. Theler..105

The 1860-1873 Mound Surveys Made by Alfred J. Hill in Minnesota, Wisconsin, and South Dakota
Fred A. Finney...145

Zooarchaeology of the Third River Bridge Site (21IC46), a Late Woodland Fishing Camp in Itasca County, Minnesota
David Mather...155

Notice to Authors

The Minnesota Archaeologist accepts submissions of original research by professional or avocational archaeologists on the anthropology and archaeology of this region. Authors should submit papers in *accessible* electronic formats (word processing files and digitized images). These may be submitted on floppy disks or CDs, sent to the address below. Internet submissions are also encouraged, with files sent as email attachments or via web download. ***However, please contact the editor by email at the address below before sending initial submissions***, in order to arrange for the most efficient transfer.

Note that figures should be scanned at a resolution of no less than 300 dots per inch (dpi) at 100 percent (full size as printed) or submitted as high-resolution, camera-ready hard copy. Figures and tables should not be embedded in word processing files. For further information on electronic formats and file preparation, please contact the managing editor, who would be happy to entertain your questions because it saves so much time and work in the long run.

Managing Editor
schoe030@tc.umn.edu

Manuscripts will be edited for content only with the consent of the author. Style will conform to the journal's style, which is based on the Society for American Archaeology's Style Guide for American Antiquity and Latin American Antiquity and on the *Chicago Manual of Style*. Copies of the Style Guide for *The Minnesota Archaeologist* are available from the editor or may be downloaded from our website at www.mnarchaeologicalsociety.org. Send materials or inquiries to:

Editor
c.diesen@att.net

The Minnesota Archaeologist
Minnesota Archaeological Society
Fort Snelling History Center
St. Paul, MN 55111
www.mnarchaeologicalsociety.org

Editor's Preface

For months I told the Minnesota Archaeological Society Board of Directors that this would be a slim volume of *The Minnesota Archaeologist*. I'm still not sure what happened, but this has become one of the larger single-year volumes we've produced in some time. And you'll also notice that we've introduced a few pages of color figures. If it works well this year, color figures may be a regular feature in the future.

In 2006 Chuck Diesen will be taking over as Editor of *The Minnesota Archaeologist*, so I can go into seclusion and finish writing my dissertation (the one about rocks). So please send him the papers that have been accumulating in the desk drawer!

Publication of *The Minnesota Archaeologist* is supported in part
by a generous bequest from the estate of William Lundquist.

Kim Breakey
1958-2004

A Passing of Note: Kim Breakey
Jeremy Nienow

The Midwestern archaeological community was deeply affected by the death of Kim Breakey in the winter of 2004. Unknown to many, Kim had been suffering from a series of medical ailments in the past few years and finally succumbed to a liver illness. She refused to let a "little thing" like that slow her down and worked up to her very last days. Like many in CRM in this region, I had the opportunity to work with her while a principle investigator with Schoell and Madson. She had an unparalleled level of confidence in her projects and crews – even when we doubted ourselves.

Kim had a career in cultural resource management that spanned over two-plus decades in which she was involved in nearly every aspect of CRM. Her career began at Minnesota State University Moorhead, where she graduated in 1980. While there, she worked on the Minnesota Statewide Survey of Clay County in 1978, and served as a field assistant during the first year of the Norman County (Red River) survey in 1980. Kim also was introduced to the contracting business on a number of small surveys MSUM conducted in the Red River region at that time.

Professor Mike Michlovic relayed to me that

She was one of the crew members who helped dig into the Archaic component at the Canning site, the first attempt to probe a buried site in the U.S. portion of the Red River Valley. A lot of informal experimenting went on with figuring the best way to work the clay through screens. Kim spent many hours sifting through the unyielding, stiff, soil of the Red River, always reminding the other crew members of how much "fun" they were having.

Kim as a student was so much like Kim the professional of later years. She was always ready with a smile and good cheer; ready to do her share of the work, and then help someone else with theirs; always looking at the bright side – unusual for an archaeologist. It's bad that we lost such a good archaeologist. It's worse that we lost such a wonderful human being.

After school, she moved full-force into the world of CRM, culminating with her serving as President of Hemisphere Field Services. Her clients ranged from residential developers to the U.S. government, with projects from the simplest SHPO initial research to the management of 2,300 miles of proposed pipeline construction. Beyond this, she also served as Vice President of the Council for Minnesota Archaeology and was a member of the Core Organizing Committee for the Joint Midwest/Plains Conference at St. Paul in 2000.

I met Kim in February 2002. As anyone can tell you, finding work in the dead of winter is never easy. Kim invited me out to her Schoell and Madson office to size me up. She knew I was more than willing and after a lunch at the steak house in front of Schoell and Madson (which some of you know became her perennial meeting spot), she told me the work would come. She was good to her word. She introduced me around, got me the experience I needed to get qualified as a principal investigator, and gave me all the opportunities for field work throughout the Midwest that I could handle. In addition to having a knack for getting fieldwork, it was amazing to see how quickly she befriended new clients, contractors, government officials, and archaeologists alike.

Kim was very supportive of my decision to complete my Ph.D. work at the University of Minnesota, as well as to find time for my family – although she always seemed to find that perfect time to call and convince me to take one last small job. After hearing of her death and sending out that first round of emails, I was amazed not only by the number of well wishers that contacted me and later attended her funeral, but by the level of sincere admiration that many had for this CRM maverick. My experiences with Kim were certainly not unique.

Frank Florin sent me this shortly after her death and I think it pretty much sums it all up:

> I worked for Kim at IMA Consulting and HFS for several years. I had not seen Kim in a couple years, but I ran into her last month at SHPO. We shared a hug and a brief conversation. I sensed she was not in good health and feel fortunate to have connected with her prior to her passing. IMAC was the first archaeological company I worked for, and while I was an undergraduate Kim gave me the opportunity to begin a career in archaeology. After completing my master's degree, she hired me as supervisor even though I had no previous experience in this capacity. I appreciated her faith in my abilities and feel that she provided me with valuable professional experience. She was friendly and interested in how things were going in my life.

Kim Breakey and the Art of Can-Do
Jim Wilson

I was the last in a long line of principal investigators to work with Kim over her years of cultural resource management (CRM) work in the upper Midwest. Among those who worked with her, I won't be the last to remember her. Not by a long shot. For me, Kim is particularly memorable because her can-do approach to life persuaded me to come along for the ride with her, and to get things done on her behalf.

I remember getting a call in the summer of 2003 with a buoyantly optimistic voice on the other end saying, " Hey Jim, I'm Kim Breakey and I understand you're looking for CRM work in Minnesota. Well, I've got lots of work to do for the Corps of Engineers up at Camp Ripley, and I need a principal investigator to help me there this fall."

Not sure how to respond, I began with a high-toned, "Hmm…."

Kim must have sensed the excitement in my tone, because she delivered her closing line before I could squeeze in a question, saying, "Well what do you say? Are you interested?"

Coming from a generation of the service economy where businesses were owned and run almost exclusively by men, Kim's can-do ethic served her well as she started and managed a series of large CRM firms in the Twin Cities. It's a sadness to me as an archaeologist that she won't be around any longer to recount her dramatic perspective on those experiences.

Many of her colleagues will also remember Kim for her willingness to give new people an opportunity to work with her. I had some learning to do for Minnesota archaeology, because most of my project experience had been out east in the Ohio valley, mid-South and mid-Atlantic regions. For Kim, however, the primary qualifications were work ethic as much as résumé. That showed in the people she'd hired along with me. Whether with Jeremy, Melissa Baltus, or others who joined our projects for shorter stints, Kim made sure that I worked with motivated archaeologists. Jeremy has since moved on for graduate studies at the University of Minnesota and Melissa to the University of Illinois, but both gained extensive upper-Midwestern fieldwork and reporting experience because of the opportunity extended to work in Kim's CRM projects.

Whether archaeologists or others who crossed paths with Kim in their professional lives, many who knew her comment on the no-nonsense practicality regarding work, mixed with the Can-do optimism for people. Because of her overabundance of practicality and optimism, Kim was probably more shocked than any of us at the sudden strength of the illness that overtook her Sunday, December 19th. As I mentioned at the beginning, Kim seldom accepted a "no" without trying to cajole or persuade her boss, or partner, or client, or employee, or child into doing what she wanted. By all accounts of her last few days, when it was her own body telling her "no!" in no uncertain terms, she was apparently more surprised than any of us at such adamant refusal.

There are strategic lessons for me to learn from losing Kim so suddenly, lessons about *lengthening* my own life through more consciously healthful choices. Indeed, Kim herself told me last year after nearly succumbing to a lingering gall bladder illness, "When it comes to your health, be smart Jim. Don't do like me, waiting to the last minute to see a doctor." But such a conclusion is drawn at her expense, and I know she wouldn't be satisfied with my leaving it at that.

That's why I'd like to think that there is an even bigger moral lesson for me to learn from my all-to-brief association with Kim, a lesson that adds to my account of her. A lesson about *furthering* my life and the lives of those I am thrown in with, no matter how long I may live. A lesson that I will go a lot further in life with her kind of can-do optimism than I will without it.

If she could come back, even momentarily to be among us, that's a lesson I think she'd be very proud to see us learn on her behalf.

Timothy Fiske
1928-2005

He Will Be Missed
Debbie Schoenholz

Tim Fiske was a fixture in Minnesota archaeology, always working, always reliable, and unfailingly helpful and accommodating to those who asked his advice. My experience with Tim was during his volunteer years at the Science Museum of Minnesota, where twice a week his smiling face was turned toward whatever project curator Orin Shane had in store for him. He worked with equal dedication on cataloging sherds or designing exhibits. He was also a mainstay of the Archaeology Department through the rigors of packing and moving the collections across St. Paul to the Science Museum's grand new facility, where he just as diligently unpacked the collections and put them away. Tim was a collection manager's dream, on top of being the repository of quantities of archaeological information that could be called upon for identification or research. I am sure that I speak for all of us who worked with him I say he will be sorely missed.

From the memorial service program:

Scofield Timothy Fiske (Tim), age 76, Wayzata, died on July 24, 2005. Tim graduated from Blake School in 1946 and Princeton University in 1950. He then served three years as an officer in the U.S. Navy, with two years in the Seventh Fleet off Korea during that war. After his discharge, he pursued graduate studies at the University of Minnesota and then worked as an archaeologist in Guatemala for the Peabody Museum, in Canada and Ecuador for the University of Manitoba, and in Minnesota for the Minnesota Historical Society. In 1967, he joined the Science Museum of Minnesota as Curator of Anthropology. In the mid-1970s, Tim and his wife Carol moved to Portugal, where they converted a coastal fort built in 1716 into a restaurant. Returning to the U.S. in 1977, Tim joined the Minneapolis Institute of Arts where he worked until he retired in 1996, as Associate Directory and Chief Operating Officer. After retirement, he worked as a volunteer at the Science Museum and the Wayzata Community Library.

Theodore H. Lewis (1856-1930): An Obituary

Fred A. Finney
fafinney@aol.com
Upper Midwest Archaeology, PO Box 106, St. Joseph, IL 61873

From the perspective of the twenty-first century, Theodore Hayes Lewis (1856-1930) is arguably one of the most important late nineteenth century archaeologists in the Midwest. Personal details of his life are scarce. An excellent summary is contained in Dunbar Rowland's (1902) editorial comments at the beginning of a Lewis (1902) article published by the Mississippi Historical Society. Rowland's brief text is reproduced below section by section in boldface type[1] separated with annotations of additional explanation. This brief biography contains virtually all that is known about Lewis' background outside the NAS. It has information not included in his entries in Marquis' *Who's Who* (Marquis 1899, 1901, 1903, 1906, 1908, 1910, and 1912).

Early Years

Theodore Hayes Lewis was born at Richmond, Va., December 15, 1856. After a residence of one year (1865) in Columbus, Ohio, his parents removed to Little Rock, Ark. [Rowland 1902:449]

A number of later writers list his year of birth. This is one of the few sources that gives the exact date (see also Marquis 1907; Upham and Dunlap 1912). Several researchers have been unable to find Lewis, his parents, or siblings in either the 1860 Richmond, Virginia, or the 1870 Little Rock, Arkansas, federal census population schedules. One potential problem for finding Lewis in the census is the fact that he was raised by an aunt and uncle for at least part of his youth.[2]

Until 2005, the names of his immediate relatives were unknown. The circumstances surrounding his family were unraveled by tracing Lewis through early twentieth century censuses. First, Lewis conclusively appears in the 1900 federal census as renting Hill's former residence at 406 Maria Avenue, St. Paul, Minnesota. In particular the 1900 entry lists Lewis as an archaeologist. This entry further indicates that his father was born in Virginia and his mother in New York (U.S. Bureau of the Census 1900). In addition to the correct name and age,[3] the birth places of his parents serve as the diagnostic marker for making a positive identification of Lewis in the 1920 and 1930 censuses as a resident of St. Louis, Missouri (U.S. Bureau of the Census 1920, 1930). The 1900, 1920, and 1930 census entries and his death certificate had the same place of birth profile for Lewis (Virginia), his father (Virginia), and his mother (New York). The death certificate for Theodore H. Lewis is the only source for his parents' names, Hiram and Marie Curdy Lewis (City of St. Louis 1930). The age listed in the death certificate indicates that Lewis was born in 1854. There is enough variation on other documents to suggest that he might have been born in 1854, 1855, or 1856. These differences suggest that Lewis might have shaved a year or two off his age when convenient; on the other hand it is possible that he simply did not know the correct year.

Lewis finished his public school education from 1866 to 1872 in Little Rock, Arkansas.

Upon completion of his common school education at this place, he took a commercial course at the Miami Commercial College, Dayton, O. (1874). [Rowland 1902:449]

It is reported that Lewis spent one or two years as a school teacher near Chillicothe, Ohio, where he observed mound excavations and apparently learned to use a surveyor's level (Keyes 1928).

Surveys

From 1876-8 he made archaeological excavations for Prof. William A. Muller, of Dresden, Germany, in Arkansas, Mississippi, and Tennessee. During the winters of 1878-95 he continued his archaeological work, surveying 10,000 mounds.

> This was a private enterprise, the results of which are still unpublished. [Rowland 1902:449]

Marvin Jeter (1990, 2001) provides some details of Lewis' excavations in Arkansas mounds, but did not find additional information on Prof. Muller. Lewis' private enterprise was called the Southern Archaeological Survey. It is evident from the Lewis-Hill correspondence that the latter provided funding for the winter surveys. Virtually nothing else is known of the Southern Archaeological Survey and, like the NAS, it remains unpublished. Unfortunately there are no extant field notes for the Southern Archaeological Survey. However, selected articles by Lewis had subjects that must comprise part of that effort. These include sites in Kentucky (Lewis 1887), Mississippi (Lewis 1891), Arkansas (Lewis 1894), and Alabama (Lewis 1895). Lewis rarely made artifact collections during his surveys. However, at least some of the materials he collected for the Southern Archaeological Survey are held at the Science Museum of Minnesota in St. Paul (Finney 2004).

> In the meantime (1880-95) he conducted the "Northwestern Archaeological Survey" under the auspices of the late Alfred J. Hill. The results of these explorations embracing over 12,000 mounds are also unpublished. [Rowland 1902:449]

Lewis (1898) used this 12,000 mound total in his brief NAS summary, and later writers (Keyes 1928, 1930, 1977; Irwin 1964) repeated this figure. However, this total is too low. Dobbs (1991) lists over 17,000 mounds and earthworks (ca. 1,000 of the latter) from over 2,000 sites in his comprehensive site finder aid for the NAS notebooks.

> Prof. Lewis has made a special study of the Spanish and French explorations and settlements in the Mississippi valley and the Gulf States during the past twenty-five years. [Rowland 1902:449]

These investigations undoubtedly comprised part of the Southern Archaeological Survey. More importantly they set the stage for his post-NAS career as an ethnohistorian. It follows up a joint interest in this subject held with Hill. By at least 1886, Lewis had acquired the title "professor" (Finney 2005).

> His writings are mostly archaeological, and are published in the *American Antiquarian*; *American Anthropologist*; *American Naturalist*; *American Journal of Archaeology*; *Magazine of American History*; *The Archaeologist*; *Science*; *National Magazine*; *Macalester Monthly*; *Macalester Contributions*; *The Anthropologist*;[4] *De Lestry's Western Magazine*; *Speaking Leaf (Order of Red Men)*; and *Appleton's Annual Cyclopedia* (1889). He published the first English translation (abbreviated) of the Rangel Narrative [on the De Soto Expedition]. Prof. Lewis is a life member of the Minnesota Historical Society and an honorary member of the Mississippi Historical Society. [Rowland 1902:449]

Ultimate Fate

The most enduring NAS mystery is the ultimate fate of Lewis himself. Despite the attempts by several generations of archaeologists, it had remained unsolved. Lewis is listed in the first seven volumes of *Who's Who*. The first two indicate his address as 406 Maria Avenue, St. Paul, which was Hill's house (Marquis 1899, 1901), and Lewis' place of residence during the Northwestern Archaeological Survey (Lewis 1898).[5] According to the 1900 federal census, Lewis rented the house at 406 Maria Avenue and lived alone. *Who's Who* Volumes 3 and 4 merely list Lewis' residence as St. Paul (Marquis 1903, 1906). Only one other address can be found for Lewis in St. Paul. The 1903 city directory indicates that Prof. T. Hayes Lewis had rooms at 467-1/2 Wabasha Street (Polk 1903).

After the NAS fieldwork ceased, Lewis became a partner in a St. Paul publishing business (Dobbs 1991; Keyes 1928). He was elected a life member of MHS in 1898 and was listed as a St. Paul resident from 1899 to 1907 in the society records (Anonymous 1898; MHS 1899, 1903, 1905, 1907). It is known that Lewis left St. Paul in 1905 when it became obvious that the NAS notes would remain beyond his reach (Anonymous 1905).[6] He sold his scrapbooks of archaeological newspaper clippings to MHS and his artifact collection to Edward Mitchell of St. Paul, who later donated these materials to MHS (Finney 2000; Mitchell 1908).

After 1905, his whereabouts become increasingly murky as Lewis began a long decline into obliv-

ion (Dobbs 1991; Keyes 1928; Winchell 1911). He can be traced until around the beginning of World War I when he disappears completely from view. The final article by Prof. Lewis (1907) lists his affiliation as an Honorary Member of the Mississippi Historical Society. Volumes 5 to 7 of *Who's Who* have one line entries, without address, that refer the reader to the detailed entry for 1906-1907 (Marquis 1906, 1908, 1910, 1912). His final entry in *Who's Who* appears in the 1912-1913 edition (Marquis 1912). Winchell (1911) merely indicates that Lewis had been reported to be in Ouray, Colorado at some point after leaving St. Paul.

Mr. Lewis, who for years was a resident of St. Paul, is said to have been more thoroughly versed in Indian lore than any other white man. He made the study his life work and from 1874 to 1907 he explored more than 12,000 Indian mounds in the United States. Lewis' mounds, on the site of the old Indian village near Lake Itasca, were discovered by him and named for him. When last heard of by St. Paul friends Mr. Lewis was conducting an exploration trip among Indian mounds near Ouray, Colo., four years ago. Since that time, all trace has been lost of him, according to Warren Upham of the State Historical society. It is believed that he perished on the trip. [Anonymous 1913]

This newspaper article must be the source of the reports that Lewis disappeared in Colorado during 1909. However, a review of the membership records in the MHS biennial reports discloses that Lewis used Ouray as his address from 1909 to 1915 (MHS 1909, 1911, 1913, 1915). In the 1917 biennial report his address is listed as unknown and Lewis is absent from the 1919 and subsequent reports (MHS 1917, 1919).

According to the 1900 federal census and *Who's Who*, Lewis was a bachelor and for this reason may have lived with relatives after leaving St. Paul. This hypothesis does not explain his 1905 to ca. 1916 residence in Colorado, but may be the rationale for his appearance in the 1920 and 1930 federal censuses for the City of St. Louis, Missouri.[7] The aunt who raised him had relatives in the St. Louis area.[8] In the 1920 census he was listed as being a retail merchant in the newspaper business (U.S. Bureau of the Census 1920). The population schedule further indicated that he was a lodger in a boarding house owned by Fredricka Heinrich at 401 South Broadway Avenue, in St. Louis. This implies that Lewis had a news stand, presumably located near his boardinghouse. Attempts to find Lewis in the St. Louis City Directories have proved futile.

The April 1930 census entry provided the missing clue to his final fate. He was listed as being an inmate at the St. Louis City Infirmary at 5800 Arsenal Drive (U.S. Bureau of the Census 1930). This institution served as the poor hospital and insane asylum for the City of St. Louis and St. Louis County. According to his death certificate, Lewis died July 17, 1930, from a heart condition recorded as "chronic myocarditis" (City of St. Louis 1930). No relatives were known and Lewis was buried in an unmarked grave for which no records exist. The Potter's Field, or St. Louis Municipal Cemetery, was located on the city and county farm at Hampton and Fyler Roads. His placement in the St. Louis City Infirmary would imply that the City of St. Louis received whatever assets that Lewis possessed. No will was ever filed with the city or county. Unfortunately the fate of the archaeological records that he retained in 1895 remains unknown.[9]

Lewis' ultimate fate is a stark reminder about the problems of human aging – particularly for those individuals without children – prior to social security. A final indignity occurred in the summer of 1950. The former city and county farm was sold for development and the human remains from the Potter's Field were moved to the Mt. Lebanon Cemetery in St. Ann, Missouri (Anonymous 1950).

The above description of his post-St. Paul period is lacking in precise details for Lewis' activities. In retrospect, what Lewis accomplished as a field archaeologist and ethnohistorian is more important than documenting his ultimate fate (Finney 2001). Lewis produced a significant body of archaeological research for prehistoric site studies that emphasized mounds and rock art, the exposure of mound builder fantasies and other fraudulent claims, and a pioneering approach that combined field surveys with historic documents in ethnohistorical studies of the De Soto route (see Lewis' bibliography). For these reasons Lewis deserves a more prominent acknowledgment in the history of American archaeology (Finney 2005).

Acknowledgments: Part of the Lewis background information has appeared in *Illinois Archaeology*, *The Minnesota Archaeologist*, and *The Wisconsin Archeologist*. Amy Rosebrough (Wisconsin Historical Society) suggested that I look for Lewis in the 1920 St. Louis census. The 1930 census had just been released to the public for less than a week (75 year privacy rule) when I made that search. Kathy Stevenson (University of Wisconsin–La Crosse) supplied the 1913 newspaper article. Robert G. McKinnell (University of Minnesota) helped me obtain the death certificate from the City of St. Louis.

Notes

1. A subsequent quote from a different source is also presented in boldface type.

2. In various letters to Hill, Lewis disclosed that it was the reason he wished to financially support the aunt in her old age.
3. Lewis' age is incorrect in the 1920 census entry.
4. A review of a brief-lived 1890-1891 monthly journal entitled "*The Anthropologist: A Journal for Thinkers*" did not find any contribution by Lewis.
5. Today the site of Hill's house is part of a large parking lot for Metropolitan State University.
6. Brower bought the NAS records from Hill's heirs in 1905.
7. Lewis can be found only in the 1900, 1920, and 1930 federal censuses. The 1900 entry provided the first listing for his parents' place of birth. This critical and diagnostic information is repeated in the 1920 and 1930 entries.
8. Lewis-Hill correspondence, Archives, Minnesota Historical Society, St. Paul.
9. Lewis retained as his property the SAS fieldnotes, the Hill to Lewis letters, and his scrapbooks of archaeological clippings. He sold the scrapbooks to the MHS before leaving St. Paul, but the final fate of the SAS fieldnotes and Hill to Lewis letters is unknown. This situation remains a potential problem for consulting archaeologists unaffiliated with an institution.

References Cited

Anonymous
1898 St. Paul in Its Cradle Days. *St. Paul Pioneer Press*. September 13, p. 3.
1905 Northwestern Archaeological Survey: State Historical Society will get Possession of the Result of the Work of Mr. Hill and Prof. Lewis. *St. Paul Pioneer Press*. August 6, Section 2, p. 2.
1913 Noted Archaeologist, Missing Since 1909, Found Snakes on the Walls. *St. Paul Pioneer Press*.
1950 July 1950 newspaper clipping in the St. Louis Municipal Cemetery file. Genealogy Room, St. Louis Public Library, City of St. Louis

City of St. Louis
1930 Theodore H. Lewis, Certificate of Death, Registered No. 7291. Bureau of Vital Statistics, Missouri State Board of Health, City of St. Louis, Missouri.

Dobbs, Clark A.
1991 *The Northwestern Archaeological Survey: An Appreciation and Guide to the Field Notebooks*. Reports of Investigation No. 135. Institute for Minnesota Archaeology, Minneapolis.

Finney, Fred A.
2000 Theodore H. Lewis and the Northwestern Archaeological Survey's 1891 Fieldwork in the American Bottom. *Illinois Archaeology* 12(1-2):244-276.
2001 An Introduction to The Northwestern Archaeological Survey by Theodore H. Lewis. *The Minnesota Archaeologist* 60:13-29.
2004 Reconstructing the 1878-1895 "Southern Archaeological Survey" of Theodore H. Lewis. Paper presented at the joint Meeting of the Southeastern Archaeological Conference and the Midwest Archaeological Conference, St. Louis.

Finney, Fred A. (editor)
2005 *Mounds, Humbugs, and De Soto: The Archaeological Legacy of Theodore H. Lewis from North Dakota to Florida*. Manuscript accepted for publication in *The Wisconsin Archaeologist* 86.

Irwin, Annabelle
1964 An Archaeological Triumph From Fifteen Years at $3 A Day. *The Iowan* 13:40-46, 53.

Jeter, Marvin T. (editor)
1990 *Edward Palmer's Arkansaw Mounds*. University of Arkansas Press, Fayetteville.
2001 Edward Palmer and Other Victorian Pioneers in Midsouth Archaeology. In *Historical Perspectives on Midsouth Archaeology*, ed. by Martha Ann Rolingson, pp. 23-50. Research Series No. 58. Arkansas Archeological Survey, Little Rock.

Keyes, Charles R.
1928 The Hill-Lewis Archaeological Survey. *Minnesota History* 9:96-108.
1930 A Unique Survey. *The Palimpsest* 11(5):214-226.
1977 The Hill-Lewis Archaeological Survey. *The Minnesota Archaeologist* 36(4):146-155. Reprinted. [Originally published 1928, *Minnesota History*.]

Lewis, Theodore H.
1887 The "Old Fort" Earthworks of Greenup County, Kentucky. *The American Journal of Archaeology* 3(3-4):375-382.
1891 De Soto's Camps in the Chickasaw Country in 1540-1. *The National Magazine* 15(1):57-61.
1894 The 'Old Fort' of Cross County, Arkansas. *The Archaeologist* 2(11):319-325.

1895 Description of the Site of "Old Coosa," Talladega County, Alabama. *The American Antiquarian* 17(3):171-174.

1898 *The Northwestern Archaeological Survey.* Pioneer Press, St. Paul.

1902 Route of De Soto's Expedition from Taliepacana to Huhasene. *Publications of the Mississippi Historical Society* 6:449-467.

1907 The Narrative of the Expedition of Hernando de Soto by the Gentleman of Elvas. In *Spanish Explorers in the Southern United States, 1528-1543*, ed. by Frederick W. Hodge and Theodore H. Lewis, pp. 127-272. Charles Scribner's Sons, New York.

Marquis, Albert N. (editor)
1899 *Who's Who in America, 1899-1900, Volume 1.* A.N. Marquis, Chicago.

1901 *Who's Who in America, 1901-1902, Volume 2.* A.N. Marquis, Chicago.

1903 *Who's Who in America, 1903-1905, Volume 3.* A.N. Marquis, Chicago.

1906 *Who's Who in America, 1906-1907, Volume 4.* A.N. Marquis, Chicago.

1907 *The Book of Minnesotans.* A.N. Marquis, Chicago.

1908 *Who's Who in America, 1908-1909, Volume 5.* A.N. Marquis, Chicago.

1910 *Who's Who in America, 1910-1911, Volume 6.* A.N. Marquis, Chicago.

1912 *Who's Who in America, 1912-1913, Volume 7.* A.N. Marquis, Chicago.

MHS (Minnesota Historical Society)
1899 *Tenth Biennial Report of the Minnesota Historical Society to the Legislature of Minnesota, Session of 1899.* Pioneer Press, St. Paul.

1903 *Eleventh and Twelfth Biennial Reports of the Minnesota Historical Society to the Legislature of Minnesota, Session of 1903.* Pioneer Press, St. Paul.

1905 *Thirteenth Biennial Report of the Minnesota Historical Society to the Legislature of Minnesota, Session of 1905.* Great Western Printing, Minneapolis.

1907 *Fourteenth Biennial Report of the Minnesota Historical Society to the Legislature of Minnesota, Session of 1907.* Harrison and Smith, Minneapolis.

1909 *Fifteenth Biennial Report of the Minnesota Historical Society to the Legislature of Minnesota, Session of 1909.* Syndicate Printing, Minneapolis.

1911 *Sixteenth Biennial Report of the Minnesota Historical Society to the Legislature of Minnesota, Session of 1911.* Volkszeitung Printing, St. Paul.

1913 *Seventeenth Biennial Report of the Minnesota Historical Society to the Legislature of Minnesota, Session of 1913.* Volkszeitung Printing, St. Paul.

1915 *Minnesota Historical Society Eighteenth Biennial Report for the Years 1913 and 1914.* Minnesota Historical Society, St. Paul.

1917 *Minnesota Historical Society Nineteenth Biennial Report for the Years 1915 and 1916.* Minnesota Historical Society, St. Paul.

1919 *Minnesota Historical Society Twentieth Biennial Report for the Years 1917 and 1918.* Minnesota Historical Society, St. Paul.

Mitchell, Edward C.
1908 Archaeological Collections Recently Donated to this Society. *Collections of the Minnesota Historical Society* 12:305-318.

Polk, R.L.
1903 *St. Paul City Directory*, Volume 39. R.L. Polk, St. Paul.

Rowland, Dunbar
1902 Editorial Comments. *Publications of the Mississippi Historical Society* 6:449.

Upham, Warren, and Rose Barteau Dunlap
1912 Minnesota Biographies, 1655-1912. *Minnesota Historical Society Collections* Vol. 14.

U.S. Bureau of the Census
1900 *12th Census of the United States, 1900.* Minnesota, Schedule 1, Population, City of St. Paul, Ramsey County. Microfilm on file, Minnesota Historical Society, St. Paul.

1920 *14th Census of the United States, 1920.* Missouri, Schedule 1, Population, City of St. Louis. Microfilm on file, St. Louis Public Library, St. Louis.

1930 *15th Census of the United States, 1930.* Missouri, Schedule 1, Population, City of St. Louis. Microfilm on file, St. Louis Public Library, St. Louis.

Winchell, Newton H.
1911 *The Aborigines of Minnesota: A Report Based on the Collections of Jacob V. Brower, and on the Field Surveys and Notes of Alfred*

J. Hill and Theodore H. Lewis. Minnesota Historical Society, St. Paul.

Publications of Theodore H. Lewis

Finney, Fred A. (editor)
2005 *Mounds, Humbugs, and De Soto: The Archaeological Legacy of Theodore H. Lewis from North Dakota to Florida.* Upper Midwest Archaeology, St. Joseph, Illinois.

Hodge, Frederick W. and Theodore H. Lewis (editors)
1907 *Spanish Explorers in the Southern United States, 1528-1543.* Charles Scribner's Sons, New York.
1925 *Spanish Explorers in the Southern United States, 1528-1543, Original Narratives of Early American History.* Reprinted. Charles Scribner's Sons, New York. [Originally published 1907, Charles Scribner's Sons, New York.]
1946 *Spanish Explorers in the Southern United States, 1528-1543, Original Narratives of Early American History.* Reprinted. Barnes and Noble, New York. [Originally published 1907, Charles Scribner's Sons, New York.]
1959 *Spanish Explorers in the Southern United States, 1528-1543, Original Narratives of Early American History.* Reprinted. Barnes and Noble, New York. [Originally published 1907, Charles Scribner's Sons, New York.]
1977 *Spanish Explorers in the Southern United States, 1528-1543, Original Narratives of Early American History.* Reprinted. Barnes and Noble, New York. [Originally published 1907, Charles Scribner's Sons, New York.]
1984 *Spanish Explorers in the Southern United States, 1528-1543.* Reprinted. Texas State Historical Association, Austin. [Originally published 1907, Charles Scribner's Sons, New York.]
1990 *Spanish Explorers in the Southern United States, 1528-1543.* Reprinted. Texas State Historical Association, Austin. [Originally published 1907, Charles Scribner's Sons, New York.]

Lewis, Theodore H.
n.d.a Unpublished Field Notes in 41 Notebooks. Manuscripts on file, Minnesota Historical Society, St. Paul.
n.d.b Scrapbooks No. 1-8. Manuscripts on file, Minnesota Historical Society, St. Paul.
n.d.c Lewis-Hill Correspondence. Manuscripts on file, Minnesota Historical Society, St. Paul.
1880 Prehistoric Fire-Place and Human Bones found at St. Paul. *St. Paul and Minneapolis Pioneer Press* 27(38):7, February 7.
1891 *Tracts for Archaeologists, Being Reprinted from Various Periodicals.* Series 1, No. 1-25. T.H. Lewis, Tupelo, Mississippi. Copy on file, Minnesota Historical Society Library, St. Paul.
1881 The Mound Builders in Minnesota. *The American Antiquarian* 3(2):153.
1883a Ancient Mounds of Minnesota. *St. Paul At Home* 1(8):11, May 12.
1883b In the Mandan Country. *St. Paul and Minneapolis Pioneer Press* 30(329):12, November 24.
1883b In the Mandan Mounds: T. H. Lewis, the Archaeologist, Reports the Result of His Recent Delvings on the Missouri's Banks. *St. Paul and Minneapolis Pioneer Press* 30(329):12, November 24.
1883c Mounds of the Mississippi Basin. *Magazine of American History* 9(3):177-182.
1883d Swamp Mounds. *The American Antiquarian* 5(4):330-331.
1883e Mandan News. *Bismarck Tribune.* Reprinted. [Originally published 1883 as "In the Mandan Country," *St. Paul and Minneapolis Pioneer Press* 30(329):12, November 24.]
1884a Mounds in Minnesota. *The American Antiquarian* 6(4):286.
1884b The Camel and Elephant Mounds at Prairie du Chien. *The American Antiquarian* 6(5):348-349.
1885a Notice of Some Recently Discovered Effigy Mounds [in Minnesota]. *Science* o.s. 5(106):131-132.
1885b Effigy Mounds in Iowa. *Science* (O.S.) 6(146):453-454.
1885c Mounds of the North-West. In Archaeological News, ed. by A.L. Frothingham and A.R. Marsh. *American Journal of Archaeology* 1(4):462.
1886a The "Monumental Tortoise" Mounds of "De-Coo-Dah." *The American Journal of Archaeology* 2(1):65-69.

1886b Ancient Rock Inscriptions in Eastern Dakota. *The American Naturalist* 20(5):423-425.

1886c Ancient Fire-Places on the Ohio. *The American Antiquarian* 8(3):167-168.

1886d Stone Paddle and Copper Spade. *The American Antiquarian* 8(5):296.

1886e The Red Wing Elephant. *The American Antiquarian* 8(5):289-290.

1886f Mounds on the Red River of the North. *The American Antiquarian* 8(6):369-371.

1886g Mounds of the North-West. In Archaeological News, ed. by A.L. Frothingham. *American Journal of Archaeology* 2(4):506.

1887a Quartz-Workers of Little Falls [Minnesota]. *The American Antiquarian* 9(2):105-107.

1887b "Old Fort" in Kentucky. *The American Antiquarian* 9(3):169.

1887c The Silver Find in Kentucky. *The American Antiquarian* 9(4):234-236.

1887d Snake and Snake-Like Mounds in Minnesota. *Science* o.s. 9(220):393-394.

1887e Incised Boulders in the Upper Minnesota Valley. *The American Naturalist* 21(7):639-642.

1887f The "Old Fort" Earthworks of Greenup County, Kentucky. *The American Journal of Archaeology* 3(3-4):375-382.

1888a Survey of Western Mounds. In Archaeological News, ed. by A.L. Frothingham. *American Journal of Archaeology* 4(1):123-124.

1888b Effigy Mounds of Northern Illinois. *Science* (O.S.) 12(292):118-119.

1889a A New Departure in Effigy Mounds [in Wisconsin]. *Science* o.s. 13(318):187-188.

1889b Stone Monuments in Southern Dakota. *American Anthropologist* o.s. 2(2):159-165.

1889c Sculptured Rock at Trempealeau, Wisconsin. *The American Naturalist* 23(9):782-784.

1889d Old French Post at Trempealeau, Wisconsin. *Magazine of American History* 12(3):204-208.

1889e Copper Mines Worked by the Mound-Builders. *The American Antiquarian* 11(5):293-296.

1890a *Description of Some Copper Relics in the Macalester Museum of History and Archaeology*. Macalester Contributions No. 6. Macalester College, St. Paul.

1890b Cave Drawings. *Appleton's Annual Cyclopedia and Register of Important Events, 1889* 14:117-122.

1890c Effigy Mound in the Valley of the Big Sioux River. *Science* o.s. 15(378):275.

1890d Stone Monuments in Northwestern Iowa and Southwestern Minnesota. *American Anthropologist* o.s. 3(3):269-274.

1891a Boulder Outline Figures in the Dakotas, Surveyed in the Summer of 1890. *American Anthropologist* o.s. 4(1):19-24.

1891b The Effigy Mounds of Buffalo Lake, Marquette County, Wisconsin. *The American Antiquarian* 13(2):115-117.

1891c Lewis and Clark and the Antiquities of the Upper Missouri River. *The American Antiquarian* 13(5):288-293.

1891d Cup Stones Near Old Fort Ransom, N.D. *The American Naturalist* 25(5):455-461.

1891e De Soto's Camps in the Chickasaw Country in 1540-1. *The National Magazine* 15(1):57-61.

1891f Itasca: A Night Vision. *St. Paul Sunday Globe* 13(214):4, August 2.

1891g Glazier Chestnuts. *St. Paul Sunday Globe* 13(214):4, August 2.

1892 *Tracts for Archaeologists, Being Reprinted from Various Periodicals*. Series 2, No. 1-4. T.H. Lewis, Tupelo, Mississippi. Copy on file, Minnesota Historical Society Library, St. Paul.

1892 The "Old Fort" of Saline County, Missouri. *The American Antiquarian* 14(3):159-166.

1893 Intaglio Effigies of Wisconsin. *The American Antiquarian* 15(3):164-168.

1894a Effigy Mounds near Aurora, Illinois. *The Archaeologist* 2(3):85-89.

1894b The 'Old Fort' of Cross County, Arkansas. *The Archaeologist* 2(11):319-325.

1894c The "Aztalan" Enclosure Newly Described. *The American Antiquarian* 16(4):205-208.

1894d Enclosures in Wisconsin. *The American Antiquarian* 16(6):357-361.

1895a Description of the Site of "Old Coosa," Talladega County, Alabama. *The American Antiquarian* 17(3):171-174.

1895b Ancient Mounds in Northern Minnesota. *The American Antiquarian* 17(6):316-320.

1895c Townsite of Coosa. *Alabama Press*. Reprinted. [Originally published 1895 as "Description of the Site of 'Old Coosa,' Talladega County, Alabama," *The American Antiquarian* 17(3):171-174.

1896a Pre-Historic Remains at St. Paul, Minnesota. *The American Antiquarian* 18(4):207-210.

1896b Mounds and Stone Cists at St. Paul, Minnesota. *The American Antiquarian* 18(6):314-320.

1896c Pre-Historic Remains at St. Paul. *St. Paul Pioneer Press* October 4. Reprinted. [Originally published 1896 as "Pre-Historic Remains at St. Paul, Minnesota," *The American Antiquarian* 18(4):207-210.

1897 Skeletons and Stone Weapons: Contents of the Indian Mounds on Dayton's Bluff. *St. Paul Pioneer Press* 44(25), January 25, p. 8. Reprinted. [Originally published 1896 as "Mounds and Stone Cists at St. Paul, Minnesota," *The American Antiquarian* 18(6):314-320.]

1898a *The Northwestern Archaeological Survey.* Pioneer Press, St. Paul.

1898b [Letter to] Editor of The American Archaeologist. *The American Archaeologist* 2(12):328-329.

1898c Sculptures in Carver's Cave, St. Paul, Minn. *The Macalester Monthly* 1(2):37-42. Macalester College, St. Paul.

1900 The De Soto Expedition Through Florida. *The American Antiquarian* 22(6):351-357.

1901a The De Soto Expedition Through Florida (continued). *The American Antiquarian* 23(2):107-111.

1901b The De Soto Expedition Through Florida (continued). *The American Antiquarian* 23(4):242-247.

1901c Sculptures in Caves at St. Paul, Minnesota. *De Lestry's Western Magazine* 6(6):229-233.

1902 Route of De Soto's Expedition from Taliepacana to Huhasene. *Publications of the Mississippi Historical Society* 6:449-467.

1903 The Chroniclers of De Soto's Expedition. *Publications of the Mississippi Historical Society* 7:379-387.

1907 The Narrative of the Expedition of Hernando de Soto by the Gentleman of Elvas. In *Spanish Explorers in the Southern United States, 1528-1543*, ed. by Frederick W. Hodge and Theodore H. Lewis, pp. 127-272. Charles Scribner's Sons, New York.

1918 Effigy Mounds of Northern Illinois. *The Wisconsin Archeologist* o.s. 17(1):19-21. Reprinted. [Originally published 1888, *Science* 12(292):118-119.]

1926a Trempealeau Rock Shelter. *The Wisconsin Archeologist* 5(1):16-19. Reprinted in "Indian Caves in Wisconsin," by Charles E. Brown. [Originally published 1889 as "Sculptured Rock at Trempealeau, Wisconsin," *The American Naturalist* 23(9):782-784.]

1926b Samuel's Cave. *The Wisconsin Archeologist* 5(1):15. Reprinted in "Indian Caves in Wisconsin," by Charles E. Brown. [Originally published 1889 as part of "Cave Drawings," *Appleton's Annual Cyclopedia and Register of Important Events* 14:117-122.]

1926c Minnesota and Iowa Caves. *The Wisconsin Archeologist* 5(1):24-29. Reprinted in "Indian Caves in Wisconsin," by Charles E. Brown. [Originally published 1889 as part of "Cave Drawings," *Appleton's Annual Cyclopedia and Register of Important Events* 14:117-122.]

1927a The Chroniclers of De Soto's Expedition. Reprinted. In *A Symposium on the Place of Discovery of the Mississippi River by Hernando de Soto*. Special Bulletin No. 1, ed. by Dunbar Rowland, pp. 1-11. The Mississippi State Department of Archives and History, Jackson. [Originally published 1903, *Publications of the Mississippi Historical Society* 7:379-387.]

1927b Route of De Soto's Expedition from Taliepacana to Huhasene. In *A Symposium on the Place of Discovery of the Mississippi River by Hernando de Soto*. Special Bulletin No. 1, ed. by Dunbar Rowland, pp. 12-30. The Mississippi State Department of Archives and History, Jackson. [Originally published 1902, *Publications of the Mississippi Historical Society* 6:449-467.]

1936a Mounds of the Mississippi Basin. *The Minnesota Archaeologist* 2(7):1-5. Reprinted. [Originally published 1883, *Magazine of American History* 9(3):177-182.]

1936b Cave Drawings. *The Minnesota Archaeologist* 2(8):2-8. Reprinted. [Originally published 1890, *Appleton's Annual Cyclopedia and Register of Important Events*.]

1936c Copper Mines Worked by the Mound Builders. *The Minnesota Archaeologist* 2(11):1-3. Reprinted. [Originally published 1889, *The American Antiquarian* 11(5):293-296.]

1937a Quartz Workers of Little Falls. *The Minnesota Archaeologist* 3(2):15-16. Reprinted. [Originally published 1887, *The American Antiquarian* 9(2):105-107.]

1937b Mounds on the Red River of the North. *The Minnesota Archaeologist* 3(2):17-19. Reprinted. [Originally published 1886, *The American Antiquarian* 8(6):369-371.]

1937c De Soto's Camps in the Chickasaw Country in 1540-1541. *The Minnesota Archaeologist* 3(3):29-32. Reprinted. [Originally published 1891, *The National Magazine* 15(1):57-61.]

1937d Stone Monuments in Northwestern Iowa and Southwestern Minnesota. *The Minnesota Archaeologist* 3(5):43-46. Reprinted. [Originally published 1890, *American Anthropologist* o.s. 3(3):269-274.]

1937e Lewis and Clark and the Antiquities of the Upper Missouri River. *The Minnesota Archaeologist* 3(5):47-50. Reprinted. [Originally published 1891, *The American Antiquarian* 13(5):288-293.]

1937f Prehistoric Fire-Place and Human Bones Found at St. Paul. *The Minnesota Archaeologist* 3(10):3. Reprinted. [Originally published 1880, *The St. Paul Pioneer Press* 27(38):7, February 7.]

1937g Ancient Mounds of Minnesota. *The Minnesota Archaeologist* 3(10):3-5. Reprinted. [Originally published 1883, *The St. Paul Pioneer Press* 30(132), At Home Section, May 12.]

1937h Meadow Mounds. *The Minnesota Archaeologist* 3(10):5-6. Reprinted. [Originally published 1883, *The American Antiquarian* 5(4):330-331.]

1937i In the Mandan Country. *The Minnesota Archaeologist* 3(10):6-7. Reprinted. [Originally published 1883, *The St. Paul Pioneer Press* 30(329):12, November 24.]

1937j Effigy Mound in the Valley of the Big Sioux River, Iowa. *The Minnesota Archaeologist* 3(12):3-4. Reprinted. [Originally published 1890, *Science* o.s. 15(378):275.]

1938a Description of Some Copper Relics of the Collection of T.H. Lewis in the Macalester Museum of History and Archaeology. *The Minnesota Archaeologist* 4(3):25-29. Reprinted. [Originally published 1890, *Macalester College Contributions No. 6.*]

1938b Boulder Outline Figures in the Dakotas, Surveyed in the Summer of 1890. *The Minnesota Archaeologist* 4(8):61-63. Reprinted. [Originally published 1891, *American Anthropologist* o.s. 4(1)19-24.]

2001 The Northwestern Archaeological Survey. *The Minnesota Archaeologist* 60:13-29. Reprinted. [Originally published 1898, Pioneer Press, St. Paul.]

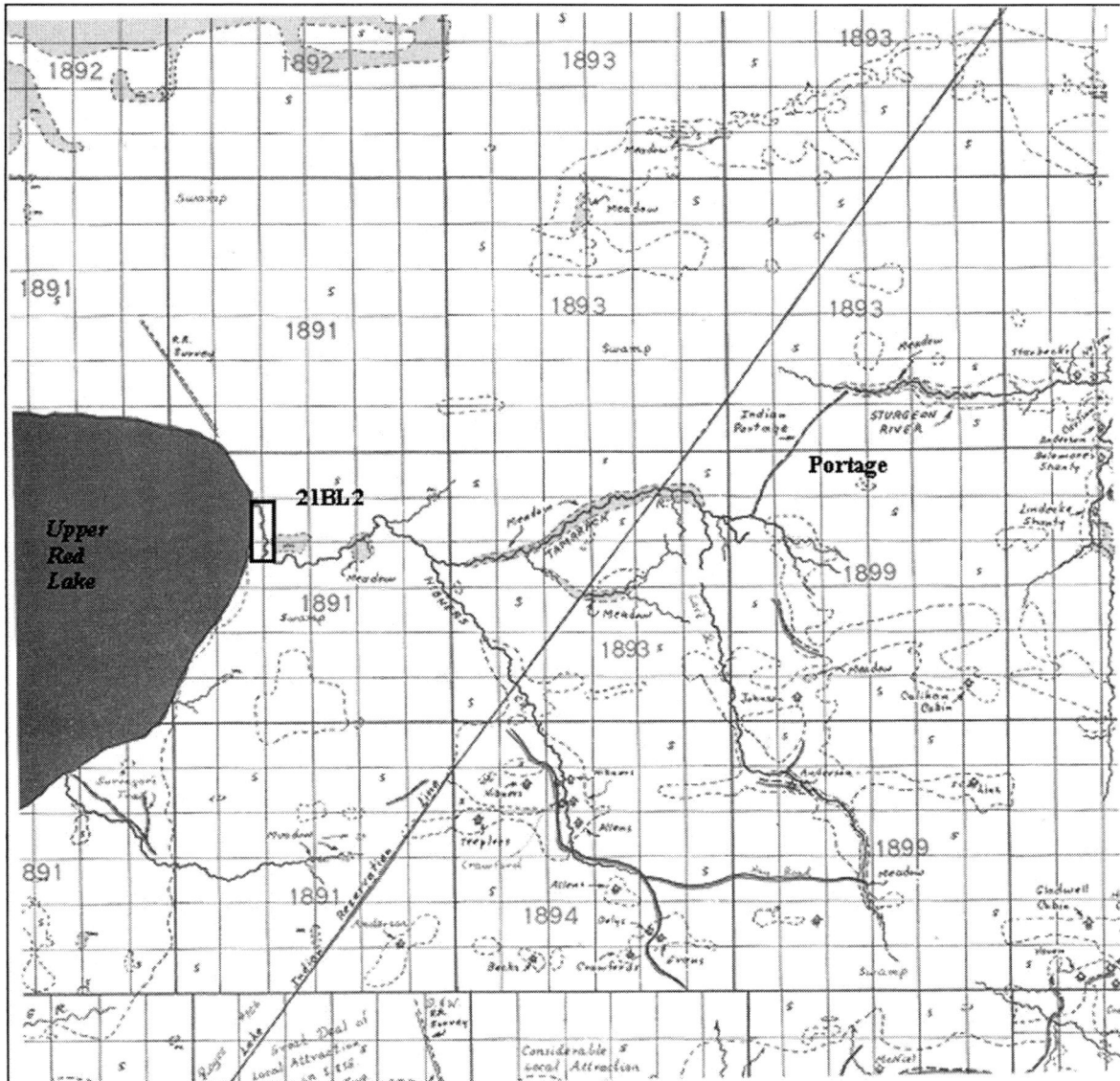

Figure 5. Trygg map showing the location of the portage between the Tamarac River and the Sturgeon River approximately 13 miles upstream from the Waskish site (21BL2) (from Trygg 1967:Sheet 19).

Natural Resources (MnDNR), Division of Parks and Recreation development of the new Big Bog State Recreation Area, Southern Unit on Upper Red Lake (Gonsior et al. 2002; Gonsior and Radford 2004). Areas of dense cultural deposits, including subsurface pit features and a Woodland lithic activity area, were identified in reconnaissance survey and intensive testing that included 203 shovel tests (Fig. 2) and 21 square meters of excavation (Fig. 3). This investigation found that the site is focused along the shoreline of the Tamarac River. Much of the site appears to remain intact, even though there has been substantial twentieth-century development. The cemetery area, which is thought to be the best location for habitation deposits, was not examined by the MSPCRMP, as this area will be protected from development. Along with the precontact components, there is a Euro-American presence at the site associated with the former town of Waskish, established in 1902 on the north bank of the Tamarac River. Within the northern end of the site are the former Forestry and Game and Fish building developments, which date to the 1920s. Creation of later lease lots also adversely affected portions of the Waskish site.

Although the general site area is thought to be the potential location of several eighteenth-century and nineteenth-century fur trade posts, thus far a limited Contact period site occupation is hinted at only by the recovery of a single spall-type gunflint.

Physical Setting

The Waskish site is situated along the Tamarac River at the junction to Upper Red Lake. The combined Lower and Upper Red lakes, remnants of Glacial Lake Agassiz, form the largest lake entirely within Minnesota, encompassing 288,800 acres. The Tamarac River is the third largest river entering the combined lakes, and the largest tributary of Upper Red Lake. Its waters are stained brown by the black spruce and tamarack bogs through which it flows (Waters 1977:117). During the spring, one of the largest historic spawning runs of walleye in the state used to occur here, with peak numbers at the old Waskish fish hatchery estimated to be in the range of 10,000 fish per day and lasting for approximately 10 days. The walleye spawning runs are preceded by impressive numbers of northern pike and suckers. Little is known about any historic sturgeon populations. The Tamarac River was formerly known as the Sturgeon River, however, suggesting the former presence of sturgeon. The river is also noted for large stands of wild rice.

Following the demise of Glacial Lake Agassiz, the remnant Lower and Upper Red lakes receded to their present levels, forming a series of beach ridges around the perimeter of the lakes. At the mouth of the Tamarac River, the falling water level resulted in the creation of a complex mosaic of shoreline and point bar formations that were also influenced by aeolian deposits.

The complex landscape features in the project area were defined and mapped during a geomorphological investigation conducted by Soils Consulting (Goltz 2001) (Fig. 4). Goltz's investigation hypothesizes that the landscape of the Big Bog State Recreation Area, Southern Unit formed as the area of Upper Red and Lower Red lakes diminished. As the water level declined, the mouth of the Tamarac River migrated northward as the lakeshore shifted westward. The Late Holocene landscape formed approximately 2500 years ago at the southeast end of the Big Bog State Recreation Area, Southern Unit while the northernmost end of the campground and current lakeshore are more recent. The southernmost portion of the site near the Waskish airport lies on an older shoreline where it is suspected that earlier components would be found. The MSPCRMP investigation found relative dates for the point bar formations with the identification of Hannaford Ware ceramics on the "D"-designated point bar formation and Brainerd Ware on the "C"-designated point bar formation in the northern portion of the campground.

The environment around the Lower Red and Upper Red lakes is significantly influenced by the moderating effect of this large body of water. This extends the frost-free growing season, which in turn fosters a greater diversity of plant life than in the surrounding inland area. The vegetation on the south shore of Lower Red Lake in particular has a northern hardwood forest character, which differs from the surrounding boreal hardwood-coniferous forest and extensive bogs. Along the eastern shore of Upper Red Lake at the Waskish site, there is a similar diversity of plants and trees because of this lake effect. Ultimately, this diversity provided resources that made the site more attractive for human use.

The water level of Upper Red Lake is controlled by the U.S. Army Corps of Engineers at the Red Lake River outlet of Lower Red Lake. The dam has raised the natural level of Red Lake between five and eight feet, although the precise level is unknown because of a lack of records pertaining to the 1916 Bureau of Indian Affairs (BIA) dam that predates the Corps' current structure (Les Peterson, personal comm. 2000). An even higher artificial lake level in the 1920s resulted in the flooding of the town of Waskish, which ultimately resulted in the government buying the former town site and moving many of the structures to the current linear alignment to the south along TH 72. Unfortunately, the higher artificial water level of Lower and Upper Red lakes has submerged most of the Woodland period sites around the lake (Les Peterson, personal comm. 2000).

Background Research and Previous Investigations

Aside from the Waskish site and twentieth-century Waskish town site, there may be several historic fur-trading posts in the immediate location. According to Nute's research on posts in the Minnesota fur-trading area from 1660 to 1855, only three posts are located on Lower and Upper Red lakes (Nute 1930:353-385). These include two on Lower Red Lake. The first is an early British post on the west side, two miles south of the outlet of the Red Lake River; this is where Cadotte wintered in 1794 to 1795. There is also a Northwest Company post on the east side (about 1790) followed by an 1826 American Fur Company post and another establishment in 1848. On Upper Red Lake, Nute (1930) plots the post where James Grant wintered on the northeast shore prior to 1784; she locates it on the south side of the Tamarac River mouth, in what should be within the Southern Unit of the Big Bog State Recreation Area and close to the Waskish site. Later, Joseph Reaume apparently wintered at the same location in 1794 to 1795. James Grant's post is listed by the Minnesota SHPO as 21BL-aj. It is placed on the north side of the mouth of the Tamarac River, based on a review by the Minnesota Historical Society during a historic-sites archaeological survey of Minnesota in 1963 (Fiske 1966:157).

A Northwest Company post was also reportedly established near the present-day town of Waskish in 1806 (Mittleholtz 1970). It is possibly plotted on a map by Lewis and Clark in 1804 to 1806 (Biddle 1962:230-231). That map depicts Lower and Upper Red lakes as a single lake, with a separate lake to the north having a river flowing north that could represent Upper Red Lake and the Tamarac River. Different copied versions of the map however, don't portray both lakes. A single lake with a river connecting to the Rainy River is depicted with the Northwest Company post placed north of the river inlet (Tomkins 1965:21). Regardless of the possible locations, the logical place for any fur-trading post along the east side of Upper Red Lake would most likely be near the mouth of the Tamarac River transportation route but inland along the river, away from the harsh wind-swept shore of Upper Red Lake.

Historically, the Tamarac River was a well-known transportation corridor that connected to the Sturgeon River by portage and eventually to the Rainy River country. The Tamarac River was initially also called the Sturgeon River. Count Beltrami called the Tamarac River the Amenikaning River (Upham 1969:47). In 1823 Beltrami noted that from Upper Red Lake and up the Tamarac River, it took only two portages to reach the Rainy River, from which you could either travel south to Lake Superior, or north to Hudson Bay (Beltrami 1962:401). The well-known historic portage between the Tamarac River and the Sturgeon River, which is still visible on the ground and on aerial photographs, has never been designated as an archaeological site. The nearly four-mile long portage is identified on the Trygg map (Trygg 1967:Sheet 19) created from General Land Office Survey notes of the connecting townships as mapped between 1891 and 1899 (Fig. 5).

The Precontact-period habitation area of the Waskish site was first noted in records from the U of M in an inquiry letter from Sterling Brackett (1932a) to Waskish Ranger E.H. Rhodes concerning the identification of "old Indian villages" that contain pottery. In reply, Rhodes acknowledged that several people had collected handfuls of pottery from his garden, including patrolman J.N. Licke from Park Rapids. Licke allowed Brackett and a graduate student, Mr. Brown, to examine his collection of 12 to 15 sherds, which Brown identified as belonging to the "Black Duck" Culture (Brackett 1932b:8). Perhaps because of Brackett's inquiries, Wilford (1956) visited the site in 1956 and collected a few sherds from what was then Ranger Blanchard's garden. The U of M accessioned the artifacts from this limited investigation under accession number 88. The U of M accession records also indicate that one David Rose donated a surface collection of 26 sherds (Acc. No. 122).

In 1959, the U of M conducted a two and one-half day field school session at the Waskish site under the direction of graduate student Gayle Evans. Prior to Evans' investigation, TH 72 was widened in 1958 and 1959 for a distance of over one mile from the bridge south through the town of Waskish. The field school crew initially identified and collected artifacts along the TH 72 corridor and the banks of the Tamarac River. Evans then began a formal subsurface examination of the site by excavating a 10 x 10 foot square block south of the then-exist-

Figure 6. Sandy Lake rims recovered by the University of Minnesota, Waskish site (21BL2).

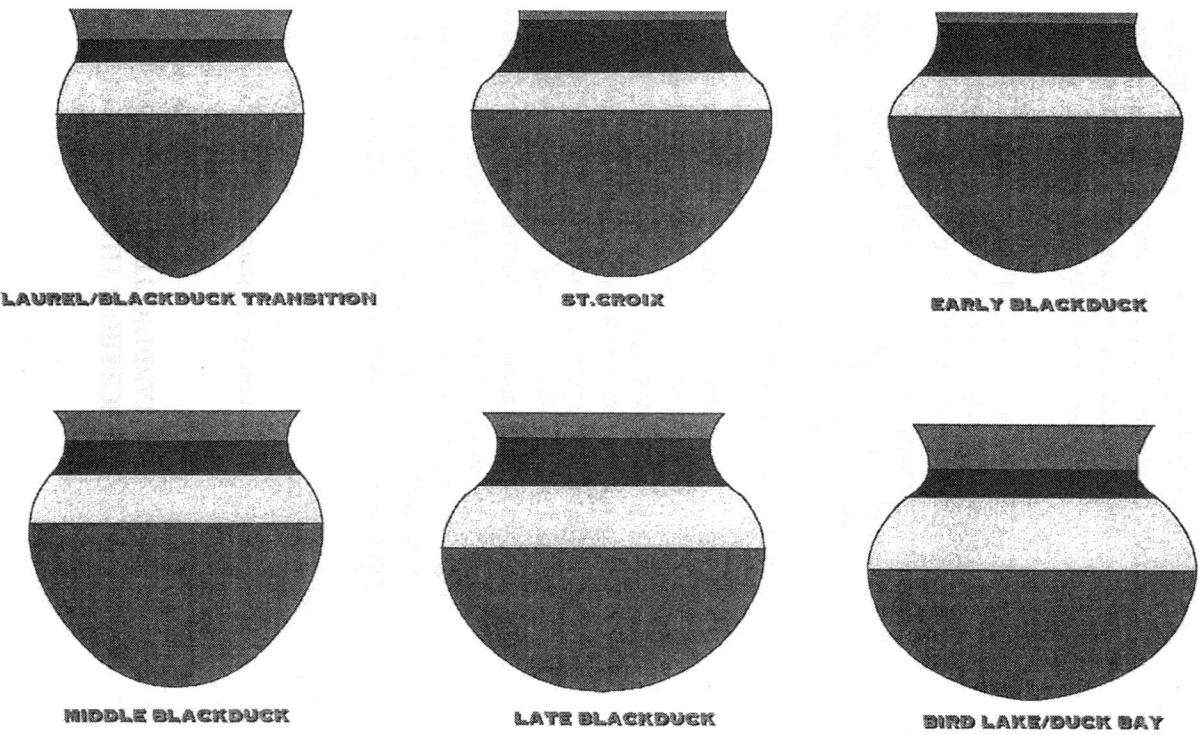

Figure 7. Middle/Late and Late Woodland vessel forms (from Hohman-Caine and Goltz 1996:Figure 26).

Figure 8. Bird Lake ceramics from the MSPCRMP investigations, Waskish site (21BL2).

Figure 9. Bird Lake ceramics from the University of Minnesota collections, Waskish site (21BL2).

Table 1. Surface Attributes of Ceramics Recovered from MSPCRMP Investigations, Waskish Site (21BL2).

SURFACE	NUMBER	PERCENTAGE
Cord Marked	549	46.4
Cord Marked Decorated	21	1.8
Smoothed Cord Marked	115	9.8
Smoothed Cord Marked/Decorated	2	0.2
Smooth Surface	30	2.5
Smooth Surface/Decorated	32	2.7
Fabric-Impressed	110	9.3
Fabric-Impressed/Decorated	10	0.8
Net-Impressed	7	0.6
Indeterminate	284	24.0
Indeterminate/Decorated	22	1.9
Totals	1182	100

Table 2. Ceramic Temper from MSPCRMP Investigations, Waskish Site (21BL2).

TEMPER	NUMBER	PERCENTAGE
Grit	1156	97.8
Grit/Sand	8	0.7
Sand	10	0.8
Shell	7	0.6
Indeterminate	1	0.1
Total	1182	100

Table 3. Lithic Material Types Recovered from MSPCRMP Investigations, Waskish Site (21BL2).

LITHIC MATERIAL	FREQUENCY	PERCENTAGE
Red River Chert	262	61.2
Swan River Chert	52	12.1
Knife River Flint	43	10.0
Quartz	16	3.7
Rhyolite	15	3.5
Basalt	13	3.0
Gunflint Silica	6	1.4
Silicified Wood	5	1.2
Tongue River Silica	4	0.9
Diorite	4	0.9
Quartzite	2	0.5
Chalcedony	2	0.5
Unidentified Chert	1	0.2
Hudson Bay Lowland Chert	1	0.2
Granite	1	0.2
Shale	1	0.2
Total	428	100

Table 4. Frequency of Lithics Recovered from the MSPCRMP Investigations, Waskish Site (21BL2).

LITHIC	FREQUENCY	PERCENTAGE
Tool	6	1.4
Core/Core Fragment	14	3.3
Complete Flake	34	7.9
Proximal Flake Fragment	48	11.2
Medial Flake Fragment	52	12.2
Distal Flake Fragment	54	12.6
Shatter	205	47.9
Unmodified Chert Pebble	15	3.5
Total	428	100

Table 5. Frequency of Lithics Recovered from the Woodland Activity Area, Waskish Site (21BL2).

LITHIC	FREQUENCY	PERCENTAGE
Tool	0	0
Core/Core Fragment	10	3.8
Complete Flake	12	4.5
Proximal Flake Fragment	16	6.0
Medial Flake Fragment	23	8.6
Distal Flake Fragment	35	13.2
Shatter	155	58.3
Unmodified Pebble	15	5.6
Total	266	100

Table 6. Frequency of Faunal Material Items Recovered from the Waskish Site (21BL2).

FAUNAL MATERIAL	FREQUENCY	PERCENTAGE
Piscine	1689	53.7
Mammalian	782	24.8
Vertebrate	596	18.9
Amphibian	37	1.2
Avian	33	1.1
Reptilian	11	0.3
Total	3148	100

ing ranger station fire tower. (The cement foundations of the fire tower still exist.) From the block, a substantial sample of 1004 Woodland period ceramic sherds was recovered, along with projectile points, lithics, and faunal material. One pit feature was identified in the excavation block, from which a number of large mammal faunal remains and ceramics were recovered. The artifacts recovered during the excavation were accessioned under U of M accession number 446.

Evans later used the field data from the Waskish site excavation and excavations at six other sites -- including Schocker (21BL1), Osufsen (21IC2), Mud Lake (21CA2), Nett Lake (21KC1), Smith Mound One (21KC3), and Hill Point (21CE2) -- as part of his 1961 U of M Master's thesis, *A Reappraisal of the Blackduck Focus or Headwaters Lakes Aspect* (Evans 1961:29-31). In this research, Evans formally identified Waskish Vertical Cord and Punctate as a variety of Blackduck ceramics at the Waskish site and other sites in northern Minnesota (Evans 1961:55). Evans' analysis of 23,750 ceramic sherds identified Blackduck, Laurel, and a third unidentified ware from the Waskish site. In defense of Evans -- who distinguished some of the undifferentiated Woodland ceramics as non-Blackduck -- Brainerd, Hannaford, Sandy Lake, and Bird Lake had not yet been identified as Woodland wares.

As part of the records review for the archaeological survey of the Big Bog State Recreation Area, Southern Unit, an examination of the University of Minnesota collections was undertaken by MSPCRMP. Examination of the earlier collections (Acc. Nos. 88 and 122) found that most of the material is missing or misplaced, with only one sherd left from collection 122 and none from 88. Most of the University's 446 collection is intact, but an exact count was not taken.

Other archaeologists have investigated the southern portion of the Waskish site. Grant Goltz and Christy Hohman-Caine conducted a reconnaissance survey on the Sunset Lodge property for the Red Lake Band of Chippewa with band archaeologist Les Peterson. This survey identified substantial Woodland period habitation debris on both sides of TH 72. The Woodland ceramics identified included Brainerd, Blackduck, and smooth shell-tempered ceramics (Les Peterson, pers. comm. 2000). The Duluth Archaeology Center identified the Waskish Airport Site 1 (21BL219) directly south of the Waskish site (Mulholland and Mulholland 2001).

The Waskish site also has a cemetery component, identified through a series of accidental discoveries during construction projects in the 1920s and 1930s. Unfortunately, the history of the recovery of burials from the Waskish site has been poorly chronicled over time. Extensive background research by MSPCRMP included the review of hundreds of Minnesota Forestry Service, Department of Conservation, and Department of Natural Resources

Figure 10. Early Blackduck rim from the MSPCRMP investigations, Waskish site (21BL2).

documents in State Archives at the Minnesota Historical Society. These documents chronicled daily staff activities and contained information on various reports from staff at the Waskish Ranger Station and Blackduck District Office, but revealed no information about burials being encountered at the Waskish Ranger Station. There are, however, a number of accounts and local stories of burials from the Southern Unit of the Big Bog State Recreation Area and the town of Waskish. Building a solid history of these occurrences has been difficult because they mostly occurred during the 1920s and 1930s and were never brought to the attention of archaeologists who could have documented the events at the time of discovery. The recollections of individuals interviewed, and the small amount of written documentation available, suggest four possible burial areas, including three areas in the Southern Unit of the Big Bog State Recreation Area and one in the southern portion of the town of Waskish.

The three burial areas in the Big Bog State Recreation Area are from the basement of the first forester's cabin, footings for the fire tower, and a borrow area just south of the campground. Wilford documented the fire tower burial after talking with Ranger Blanchard (Wilford 1956:22). In Petrowske's (1989:173) historical overview of Waskish, he documented in detail the removal of multiple burials at the south end of the Waskish site in a borrow area that was probably a mound. Other burials were found just south and west of the Waskish site. Wilford (1956) reported that he examined a beach ridge west of the Waskish Airport where burials were uncovered during the WPA period (1935-43) according to an informant, Mr. Beck. The area that was described is on the opposite (west) side of TH 72, compared to the location described by Petrowske. Wilford apparently was already aware of this burial find, as he had previously examined some remains from the site. One of the skulls apparently had a projectile point embedded in it and it was placed on display at a museum in Big Falls. Beck also reported to Wilford that he had found a stone celt in the roots of a tree there. There is also a large unrecorded burial mound west of the airport that has not been documented.

MSPCRMP Investigation of the Waskish Site

The Big Bog State Recreation Area, Southern Unit was added to the Minnesota state park system in 2000 as a result of state legislation, which transferred MnDNR Forestry land from the Red Lake State Forest to the Division of Parks and Recreation. For the development of the recreation area, CRM studies have been conducted for the different stages of MnDNR developments (Radford et al. 2001, 2002; Gonsior et al. 2002; Gonsior and Radford 2004). The development and archaeological review is ongoing. Two additional sites, the Waskish Hatchery site (21BL234) and the Waskish Timber Sale site (21BL237), were identified by CRM studies conducted by the MnDNR Division of Forestry and Trails and Waterways (Magner 2003, 2005a, 2005b; Tumberg 2005) on the opposite bank of the Tamarac River (Fig. 1). Scattered artifacts have been recovered from four beach ridges at the Waskish Hatchery site, while more substantial habitation debris has been recovered from the Waskish Timber Sale site where Magner (2005b) has identified Bird Lake ceramics.

In 2000, the initial MSPCRMP survey was focused along the bank of the Tamarac River where a

Figure 11. Selected "Classic" Blackduck rims from the MSPCRMP investigations, Waskish site (21BL2).

Figure 12. Selected unclassified Late Woodland sherds from the MSPCRMP investigations, Waskish site (21BL2).

Figure 13. Hannaford Smooth rims: a-e, University of Minnesota; f-g, MSPCRMP investigations, Waskish site (21BL2).

15-meter grid shovel testing methodology was employed as part of the proposed campground rehabilitation. Eighty-nine tests were excavated. In 2002, most of the Southern Unit of the Big Bog State Recreation Area east of TH 72 was shovel tested at 15-meter intervals for a proposed visitor center development. Instead of maintaining a shovel-test grid pattern in the dense undergrowth, the ridges of the point bar formations were shovel tested at 15-meter intervals at generally closer transect intervals than the grid system encompassed. Following completion of the reconnaissance survey, intensive archaeological testing for the campground rehabilitation and Visitor Center development was conducted; this included 21 square meters of excavation using meter-square units. The unit locations were determined by areas of development, including electrical post locations in the campsites along the Tamarac River, sewer line connections at the park office, and a five square meter block for a drain field (which identified a lithic workshop). The shovel testing (n=203) and formal excavation of 21 square meters by the MSP-CRMP recovered 4,989 items, including precontact ceramics (n=1,182), lithics (n=428), faunal remains (n=3,148), historic artifacts (n=141), fire-cracked rock (FCR) (n=46), and botanical remains (n=44).

Ceramics

Precontact ceramics (n=1,181) were the most common artifact item recovered from the Waskish site. Ceramic wares represented include Late Woodland Bird Lake, Blackduck, and Sandy Lake; transitional Middle-Late Woodland Hannaford; and Early Woodland Brainerd. Woodland wares Laurel, Selkirk, and St. Croix were anticipated but not recovered. Since the Waskish site is so large, and only about a third of the area has been examined, future research may identify such other components. The surface attributes of the ceramic sample are listed in Table 1. The ceramic sample is overwhelmingly grit tempered (97.8 percent), with just a few shell-tempered and sand-tempered sherds present (Table 2).

From the combined University of Minnesota and Minnesota Historical Society collections, there are a total of 115 rims and 104 decorated/neck sherds from the Waskish site. Unfortunately, there are only a couple of reconstructed vessel fragments that can

Figure 14. Laurel oblique rim from the University of Minnesota Collection Number 122, Waskish site (21BL2).

be classified as Blackduck or Bird Lake. More importantly, there are not enough sherds from any particular vessel to securely define the vessel form. For this analysis, the rim and decorated sherds were clustered into groups with similar attributes. Within the groupings, classic Blackduck and Bird Lake are evident in addition to Sandy Lake, Hannaford, Laurel, and Brainerd wares. These are examined chronologically from most recent to oldest. Two ceramic pipe fragments were also identified.

Sandy Lake Ware is a Late Woodland ware (A.D. 1000 - Contact) assigned initially to the Wanikan Culture (Birk 1979:175) and more recently to the Psinomani Culture (Gibbon 1994:145-147). Sandy Lake Ware has a broad distribution and was used by both the Dakota and Assiniboine (Participants 1988). Some Sandy Lake sites in Minnesota are also associated with Oneota ceramics. There were some smooth shell-tempered body sherds at the southern end of the Waskish site recovered from the Sunset Lodge property that may fit this pattern.

There are no diagnostic Late Woodland Sandy Lake rim sherds from the MSPCRMP investigations. There are, however, seven shell-tempered cordmarked body sherds that are considered assignable to Sandy Lake. In the U of M collections, there are four Sandy Lake rims and three other plain undecorated rims that may also be associated with

Figure 15. Net-impressed Brainerd body sherds from MSPCRMP investigations, Waskish site (21BL2).

Figure 16. Complex fabric-impressed body sherds from the University of Minnesota collection thought to have been mistaken as net-impressed, Waskish site (21BL2).

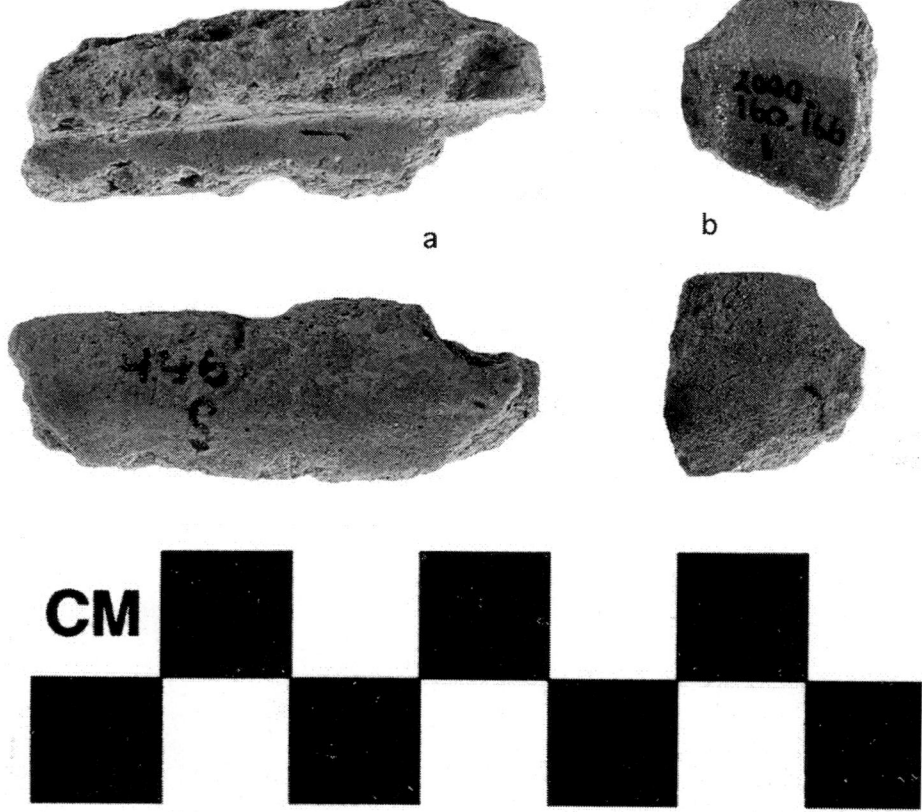

Figure 17. Interior and exterior of Woodland pipe fragments: a, pipe stem fragment from University of Minnesota collections; b, bowl fragment from MSPCRMP investigations, Waskish site (21BL2).

Figure 18. Projectile points: a-b, MSPCRMP; c-f, University of Minnesota, Waskish site (21BL2).

Figure 19. Scrapers: a, MSPCRMP; b-e, University of Minnesota, Waskish site (21BL2).

Sandy Lake (Fig. 6). The rims are notched on the inside with what appears to be a tool impression.

Late Woodland Blackduck ceramics and Bird Lake ceramics, which are associated with the Rainy River Composite, are the dominant wares recovered from the Waskish site. The Waskish site, according to the Minnesota SHPO historic contexts for the Prehistoric period, is one of the principal Blackduck sites in Minnesota. Blackduck ceramics were first described by Wilford (1937) at the Schocker site and have been studied extensively since (MacNeish 1958; Evans 1961; Dawson 1974; Carmichael 1977; Lugenbeal 1976 and 1978; Arthurs 1986; Lenius and Olinyk 1990; Hohman-Caine and Goltz 1994; Rapp et al. 1995; Thomas et al. 1996). Evans (1961) was the first American archaeologist to name varieties of Blackduck ceramics after MacNeish (1958) had done so in Manitoba. Evans' types have been, and still are, used to describe Blackduck ceramics, even though they are no longer thought to be valid. Evans' seven types included Osufsen Cord and Punctate; Nett Lake Cord and Punctate; Schocker Cord Impressed; Schocker Horizontal Cord; Waskish Vertical Cord and Punctate; Nett Lake Vertical Cord, and

Figure 20. Red River Chert bipolar cores recovered from Woodland activity area; b and e are burned, Waskish site (21BL2).

Mud Lake Punctate. Blackduck is often referred to in the "Early," "Classic," and "Late" phases, each of which are presumed to be stylistically homogenous (Lugenbeal 1978). Lugenbeal's reclassification of Blackduck identified "Late Blackduck," a fabric-impressed ware that is now associated with the Rainy River Composite and Bird Lake ceramics.

Blackduck ceramics span the period from A.D. 600 to 1000 before being replaced by the Rainy River Composite of the Western Woodland Algonkian Configuration in northern Minnesota. The Western Woodland Algonkian Configuration includes Selkirk, Duck Bay, and Bird Lake wares (Lenius and Olinyk 1990). Within the Western Woodland Algonkian Configuration, Selkirk is associated with the Cree, while Duck Bay and Bird Lake are associated with the Ojibwe. More recently, an outline by Stoltman (Rapp et al. 1995) seriates Blackduck into four chronological groupings: Early Blackduck (Transitional), Middle Blackduck, early Late Blackduck, and late Late Blackduck. This seriation was used in data recovery investigations at the Hannaford and McKinstry sites to place Blackduck occupations into a chronology (Rapp et al. 1995; Thomas et al. 1996). Neither Lugenbeal's nor Stoltman's models of Blackduck completely addresses the chronological changes in Blackduck and the emergence of the Rainy River Composite. Goltz (personal communication, 2004) believes that Stoltman's seriation is flawed because of an error in mixing vessels from different stratigraphic units from the Hannaford site. Goltz also believes that vessel form is the most im-

Figure 21. Unmodified Red River Chert pebbles recovered from Woodland activity area, Waskish site (21BL2).

portant attribute, and that the various designs evident are more likely clan related than chronologically related (Fig. 7).

The Rainy River Composite ceramics from the Waskish site are dominated by Bird Lake ceramics as defined by Lenius and Olinyk (1990), which replace Blackduck after A.D. 1000 to 1200 (Figs. 8, 9). Several sherds from the Waskish site may fall within the range of Duck Bay, which is defined by a larger stamp impression than Bird Lake. Bird Lake ceramics, which are now part of the Rainy River Composite, were formerly identified as Late Blackduck. Bird Lake vessels share some characteristics of Blackduck, such as horizontal bands of cord-wrapped object impressions and some combing. Vessel shape includes "S" shaped rims. Generally, there are vertically oriented stamps or tool impressions which can be described as small punctates that do not produce bosses. Stamps are sometimes applied at an angle and often the interior of the rim has a band of stamps. The Bird Lake Ware from the Waskish, the Hannaford, and the McKinstry sites varies only slightly from the core area to the north in Ontario and Manitoba (Goltz, personal communication 2004). Bird Lake ceramics have now been identified as far south as the Mississippi River Headwaters area of Minnesota. Possible Bird Lake ceramics are found even further south, in the Joe Neubauer collection from Knife Lake in east–central Minnesota. These are associated with Kathio/Clam River Ware and decorated with small obliquely-applied rectangular punctates.

Researchers have also recognized the close associations of Blackduck with Kathio/Clam River Ware in east-central Minnesota and western Wisconsin. Most researchers agree that the differences appear to be largely geographical. The largest collection of Kathio/Clam River Ware in Minnesota is from a series of 69 sites around the perimeter of Knife Lake in Kanabec County. Unpublished drawings from the Knife Lake ceramics, furnished by Grant Goltz, were examined. Many of the rims are identical to classic Blackduck and other sherds from the Waskish site, but there are some differences. The

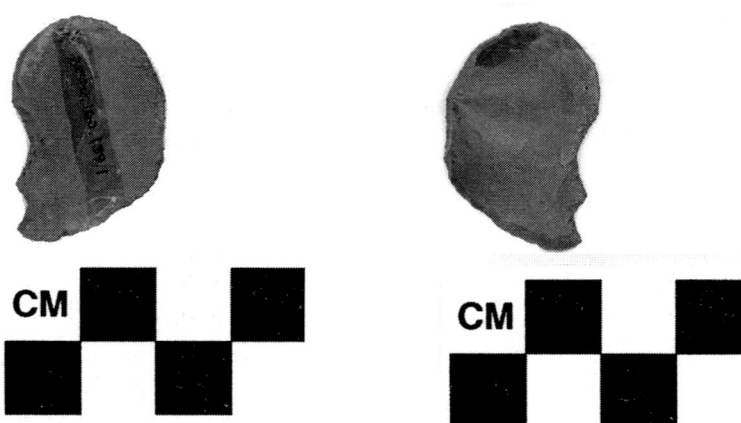

Figure 22. Spall-type gunflint, dorsal and ventral sides, Waskish site (21BL2).

use of punctates in Kathio/Clam River Ware is less frequent than with Blackduck, and there are sometimes chevrons placed below the last row of horizontal bands of cord-wrapped object impressions. Occasionally, complex geometric designs replace the typical horizontal bands of cord-wrapped object impressions. In what can be termed "Classic Blackduck," there are typically no more than four or five horizontal bands of cord-wrapped object impressions. Kathio/Clam River ceramics from the Knife Lake sites frequently have more bands of decoration and the lips are also sometimes "notched" by deeply applied cord-wrapped object impressions.

It is necessary to have a rim-to-shoulder vessel segment to place Blackduck into a chronological sequence. Since substantially-reconstructed vessels are not present in the Waskish collections, the Blackduck ceramics can only be clustered into "early" and "classic." Early Blackduck is transitional from St. Croix Ware and generally has high, thin rims with large bosses and punctates in conjunction with bands of cord-wrapped object impressions. One Early Blackduck sherd (Fig. 10) is very similar to a sherd recovered from the Third River Borrow Pit site (21IC46), which was dated at A.D. 630 (Hohman-Caine et al. 1998:Fig. 8c). Vessels having straight rims with bosses and punctates, previously described as Early Blackduck, are now thought to be associated with the St. Croix ceramic series. No St. Croix ceramics have been recovered from the Waskish site.

The "classic" Blackduck ceramics have thickened rims, decorative elements from the lip down, oblique cord-wrapped object impressions over four to five horizontal bands, in addition to one or two rows of punctates (Fig. 11). In later Blackduck, the use of punctates declines and the vessel rim changes to a short rim with thickened lips. Combing occurs throughout Blackduck and extends into the Rainy River Composite, but is not as clearly applied. The sample of Blackduck from the Waskish site differs from the Mississippi River Headwaters area to the south in that there are more horizontal bands of cord-wrapped object impressions in the ceramics from the Waskish site. Many of the sherds from the collection could not be defined as either Blackduck or Bird Lake (Fig. 12).

Transitional Late to Middle Woodland ceramics from the Waskish site appear to be related to the recently defined, but poorly understood, Hannaford Ware. Hohman-Caine and Goltz (1996, 1998) believe that this is a transition ware from the Middle Woodland Laurel to Late Woodland Blackduck, and that it dates to approximately A.D. 500. Hannaford Ware vessels are both smooth (Hannaford Smooth) and cord marked (Hannaford Vertically Corded) (Hohman-Caine and Goltz 1998:3). The vessels are thick, simple-necked jars with subconoidal bases, gently rounded shoulders, and slight to moderately flared rims. Decoration includes cord-wrapped rocker stamp, cord-wrapped simple stamp, and plain. They are grit tempered and constructed by the coiling method. Hannaford Ware has been identified at the Hannaford site (21KC25), the McKinstry site (21KC2), and the Lake Bemidji Boat Harbor site (21BL35). Three undecorated rim sherds from the MSPCRMP collections are Hannaford-like (Fig. 13f-g). The U of M collections include a three-part segment of an undecorated Hannaford vessel (Fig. 13a-c) and two other possible rims. It is suspected that Evans classified these as Laurel.

Stoltman (1973) has assigned Laurel ceramics to the Middle Woodland period (100 B.C. - A.D. 600). The Laurel component is limited to one rim sherd from the 1934 David Rose collection that was donated to the U of M (Acc. No. 122). It is uncertain from where this sherd was collected. The rim can be classified as Laurel Oblique (Fig. 14). There are only 30 smooth-surfaced sherds in the MSPCRMP collections, and many of these may be associated with decorated Late Woodland neck sherds.

Brainerd is the earliest ceramic ware in northern Minnesota, and has been attributed to the Early Woodland period (Hohman-Caine and Goltz 1995). The Brainerd component from the northern portion of the Waskish site is limited to seven net-impressed body sherds recovered during the MSPCRMP investigations (Fig. 15). The net-impressed ceramics identification noted by Evans (1961) at the Waskish site remain an enigma. There are eight sherds that resemble net-impressed from this collection, but examination of these pieces indicated that they are actually complex fabric impressions that are not assignable to Brainerd or any other ware at this time (Fig. 16).

Currently, the Minnesota SHPO has the Waskish site listed as one of the principal Brainerd sites in their outline of historic contexts for the Prehistoric period (Dobbs 1990:150). There is no archaeological data to substantiate this designation because so little Brainerd material has been recovered from the site. It should be noted that a Brainerd component was recently identified at the southern portion of the Waskish site (Les Peterson, personal comm. 2000).

Two fragments from grit-tempered Woodland ceramic pipes have been recovered from the Waskish site. One pipe stem fragment was identified in the U of M collections (Fig. 17a) and one pipe bowl fragment was recovered during MSPCRMP investigations (Fig. 17b).

Lithics

Lithics (n=428) from the Waskish site occur at a relatively low frequency. Tools are not abundant and are limited to projectile points, scrapers, and flake tools. The paucity of lithics apparently may be characteristic of Woodland fishing sites in the northern portion of Minnesota. The lithic recovery at Waskish is similar to the quantity recovered at the Hannaford site (21KC25) and McKinstry site (21KC2) (Rapp et al. 1995; Thomas et al. 1996). Most of the lithic materials from the site could have been obtained locally from within Bakken's (1997) Western Lithic Resource Region. Lithic material types recovered from the site are tabulated in Table 3. There was an overwhelming preference for Red River Chert (%=61.2). Ten percent of the lithic assemblage is exotic Knife River Flint from western North Dakota. This material was recovered primarily as small pressure flakes and finished tools. The increasing use of Knife River Flint fits a developing Late Woodland pattern in portions of northern Minnesota.

In terms of stone tools, only two projectile points, one scraper, one retouched flake, and one utilized flake were recovered from the Waskish site during the MSPCRMP investigations. Both projectile points are small, side-notched arrow points (Fig. 18a-b). The U of M excavations recovered four projectile points (Fig. 18c-f). Three of the points are small, side-notched arrow points and one is triangular. All of the projectile points are Late Woodland types presumed to be associated with bow and arrow use. The side-notched points generally fall within Kehoe's (1966) Prairie Side-notched point system and the triangular within the Madison type (Morrow 1984). Lithic materials for the projectile points included Knife River Flint (n=3), Red River Chert (n=2), and quartz (n=1).

Five scrapers were identified from the Waskish site (Fig. 19). Lithic materials included Swan River Chert (n=2), Knife River Flint (n=1), Red River Chert (n=1), and a hafted scraper of Tongue River Silica (Fig. 19f). One of the scrapers was recovered during the MSPCRMP investigation (Fig. 19a) while the other four scrapers are from the U of M collections.

An expedient lithic technology is evident at the site based on the types of debitage and low number and types of patterned tools present (Parry and Kelly 1987; Bousman 1993). All of the lithics recovered from the Waskish site by the MSPCRMP are tabulated in Table 4. Of the 428 lithics from the site, 266 were recovered from a five-square-meter block (Units 12, 13, 14, 16, and 17) in the proposed visitor center drain field location (Table 4). Analysis of this assemblage indicates that a lithic workshop emphasizing the reduction of Red River Chert pebbles by bipolar reduction is represented in this very small activity area.

The Woodland activity area is intriguing in that it appears to represent a localized pattern or phenomena in the Red Lake basin. The regional landform is the Glacial Lake Agassiz lakebed, and lithic materials are apparently difficult to procure locally, with only small pebbles being available along the shoreline in reworked lake sediments. This apparently did not dissuade Late Woodland peoples from utilizing the relatively small Red River Chert pebbles that were available. The Waskish site appears to be similar to other precontact sites in the Lower and Upper Red lakes basin because it contains few lithics, and a pattern of using what is available, including pebbles (Les Peterson, personal comm. 2000). The Red River Chert pebbles that were used appear to be between 2.0 and 5.0 cm in size based on the dimension of 10 bipolar cores (Fig. 20) and 15 unmodified pebbles (Fig. 21) that were recovered from the activity area. There were no hammer or anvil stones associated with the activity area. Perhaps this is because the activity area is not particularly large and the tools needed for bipolar reduction were taken away. It is also possible that they would have been reused for other activities. There is no local source for cobbles on the eastern end of Upper Red Lake, which is readily evident in that only 46 fragments of FCR have been recovered from all of the investigations at the Waskish site.

The MSPCRMP cataloging protocol for lithic debitage used in this study was modeled after Sullivan and Rozen (1985:755-779), debitage analysis with several minor terminology changes. The four debitage types that Sullivan and Rozen devised are complete flakes, broken flakes, flake fragments, and debris. We redefined their debris category as shatter. Experimental bipolar reduction studies by Kuijt et al. (1995) identify shatter or debris as non-orientable. In the cataloguing, identifiable flake fragments were defined as medial and distal flake fragments and renamed broken flakes as proximal flake fragments. Following the modified categories, the site activity appears to most closely represent Sullivan and Rozen's (1985) Group IB2 technological grouping, which represents intensive core reduction and tool manufacture.

Although Sullivan and Rozen's (1985) debitage analysis has been criticized by Amick and Mauldin (1989), Ensor and Roemer (1989), and Prentiss and Romanski (1989), the simplicity of this typological approach has been used by many researchers to understand what type of core and tool production is apparent in lithic assemblages. One of the major criticisms is that Sullivan and Rozen used archaeological assemblages instead of using experimental replication data. The Kuijt et al. (1995) study has furnished the experimental data that compliments and validates the Sullivan and Rozen study in regard to bipolar reduction.

Kuijt et al. (1995) conducted experimental bipolar reduction that clarified what types of debitage percentages occur using this core reduction method. They concluded that the percentages vary with what type of lithic material is used, but high percentages of shatter, in the 40 to 50 percent range, are diagnostic of bipolar reduction. In the Waskish site lithic sample, nearly 48 percent of the site debitage is shatter. In the activity area at the site, it was 58 percent. The percentages of debitage types identified in the Kuijt et al. (1995:116) study clearly indicates that bipolar core reduction activity dominates the lithic workshop at the Waskish site. The low total of complete flakes (i.e., 7.9 percent versus 12.3 percent for experimental debitage in the Kuijt et al. study [1995:122]) is an indication that many were used for flake tools or patterned tools.

Historic

A total of 141 historic artifacts were recovered from the site. The sample is dominated by recent historic debris from recreational campground activities and from the Forestry, Game and Fish, and MnDNR uses at Waskish that started in the 1920s. Historic artifacts that were obviously very recent were noted in the field notes and discarded. No historic MnDNR building foundations or other historic features of the site were affected by the development activities. A single Contact-period historic artifact was recovered, a spall-type gunflint, alluding to a late 1700s presence (Fig. 22). The gunflint is made of an undetermined lithic material. It also appears to have been in a fire, which may have changed the color. No other Contact period artifacts were recovered.

Faunal

Faunal remains (n=3,148) were the most frequent item recovered from the Waskish site (Table 5). There are two subsistence patterns evident in the faunal material from the site: The Waskish site appears to have functioned as a fishing village, likely as a spring piscary, and as a camp for big game hunting. Faunal material from the reconnaissance surveys and the intensive testing phase were examined and the number of identified specimens is indicated below. It should be noted that there are many more identifiable fish elements that have not been identified to species and that need further study. Identified mammalian elements included beaver (n=19), deer (n=2), bear (n=1), *Canis* sp. (n=1), cottontail rabbit (n=1), and moose (n=77, including a mandible fragmented into 75 pieces and two maxilla fragments from separate locations. The beaver elements are probably from only three individuals and were recovered as two clusters of bone found together. This material accounted for the majority of the identifiable beaver elements. Identified fish bone was from walleye (n=27), sucker (n=10), northern (n=8), and muskellunge (n=1). Turtle (n=11) and frog (n=16) remains, representing reptiles and amphibians, were also identified. Recent domestic animal bone, some sawn, were identified as being pig (n=10) and cattle (n=6).

Several pit features encountered during the shovel testing contained faunal remains. One large pit feature just north of the park office building was partially excavated as part of Shovel Test 91. The shovel test contained a dense layer of fish bone (n=529) that was sampled with one-quarter inch mesh. Ash and corded ceramic sherds that apparently represents some type of fish processing were also recovered. Similar features were identified at the Third River Bridge site (21IC46) where a series of pit features contained broken ceramic vessels filled with sucker bones left from making fish soup (Hohman-Caine et al. 1998; LeVasseur 2000:13).

Several small hearth-like features were also found in shovel tests. The features contained pockets of burned mammal bone fragments. The pit feature that the U of M identified at the Waskish site contained large mammal bone fragments.

Summary

Archaeological investigations in the Southern Unit of the Big Bog State Recreation Area have found that the northern portion of the Waskish site is a significant Woodland site primarily associated with the Late Woodland period. The Waskish site functioned as a fishing village at a prime spring fishing location, but also was at a significant transportation junction lying approximately 13 miles downstream from the historic Tamarac River portage. The Waskish site is dominated by Late Woodland Bird Lake and Blackduck ceramics. The emergence of Bird Lake ceramics in the archaeological record in northern Minnesota, with the inferred association that they relate ancestrally to the Ojibwe, is bringing about a better understanding of the Terminal Woodland dynamics occurring in the region. As more previously excavated sites are re-examined for Bird Lake ceramics, as was done in this study, the presence of this late Late Woodland ware will emerge and more meaningful research questions can be asked about the people who used them.

Late Woodland Sandy Lake, Middle/Late Woodland Hannaford, and Early Woodland Brainerd ceramic components are also present at the Waskish site. The Sandy Lake component is sparse and includes both grit-tempered and shell-tempered ceramics. Most of the Sandy Lake ceramics were recovered by Evans' excavation. The identification of Hannaford ceramics from the Waskish site is intriguing. The transitional Late/Middle Woodland Hannaford Ware component is poorly understood in Minnesota as it has only been recently recognized at a handful of sites along the Rainy River and south to Lake Bemidji. Interestingly, in most areas St. Croix ceramics are seen, through a gradual change, as the predecessor to Blackduck ceramics. No St. Croix ceramics have been identified at the Waskish site. Instead, the people who produced Hannaford Ware appear to occupy this area at approximately A.D. 500, rather than St. Croix ceramic users. Very little can be said concerning the Middle Woodland Laurel occupation of the site. The Early Woodland Brainerd component is minor irrespective to the Minnesota SHPO Precontact period context which list the Waskish site as one of the principal Brainerd sites in Minnesota.

Stone tools from the Waskish site are limited to Late Woodland side-notched and triangular projectile points, scrapers, and flake tools. Under Sullivan and Rozen's (1985) technological grouping, intensive core reduction and tool manufacture was identified specifically for the lithic activity area and for the site. A lithic activity area for processing pebbles of Red River Chert for flakes is indicative of some degree of sedentism (see Parry and Kelly 1987) with a shift to an expedient core technology where local materials are intensively used mostly for flake tools and a limited range of patterned tools (i.e., small projectile points and scrapers). This pattern is apparent at other sites around Upper and Lower Red lakes where suitable lithic materials are difficult to procure in the fine sediments left behind by Glacial Lake Agassiz. Aside from the intensive use of Red River Chert, Knife River Flint was a desired commodity obtained through trade or seasonal forays. A Late Woodland lithic pattern of using Knife River Flint is skewed with the inclusion of the Red River Chert activity area. Excluding the activity area, Knife River Flint accounts for 26 percent of the lithics from the site, which is remarkably high. This increased reliance on Knife River Flint is a pattern that is becoming apparent for the Late Woodland period in northern Minnesota and particularly at the Waskish site.

The Waskish site is located at the prime spring fishing location on Upper Red Lake. The limited faunal analysis suggests that the Waskish site functioned as a spring piscary. One fish processing pit feature was identified. Several small hearth-like features with burned large mammal bone were also identified.

It was thought that the Waskish site would have high potential for the location of several late nineteenth-century fur trading posts and historic Ojibwe settlements. The archaeological investigations have, however, only identified a single Contact period spall type gunflint. It is suspected that the highest, most desirable area along the Tamarac River for these components is also the location of the suspected cemetery area. This broad area was excluded from archaeological survey and park development.

Acknowledgments. The MnDNR, Division of Parks and Recreation funded the investigations at the Waskish site. The efforts of many people contributed to the site excavation, artifact processing, and editing including Stacy Allan, Douglas George, and Mike Magner. Grant Goltz generously donated his time to aid in the identification of the ceramics from the site. The project was coordinated with the Red Lake Band of Chippewa with the assistance of Les Peterson. Terry McGibbon photographed the artifacts. Kent Bakken helped identify lithic materials.

References Cited

Amick, D.S. and R.P. Mauldin
  1989 Comments on Sullivan and Rozen's Debitage and Archaeological Interpretation. *American Antiquity* 54:166-168.

Arthurs, D.A.
  1986 A*rchaeological Investigations of the Long Sault Site: A Stratified Habitation and Burial Station on the Rainy River in Northwestern Ontario.* Conservation Archaeology Report No. 7, Ministry of Citizenship and Culture, Northwestern Region, Kenora, Ontario.

Bakken, K.
  1997 Lithic Raw Material Resources in Minnesota. *The Minnesota Archaeologist* 56:51-83.

Beltrami, J.C.
  1962 *A Pilgrimage in America, Leading to the Discovery of the Secrets of the Mississippi and Bloody River; with a Description of the Whole Course of the Former, and of the Ohio.* Reprinted, first edition in 1828, London Quadrangle Books Inc., Chicago.

Biddle, N.
  1962 *The Journals of the Expedition under the Command of Capts. Lewis and Clark to the sources of the Missouri, thence across the Rocky Mountains and down the river Columbia to the Pacific Ocean, performed during the years 1804-5-6 by Order of the Government of the United States.* Volume One. The Heritage Press, New York.

Birk, D.A.
  1979 Sandy Lake Ware. In *A Handbook of Minnesota Prehistoric Ceramics*, compiled and edited by S.F. Anfinson, pp. 175–182. Occasional

Publications In Minnesota Anthropology No. 5, Minnesota Archaeological Society, St. Paul.

Bousman, C.B.
1993 Hunter-Gatherer Adaptations, Economic Risk and Tool Design. *Lithic Technology* 18:59-86.

Brackett, S.
1932a Letter to Ranger E.H. Rhodes at Waskish. Beltrami County files, Department of Anthropology, University of Minnesota, Minneapolis, Minnesota. Available at the Fort Snelling History Center, Minnesota Historical Society, St. Paul.
1932b *Black Duck Culture Geographical Distribution*. University of Minnesota student paper in Shocker site files, Beltrami County. Available at the Minnesota Historical Society, St. Paul.

Carmichael, P.H.
1977 *Descriptive Summary of Blackduck Ceramics from the Wanipogow Lake Area (EgKx-1), 1976 and 1976*. Papers In Manitoba Archaeology Miscellaneous Paper No. 5. Department of Tourism and Cultural Affairs, Historic Resources Branch, Winnipeg, Manitoba.

Dobbs, C.A.
1990 *Outline of Historic Contexts for the Prehistoric Period (ca. 12,000 B.P. – A.D. 1700)*. Institute for Minnesota Archaeology, Report of Investigations Number 37. Prepared for the Minnesota State Historic Preservation Office, Minnesota Historical Society, St. Paul.

Dawson, K.C.A
1974 The McCluskey Site. National Museum of Man, Archaeological Survey of Canada, Mercury Series Paper No. 25. National Museum of Man, Ottawa.

Ensor, H.B. and E. Roemer Jr.
1989 Comments on Sullivan and Rozen's Debitage and Archaeological Interpretation. *American Antiquity* 54:175-178.

Evans, G.E.
1961 *A Reappraisal of the Blackduck Focus or Headwaters Lake Aspect*. Unpublished Master's thesis, University of Minnesota, Minneapolis.

Fiske, T.
1966 Historic Sites Archaeological Survey. *The Minnesota Archaeologist* 28:145-193.

Gibbon, G.E.
1994 Cultures of the Upper Mississippi River Valley and Adjacent Prairies in Iowa and Minnesota. In *Plains Indians, A.D. 500-1500, The Archaeological Past of Historic Groups,* edited by K.H. Schlesier. University of Oklahoma Press, Norman and London.

Goltz, G.
2001 *Soils and Geomorphic Investigations, Big Bog Recreation Area, Waskish, Minnesota*. Prepared for the Minnesota Department of Natural Resources, St. Paul. Soils Consulting, Inc., Longville, Minnesota.

Gonsior, L, D.C. George and D.S. Radford
2002 *Cultural Resource Reconnaissance Survey of a New Visitor Center and Rehabilitation of an Existing Campground, Southern Unit, Big Bog State Recreation Area, Beltrami County, Minnesota*. Prepared for the Minnesota Department of Natural Resources, Division of Parks and Recreation, St. Paul. Archaeology Department, Minnesota Historical Society, St. Paul.

Gonsior, L. and D.S. Radford
2004 *Cultural Resource Reconnaissance Survey and Intensive Archeological Testing of the Waskish Site (21BL2) for the Visitor Center and Campground Development in the Southern Unit of the Big Bog State Recreation Area, Beltrami County, Minnesota*. Prepared for the Minnesota Department of Natural Resources, Division of Parks and Recreation, St. Paul. Archaeology Department, Minnesota Historical Society, St. Paul.

Hohman-Caine, C.A. and G.E. Goltz
1994 Descriptive Analysis of the Ceramics from the Hannaford Site (21-KC-25). In *Report of the Field Excavations: 21-KC-25, The Hannaford Site, Minnesota Department of Transportation Archaeological Data Recovery Project S.P. 3604-46 (T.H. 11)*. Prepared for the Minnesota Department of Transportation, St. Paul. Soils Consulting, Inc., Longville, Minnesota.
1995 Brainerd Ware and the Early Woodland Dilemma. *The Minnesota Archaeologist* 59:109-129.
1996 *Ceramics from the Hannaford Site: Keys to Understanding the Middle to Late Woodland Transition*. Paper presented at the Minnesota Academy of Sciences Archaeology Symposium, Hamline University, St. Paul.

1998 *Hannaford Ware: A Transitional Middle Woodland to Late Woodland Ceramic Ware In Northern Minnesota.* Manuscript available from authors.

Hohman-Caine, C.A., G.E. Goltz, and D. Mather
1998 *A Spring Piscary in the Headwaters Region: The Third River Bridge Site (21-IC-6 (CNF #09-03-01-109).* Prepared for the Chippewa National Forest. Hamline University, St. Paul.

Kehoe, T.F.
1966 The Small Side-Notched Point System of the Northern Plains. *American Antiquity* 31:827-841.

Kuijt, I., W.C. Prentiss and D.L. Pokotylo
1995 Bipolar Reduction: An Experimental Study of Debitage Variability. *Lithic Technology* 20:116-127.

Lenius, B.J. and D.M. Olinyk
1990 The Rainy River Composite: Revisions to Lake Woodland Taxonomy. In *The Woodland Tradition in the Western Great Lakes: Papers Presented to Elden Johnson,* ed. by G. Gibbon, pp. 77-112. University of Minnesota Publications in Anthropology No. 4. Department Of Anthropology, University of Minnesota, Minneapolis.

LeVasseur, A.K.
2000 10,000 Years in the Headwaters: Archeology on the Chippewa National Forest. *The Minnesota Archaeologist* 59:11-21.

Lugenbeal, E.N.
1976 *The Archaeology of the Smith Site: A Study of the Ceramics and Culture History of Minnesota Laurel and Blackduck.* Ph.D. dissertation, Department of Anthropology, University of Wisconsin, Madison.
1978 The Blackduck Ceramics of the Smith Site (21KC3) and their Implication for the History of Blackduck Ceramics and Culture History in Northern Minnesota. *Midcontinental Journal Of Archaeology* 3 (1):45-68.

MacNeish, R.S.
1958 *An Introduction to the Archaeology of Southeast Manitoba.* Bulletin No. 157. National Museum of Canada, Ottawa.

Magner, M.A.
2003 *Report of Archaeological Reconnaissance Survey: Vault Toilet Installation Adjacent to the Waskish Public Access.* Prepared for the Minnesota Department of Natural Resources, Division of Parks and Recreation, St. Paul. Archaeology Department, Minnesota Historical Society, St. Paul.
2005a *Report of Archaeological Reconnaissance Survey: Potential Public Access Development at the Waskish Hatchery.* Prepared for the Minnesota Department of Natural Resources, Division of Parks and Recreation, St. Paul. Archaeology Department, Minnesota Historical Society, St. Paul.
2005b *Report of Archaeological Reconnaissance Survey: Waskish Timber Sale.* Prepared for the Minnesota Department of Natural Resources, Division of Parks and Recreation, St. Paul. Archaeology Department, Minnesota Historical Society, St. Paul.

Mittleholtz, E.F.
1970 *Historic Site Survey, 21BL2.* Manuscript available at the Fort Snelling History Center, St. Paul.

Morrow, T.
1984 *Iowa Projectile Points.* Office of the State Archaeologist, University of Iowa, Iowa City.

Mulholland, S.C. and S.L. Mulholland
2001 *Phase I Archaeological Survey at the Waskish Airport on Upper Red Lake, Beltrami County, Minnesota.* Prepared for the Waskish Township Council. Duluth Archaeology Center, LLC, Duluth.

Nute, G.L.
1930 Posts in the Minnesota Fur-Trading Area, 1660-1855. In *Minnesota History* 11:353-385.

Petrowske, A.J.
1989 *On the Trail.* Published by the author, Bemidji, Minnesota.

Parry, W.J. and R.L. Kelly
1987 Expedient Core Technology and Sedentism. In *Organization of Core Technology,* ed. by J.K. Johnson and C.A. Morrow, pp. 285-304. Westview Press, Boulder, Colorado.

Participants of the Lake Superior Basin Workshop 1988 (Participants)
1988 Desperately Seeking Siouians: The Distribution of Sandy Lake Ware. *The Minnesota Archaeologist* 47 (1):43-47.

Prentiss, W.C. and E.J. Romanski
1989 Experimental Evaluation of Sullivan and Rozen's Debitage Typology. In, *Reduction*

Experiments and Ethnographic Observations in Lithic Technology, ed. by D. Amick and R. Mauldin, pp. 89-100. BAR International Series 528. BAR, Oxford.

Radford, D.S., L. Gonsior, D.C. George and S. Allan

2001 *Minnesota State Park Cultural Resource Management Program Annual Report-2000*. Prepared for the Minnesota Department of Natural Resources, Division of Parks and Recreation, St. Paul. Archaeology Department, Minnesota Historical Society, St. Paul.

2002 *Minnesota State Park Cultural Resource Management Program Annual Report-2001*. Prepared for the Minnesota Department of Natural Resources, Division of Parks and Recreation, St. Paul. Archaeology Department, Minnesota Historical Society, St. Paul.

Rapp, G., Jr., S.C. Mulholland, S.L. Mulholland, Z. Jing, D.E. Stoessel, C.L. Hill, O.C. Shane, S.H. Valppu, J.K. Huber, J.B. Stoltman and J.R. Shafer

1995 *Final Report: Hannaford Data Recovery Project, Koochiching County, Minnesota*. Archaeometry Laboratory Report No. 95-31. Prepared for the Minnesota Department of Transportation, St, Paul. University of Minnesota, Duluth.

Stoltman, J.B.

1973 *The Laurel Culture in Minnesota*. Minnesota Prehistoric Series No. 8. Minnesota Historical Society, St. Paul.

Sullivan, A.P. III and K.C. Rozen

1985 Debitage Analysis and Archaeological Interpretation. *American Antiquity* 50:755-779.

Thomas, M.M., D. Mather, C. Falk, E. Hajic, A. Hoppin, D. Morey, A. Newman, P. Nunnally, H. Semken, Jr., C. Shen, J. Stoltman, R. Thompson and S. Valppu.

1996 *Final Report of Phase III Investigations for MnDOT S.P. 3604-44, Replacement of T.H. 11 Bridge 5178 over the Little Fork River, Koochiching County, Minnesota*. Prepared for the Minnesota Department of Transportation, St. Paul. Loucks & Associates, Inc., Maple Grove, Minnesota.

Tomkins, C.

1965 *The Lewis and Clark Trail*. Harper & Row, New York.

Trygg, J.

1967 *Composite Map of United States Land Surveyors' Original Plats and Field Notes, Sheet 19, Minnesota Series*. J.Wm. Trygg, Ely, Minnesota.

Tumberg, T.

2005 *Trails and Waterways Cultural Resources Annual Report-2004*. Prepared for the Minnesota Department of Natural Resources, Division of Parks and Recreation, St. Paul. Archaeology Department, Minnesota Historical Society, St. Paul.

Upham, W.

1969 *Minnesota Geographic Names*, reprinted edition. Minnesota Historical Society, St. Paul.

Waters, T.F.

1977 *The Streams and Rivers of Minnesota*. University of Minnesota Press, Minneapolis.

Wilford, L.A.

1937 *Minnesota Archaeology with Special Reference to the Mound Area*. Ph.D. thesis, Harvard University, Cambridge.

1956 Lloyd Wilford 1956 notes for Beltrami County. Unpublished notes available at the Fort Snelling History Center, Minnesota Historical Society, St. Paul.

A Prairie Blackduck Site in Northwestern Minnesota

Michael G. Michlovic
Minnesota State University Moorhead

Site 21CY39 is located on an upland terrace of the Buffalo River where the river cuts through beach deposits of Glacial Lake Agassiz. It is a Late Woodland site, with a cultural horizon 20 to 35 cm below the surface. Blackduck is the only ware identified in the ceramic sample. Lithic materials consist of various finished lithic tools, including two side-notched points. Both local and exotic materials are represented in the flaking debris sample. Faunal remains are mostly bison, with a few minor species represented as well. A single radiocarbon date provides an estimated age of 1000 B.P. The site is important as one of only a few reported Blackduck sites in this part of the plains, and for insights it offers regarding the Late Woodland use of the northeastern plains environment.

Introduction

In 1981 Minnesota State University Moorhead (MSUM; formerly Moorhead State University) began planning an outdoor Science Center for education and educational outreach. This center was to be developed on property formerly comprising the Ponderosa Golf Course, land that was donated to the University by the Fargo Elks club. During the planning process, the golf course became an issue of debate, and the decision was made to save the golf facility but to plan the Science Center to the west, south and east of the course.

Part of the planning for the Science Center included an archaeological survey of the property. The survey resulted in the discovery of six archaeological sites, including one, 21CY39, that was recognized as a Late Woodland Blackduck site on the basis of a decorated rimsherd found in a golf-cart path cut on the perimeter of the site. 21CY39 was partially disturbed by the golf course, and it was on land that would be modified by golf course expansion as planned in the 1980s. For this reason, archaeological testing of the site was initiated.

The first archaeological work at the site was done in 1985 and expanded in 1991, a time when there was a desire to use the site area as a fairway. After 1991 the golf course gave up development plans for the area around 21CY39, which then reverted to the Science Center. In 2002 further excavations recovered additional information about the site. The 1985 work included 16 m² in 1 x 2 and 1 x 1 m units. More extensive excavations in 1991 consisted of 37 m² including a block of about 18 m². Additional extensive digging in 2002 involved 21 m². The 2002 work completed digging at the site to this point. Altogether 74 m² have been excavated over various portions of the site. This represents less than 2 percent of the total site area. All of the archaeological work was performed by MSUM field schools in archaeology under direct supervision of the author. Total labor devoted to the excavations over the three seasons was about 3,500 person hours. Laboratory work associated with the field projects has not been calculated, but includes at least as many hours as the excavations.

Site Location and Environment

21CY39 is located on a terrace above the wooded floodplain of the Buffalo River, about 400 m south of the present stream. The river cuts through the beach deposits of Lake Agassiz at this point. The site is approximately 25 km east of Moorhead, Minnesota (see Figs. 1-3). Its coordinates are the NE, SE, Section 11, T139N, R46W, Riverton Township, Downer, MN Quad, 7-1/2°, Clay County. Datum is at approximate latitude N46° 51' 57", longitude W96° 26' 2". UTM coordinates are easting 694,940, northing 5,193,200, zone 14. The site dimensions are about 150 m on an east-west axis and 50 m north to south. The site area is about 7500 m² (Figs. 4, 5).

The Buffalo River is a tributary of the Red River, whose drainage basin covers the border area between Minnesota, North Dakota and Manitoba. The region is characterized by a continental climate and is on the border of cold, semi-arid steppes to the *num* spp), and others. Along the river and in places of high moisture, cottonwood (*Populus deltoides*) and quaking aspen (*Populus tremuloides*) trees occur. On the highlands bur oak (*Quercus macrocarpa*) stands are common (Williams 1982:7). Beach ridge prairies are typically classified as dry prairie, and grasses and sedges are dominant.

Native mammals include the eastern cottontail (*Sylvilagus floridanus*), jackrabbit (*Lepus townsendii*), white-tailed deer (*Odocoileus virginiana*), beaver (*Castor canadensis*), raccoon (*Procyon lotor*), striped skunk (*Mephitis mephitis*), woodchuck (*Marmota monax*), weasel (*Mustela* spp), squirrel (*Sciurus* spp), red squirrel (*Tamiasciurus hudsonicus*), pocket gopher (*Geomys bursarius*), and various ground squirrels (*Spermophilous* spp). It is probable that before Europeans settled in the area, other large mammals, such as bear (*Ursus* sp), wolf (*Canis lupus*), wapiti or elk (*Cervus elaphus*), and moose (*Alces alces*) also lived in the area. Bison (*Bison bison*) is indicated by numerous historical sources, and by faunal remains recovered from the site (Hazard 1982).

The terrain in the vicinity of the site consists of three features: the lacustrian plain of ancient Lake Agassiz west of the site, the beach ridges that bound this plain, and alluvial features created by the Buffalo River. The site is located adjacent to one of the

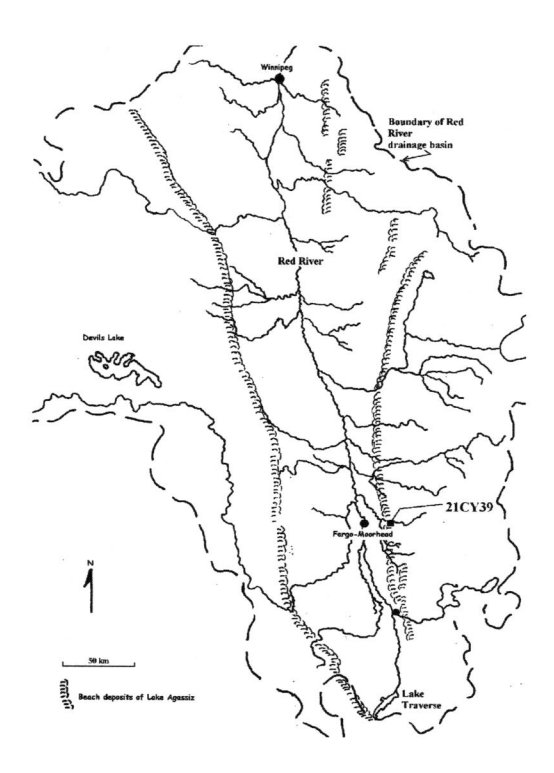

Figure 1. 21CY39, Lake Agassiz basin and Red River drainage.

west, and cold, subhumid forests to the east. Most precipitation occurs in the spring and summer, much of it in the form of convective storms. Mean annual precipitation is 53 cm (21 inches). Winds are common and average 17 to 23 km/hr (10-14 mph). Temperature averages range from −15.4° C in January to 21.5° C in July (4.3-71° F) (NOAA 2003).

21CY39 is located near the eastern boundary of the North American Grasslands as defined by Borchert (1950). Grasses such as blue grama (*Bouteloua gracilis*) and big and little bluestem (*Agropogon geradi* and *Agropogon scoparius*, respectively) are dominant over wide areas (Williams 1982:7). These open stretches host many flowering meadow plants, as well as various edible plants such as wild onion (*Allium stellatum* and *Allium testile*), prairie turnip (*Psorilea esculenta*), ground plum (*Astragalus caryocarpus*), goosefoot (*Chenopodium album*), wild plum and chokecherry (*Prunus* spp), dandelion (*Taraxacum officinale*), bush cranberry (*Vibur-*

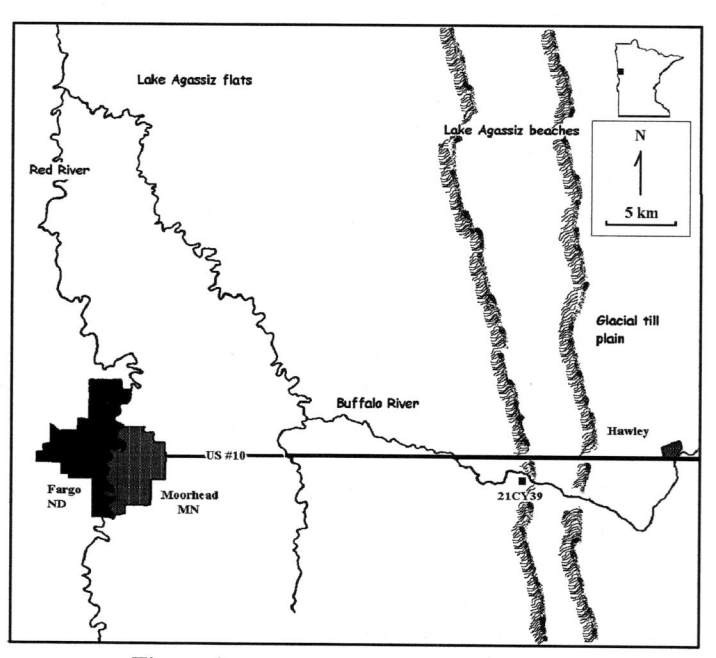

Figure 2. 21CY39 and regional features.

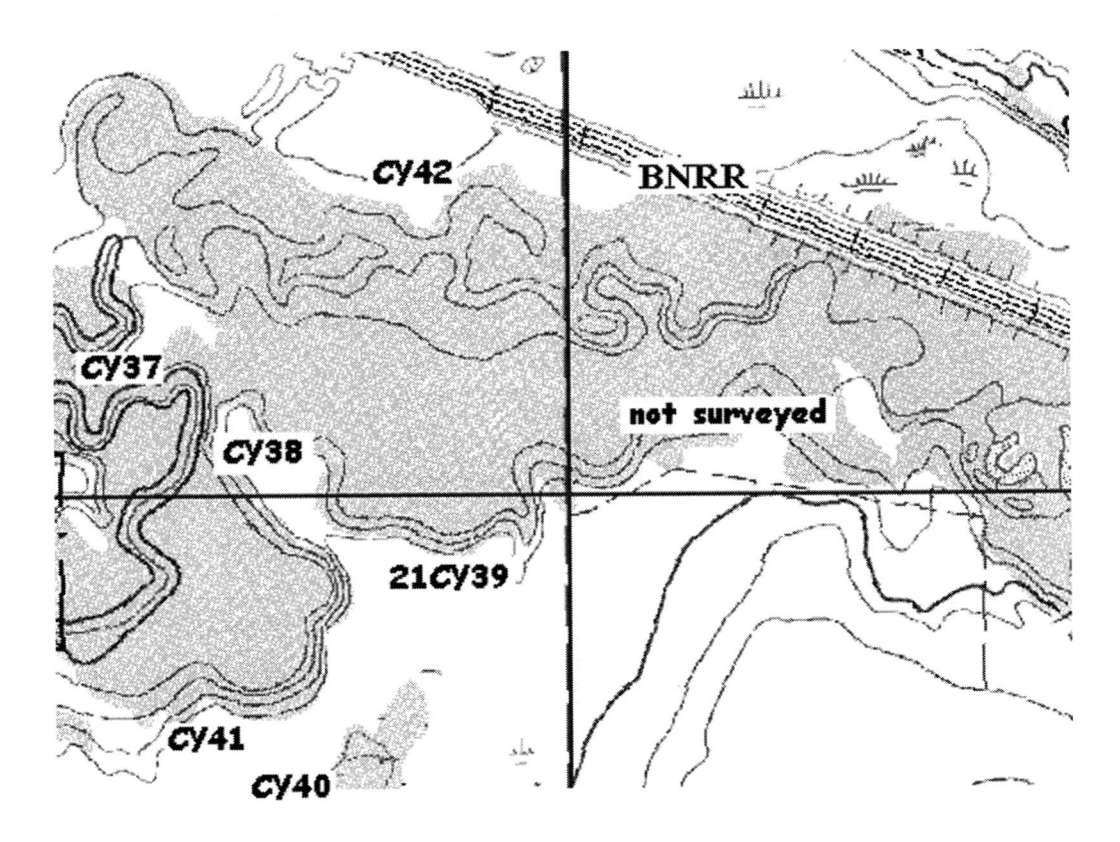

Figure 3. 21CY39 and nearby archeological sites.

strandlines or beach ridges of Lake Agassiz. To the east of the site, a prominent ridge rises about 15 m above the site surface. This is the summit of the local Lake Agassiz beach. Most local authorities regard this as the Campbell beach, abandoned about 9300 years ago (Bluemle 1977:52). The matrix in which the site is deposited may be a minor beach fronting this larger strandline, or it may be a terrace carved by the Buffalo River into outwash materials deposited on the shore of Lake Agassiz by the late-Pleistocene Buffalo River.

On the north edge of the site, the ground slopes sharply down to the floodplain about 10 m below. The site thus lies above the floodplain and some distance away from the river. However, its location on the edge of these uplands places it immediately adjacent to the river lowland, thus allowing the occupants of the site easy access to the riparian resources (see Fig. 4).

The soil of the site area is mapped as Lohnes coarse sandy loam (Jacobson 1982:42), although Soil Conservation field workers who visited the site in 1991 felt the soils were not typical of Lohnes. The loam at the site fines upward from a coarse bed of parent material, and may be described as a mollisol. The profile includes A1, A2, Bw and C horizons. The A and Bw horizons are leached; the C horizon is calcareous, producing a weak reaction. The solum (0 to 60 cm) is a zone of active faunalturbation, and numerous animal burrows may be seen in profiles.

Environment and Archaeology

These environmental features are important for understanding the natural setting of the site, but they are also relevant to understanding the disposition of the cultural assemblage. The relatively coarse sediment the soil is formed in, and the activity of burrowing animals, have obviously moved artifacts from their original place of deposition. Burrowing transports small artifacts both above and below the original occupation, and it tends to allow larger artifacts to sink lower in the profile over time as burrows collapse. Presumably burrowing does not entirely disrupt patterning, and the stratigraphic position of the high-

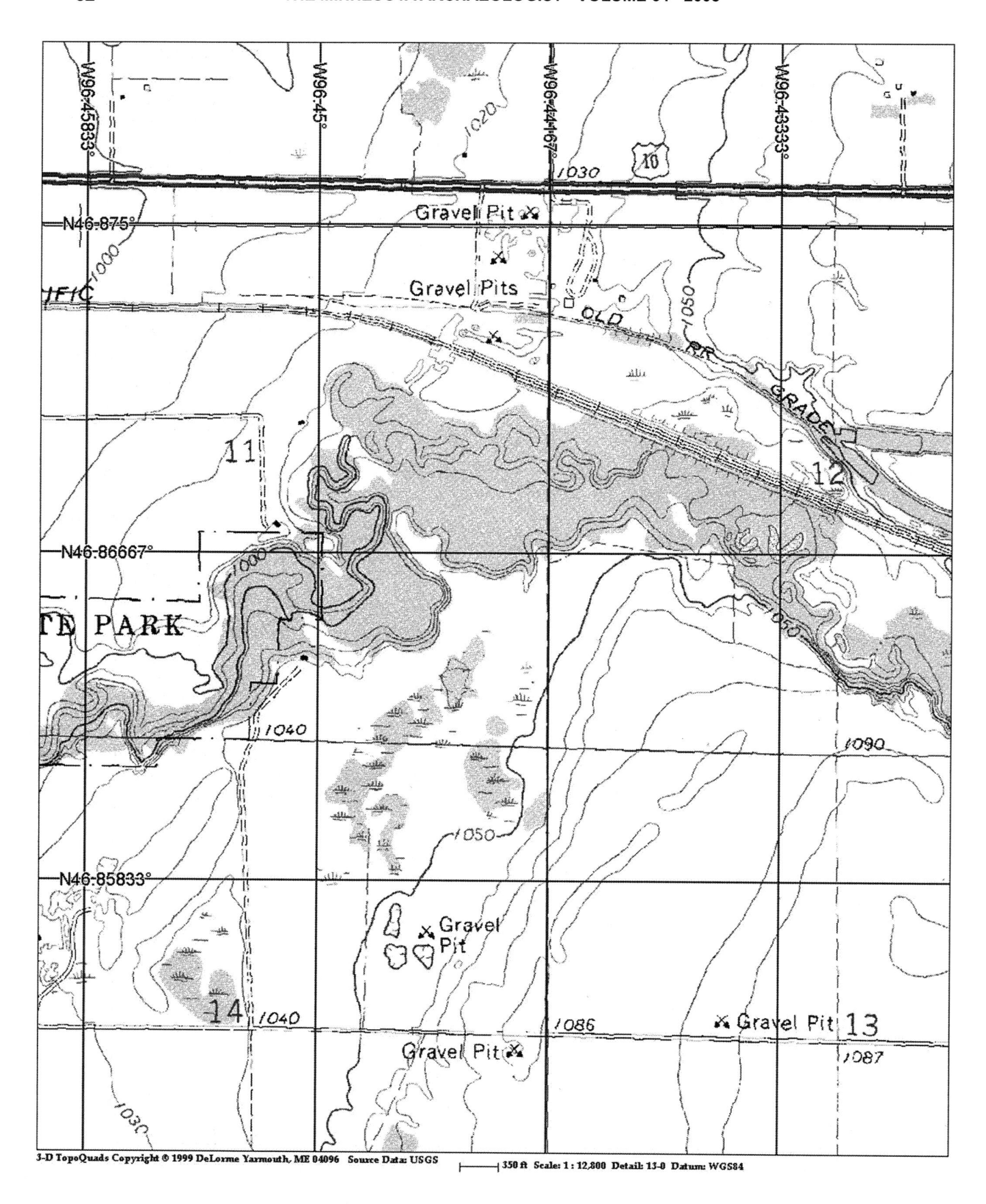

Figure 4. Topography of 21CY39.

Figure 5. View of 21CY39 to the north.

However, the presence of these features did aid in the identification of an occupation zone or living floor. For example, a disturbed hearth, with charcoal flecks and scattered fire-cracked rock, was found at a depth of about 25 cm. About 5 m distant from this and only slightly more deeply buried in the profile was the top of a refuse pit. This was obviously the living surface at the site when these cultural materials were deposited, since features such as these may be disturbed -- but not moved vertically through -- the profile.

While natural processes have heavily impacted the living floor; the soil pH in the B and C horizons is slightly elevated (Jacobson 1982:108), a feature typical of prairie soils. This condition has resulted in very good preservation of bone at the site, even though rodents have gnawed some of it. On the other hand, the thick mollisol found here has a very well developed A horizon that extends below the level of the occupation. The black soil color makes cultural disturbances in the subsoil very dif-

est artifact frequencies is regarded as a signature of the original occupation level. Plotting artifact and ecofact frequencies throughout the deposit indicates that the location of the original occupation surface was probably 20 to 35 cm below surface.

Of the three cultural features identified at the site, two were heavily disturbed by faunalturbation.

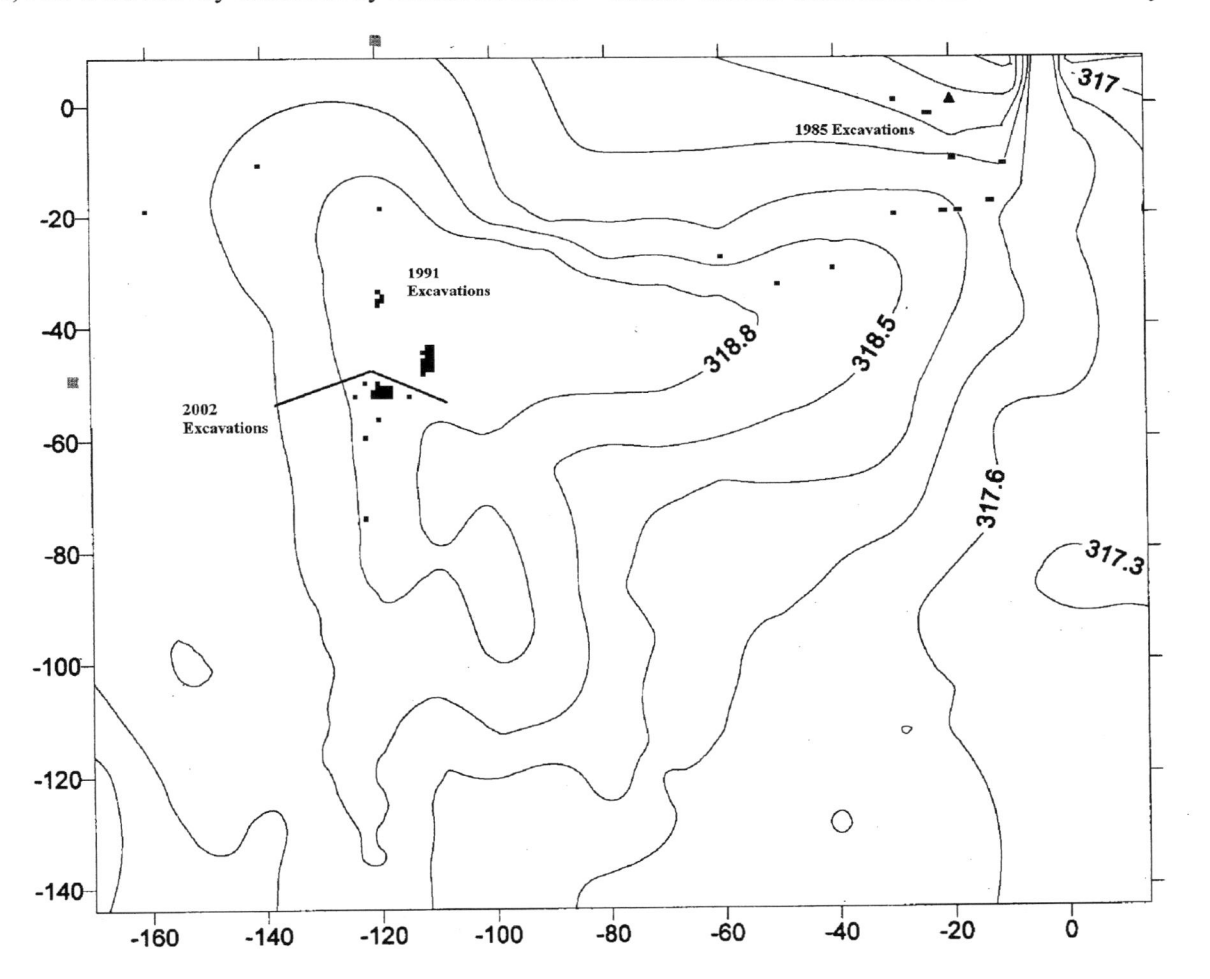

Figure 6. Excavations at 21CY39.

Figure 7. Soil profile showing beach or terrace sands,

ficult to identify. In fact, only a single feature was identified in the subsoil -- feature 2, a deep pit. Feature 1, in a slightly shallower position, was defined on the basis of rock and charcoal, and feature 4 on the basis of rock and artifacts. Dark staining of the subsoil, typically used in feature identification, was not involved in the definition of any features at the site. So while the rich prairie soil preserved bone, it probably masked some features that might otherwise have been recognized.

The tall grass prairie found in this part of the plains has sometimes been regarded as being less attractive to bison than the more nutrient rich short grasses of the western plains. While this may be accurate insofar as the productivity of individual grass plants is concerned, it misses the obvious point that the tall grass prairie had much more total forage available for bison. Bison were abundant on these northeastern plains grasslands in the early historic period. In 1800-1801, Alexander Henry reports enormous herds along the Red River from late summer through the winter months. One herd, which he states was in constant motion, took several days to pass by his camp (Coues 1897:65, 86-87, 99, 145, 150-151, 167). Henry also reports large numbers of black bears and many elk. Surprisingly, he makes little note of white-tailed deer, common in the area today.

The various roots, tubers, berries, seeds and greens that may be used for food were very likely used sparingly by the occupants of the site. 21CY39 does not have any of the characteristics of a permanent settlement. This is true even though the ceramics apparently contain phytoliths from maize, a domestic plant that must have been brought to this place. It is most likely that people came to this site to use the most abundant resource to be found here, and that was bison. Various other food resources could be obtained locally, but these were relatively sparse and would have required a great deal of acquisition time. The only animals found besides bison were turtle and hawk, as well as a very few clamshells. On the other hand, bison, if they were located, could be had in great numbers. From the remains found at the site, it would appear that this was the primary attraction for the Blackduck people who used this place.

Archaeological Work at 21CY39

A survey crew from MSUM discovered 21CY39 in May of 1982 (Michlovic 1982). A number of other sites were also located during this survey, all within

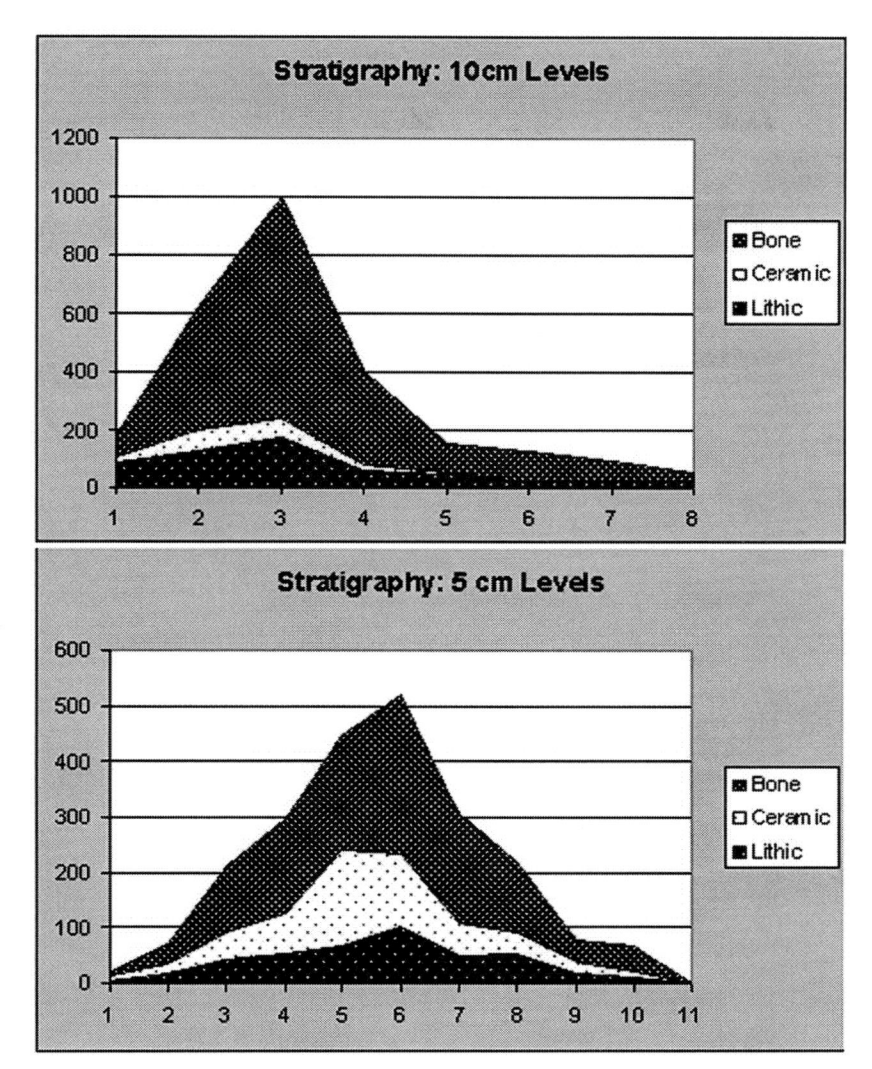

Figure 8. Cultural materials stratigraphy by 10 and 5 cm arbitrary levels, 21CY39.

the boundaries of the Regional Science Center property (Table 1, Fig. 3). At that time the Science Center property consisted of about 100 acres (Fig. 5). Although no dates were obtained for these sites, several diagnostic artifacts (ceramic rims) which were recovered demonstrate an affiliation with 21CY39, if not a direct connection. The materials recovered from these sites during survey, including 21CY39, are listed below.

The initial excavations in 1985 demonstrated the presence of subsurface cultural materials, provided profile views of the soil, and suggested that the site area had not been cultivated. This was later confirmed by soil scientists who visited the site, and by one informant who remembered the area as a pasture but never a cropland. Nine units were excavated during the 1985 field season, mostly in the eastern portion of the site. These units were 1 m² and 2 m². Arbitrary levels of 10 cm were used. Soil was screened through 1/4 inch mesh.

This work produced a total of 729 pieces of lithic material, a far greater amount of lithic material than recovered during either the 1991 or 2002 field seasons (Fig. 6, Table 2). Several tools and worked flakes are present in this assemblage. Two separate point fragments were found; however, neither could be used for typological classification. A single small piece of copper was also found. It is probably cultural, although it is not an artifact. The 1985 excavations recovered a small sample of ceramic material, totaling 201 sherds. All of this is grit tempered, and almost all is cordmarked. Surface treatment and tempering in these sherds is consistent with other Blackduck ceramic assemblages.

Table 1. Archaeological Survey Results in the Vicinity of 21CY39 (see Fig. 3)

Site	Materials Recovered
21CY37	1 biface fragment, 48 flakes, 1 Blackduck rim, 4 sherds, 111 bone fragments
21CY38	1 notched point (Middle Woodland?), 1 flake, 4 FCR, 1 sherd, 8 bone fragments (4 burnt)
21CY39	6 flakes, 1 Blackduck rim, 15 bone fragments
21CY40	20 flakes, 21 bone fragments
21CY41	1 core, 54 flakes
21CY42	1 point, 1 scraper, 1 biface, 1 core, 33 flakes, 35 bone fragments (3 burnt)

(FCR = fire cracked rock)

Table 2. Excavation Unit Size/Coordinates from Datum, 21CY39

$1 m^2$	$2 m^2$	
S30W20	S52W101	S32W99
S25W40	S53W95	S33W100
S30W60	S53W97	S46W90
S25W80	S53W98	S45W89
S30W100	S53W99	S47W89
S20W120	S53W100	S45W88
S10W140	S53W101	S48W90
S20W160	S53W105	S47W88
S43W90	S58W100	S43W88
S6E6	S62W103	S43W89
S30E80	S30W103	S20E4
S50W100	S18E5	
S50W104	S16E6	
S51W97	S14E5	
S51W98	S33W30	
S51W99	S20W10	
S51W100	S20E0	
S52W97	S10W5	
S52W98	S10E0	
S52W99	S6E5	
S52W100	N0E14	

Additional evidence for designating these ceramics as Blackduck Ware was provided by five rims. Three have cordwrapped-stick impressions on the lip. A total of 1,859 pieces of bone were recovered during the 1985 field season. Of this total 369 pieces are burned. Most of the faunal material is non-identifiable bone (1,441 pieces), although 48 pieces of bone are from large mammals, while 2 are from small mammals.

During the excavations in 1991, an additional 37 m^2 was excavated. This included several 1 m^2 test units along the tree line on the northern side of the site, and major block excavations at two loci in the center of the field containing the site. Both blocks were intended to expose a large area that might provide a view of the living floor at the site. Five-centimeter arbitrary levels were used, a change from the 1985 season when 10 cm levels were used. However, as in the previous season, 1/4 inch mesh was used to screen soil. The features encountered during 1991 were treated as discrete deposits. Each was plotted in situ and collected in its entirety. Soil matrix was floated for small artifacts and organic matter, and all size fractions were examined.

The major finds in 1991 included a sizable artifact collection of over 4,000 items related to the cultural deposit, consisting of 415 flakes, 937 potsherds, and over 2,700 bones and bone fragments. The cultural materials, although from different areas on the site, were essentially similar to those found in 1985. The raw materials in the lithic collection included Swan River Chert, Knife River Flint, Tongue River Silica, and a variety of quartz, quartzite, jasper, and miscellaneous fine-grained rocks such as rhyolite and siltstone. The ceramic collection was larger than that found in 1985, and included classic Blackduck rims and a large number of grit-tempered, cordmarked body sherds. The bone was almost entirely of large mammal remains, along with two claws from a large raptor, probably a red-tailed hawk. The identifiable mammal remains included 56 elements, and were all bison. These were almost exclusively leg fragments and teeth. Cut marks and spiral fractures indicate butchery at this location (Haury 1991).

Two features were identified in 1991; both appeared at a depth of about 25 cm. Feature 1 was a disturbed hearth with burnt bone, charcoal flecks, and fire-cracked rock. The feature was probably disturbed by rodents, which are very common in the area. Feature 2 was a pit filled with bison bone and Blackduck pottery. No charcoal was recovered in quantities sufficient for C-14 dating from either of the features. Both features rested on a level about 25 cm below the surface, and this depth is regarded as the living floor at the site. Cultural materials from above or below this depth were moved there by soil disturbing processes, mostly faunalturbation.

The 2002 excavations included 21 1-m² units. All units were excavated in 5 cm levels and 1/4 inch mesh screening was used. Many of the units were placed adjacent to one another in the vicinity of S50W100, and constituted a block excavation of about 15 m². This block was placed to the west of the 1991 block in the hope that some additional features might be identified to shed further light on the nature of the living floor at the site. Unfortunately, no real floor was observable in these units, although all of them yielded some artifacts and animal bone. The total recovery during 2002 included about 417 lithic items, 577 ceramic, and 1,237 animal bone fragments. Two side-notched points were also found, along with a few clamshell fragments and two pieces of turtle plastron or carapace. The pottery fragments from the units included some with a relatively thick coating of burned residue on the interior of the sherds. An analysis of the entire cultural assemblage from all three seasons at the site is presented below.

Two features were also recorded in the 2002 excavations. One of these was a stain, and one (Fea. 4) was an association of artifacts with cracked rock, interpreted to be a discard event. Feature 3, a light colored stain, was immediately below the sod and it probably was not cultural. Feature 4, along with features 1 and 2 (found in 1991), were all at about the same depth. They indicate a living surface with associated materials from 25 to 35 cm below the present surface. Only small amounts of charcoal were found in either of these. Although this charcoal was sufficient for AMS dating, the nearness of the features to the surface, and the widespread evidence of rodent disturbance, raised concerns about the possibility of intrusion from later, perhaps natural, events.

Stratigraphy

No natural depositional facies were identified in the profile of 21CY39. The solum is developed in a sandy matrix of terrace or beach deposits dating to the time of Lake Agassiz (before 9300 B.P.). The very thick A horizon, extending in some parts of the site to about 50 cm below the surface, suggests a long period of development. There is a gravel deposit at the base of the B horizon, about 90 cm deep; however, this is well below the cultural deposit (Fig. 7).

Recovery of cultural materials at 21CY39 was by 2 x 1 m and 1 x 1 m units, each excavated by arbitrary levels. A 10 cm level was used in 1985, while 5 cm levels were used in subsequent seasons. The results of this procedure are shown in Figure 8 and Table 3. On the basis of the stratigraphic distribu-

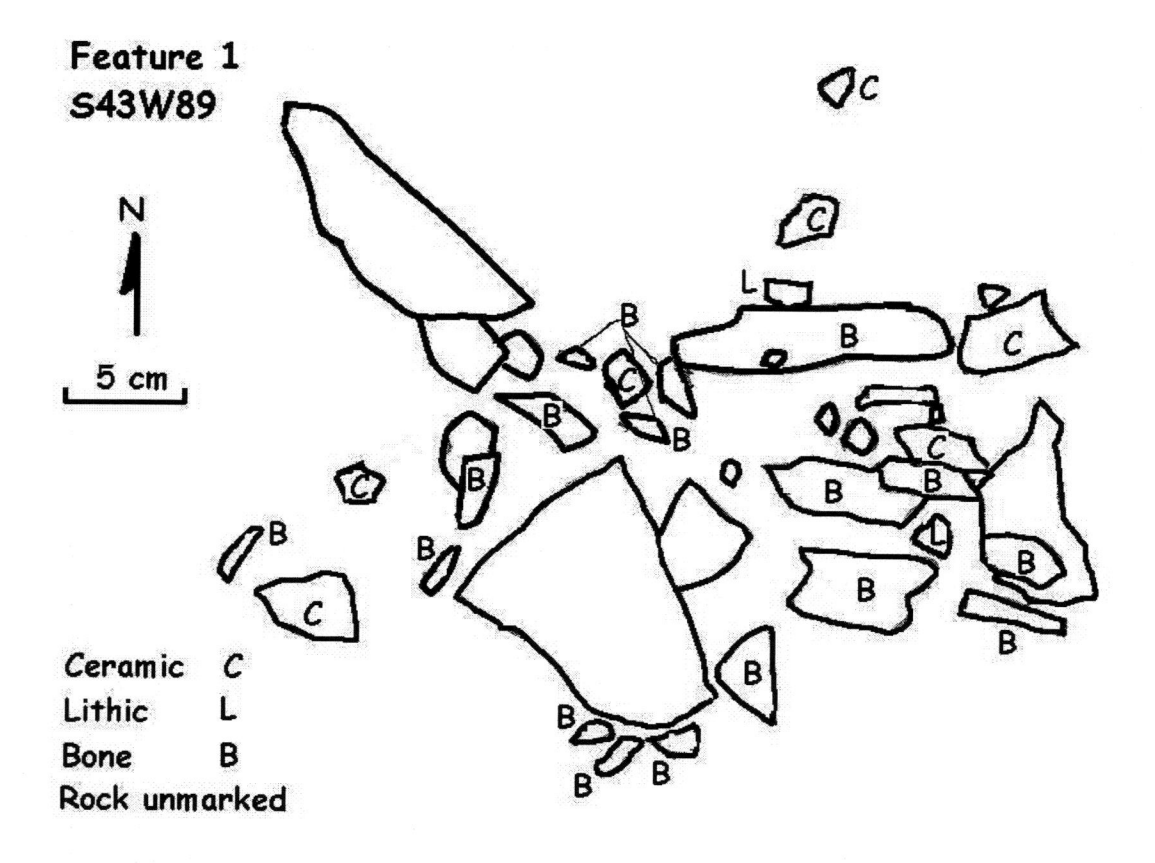

Figure 9. Feature 1 plan view, 21CY39.

tion of cultural materials, this is a single-component site. The occupational materials lie within a 30 cm horizon from 15 to 45 cm below the surface of the field. The results also show that in this naturally disturbed, near-surface cultural deposit there is no real difference in results produced by use of 5 and 10 cm recovery procedures. Both show a peak from 20 to 35 cm below surface. Five-centimeter levels show the peak at 25 to 30 cm, while 10 cm levels show the peak at 20 to 30 cm (Fig. 8). This would be on the living floor at the site as determined from features. The 5 cm levels excavated in 2002 show some small difference in the peak for ceramics as against lithic and bone materials. It is not clear that this is significant. A major operational difference between the two methods is that the 5 cm levels are more time consuming to excavate, generate a larger quantity of paper, and are more cumbersome to handle in the lab.

Living Floor

The living floor, or the surface on which people presumably lived, is identified as that portion of the profile where most of the artifacts were found, and which contained the identified features at the site. As already mentioned, the black A horizon obscures cultural disturbances in the upper 45 cm of the profile, which often show up as dark stains intruded into lighter-colored subsoil. Even so, two features were found during the 1991 season, and one additional feature during the 2002 work. These were defined at about 25 to 35 cm below the surface (feature 3 could not be regarded as cultural). Feature 1 is considered a disturbed hearth, feature 2 a pit, and feature 4 possibly a discard event. No charcoal fragments large enough for dating were found in this feature. Figure 9 shows feature 1. Figure 10 illustrates a por-

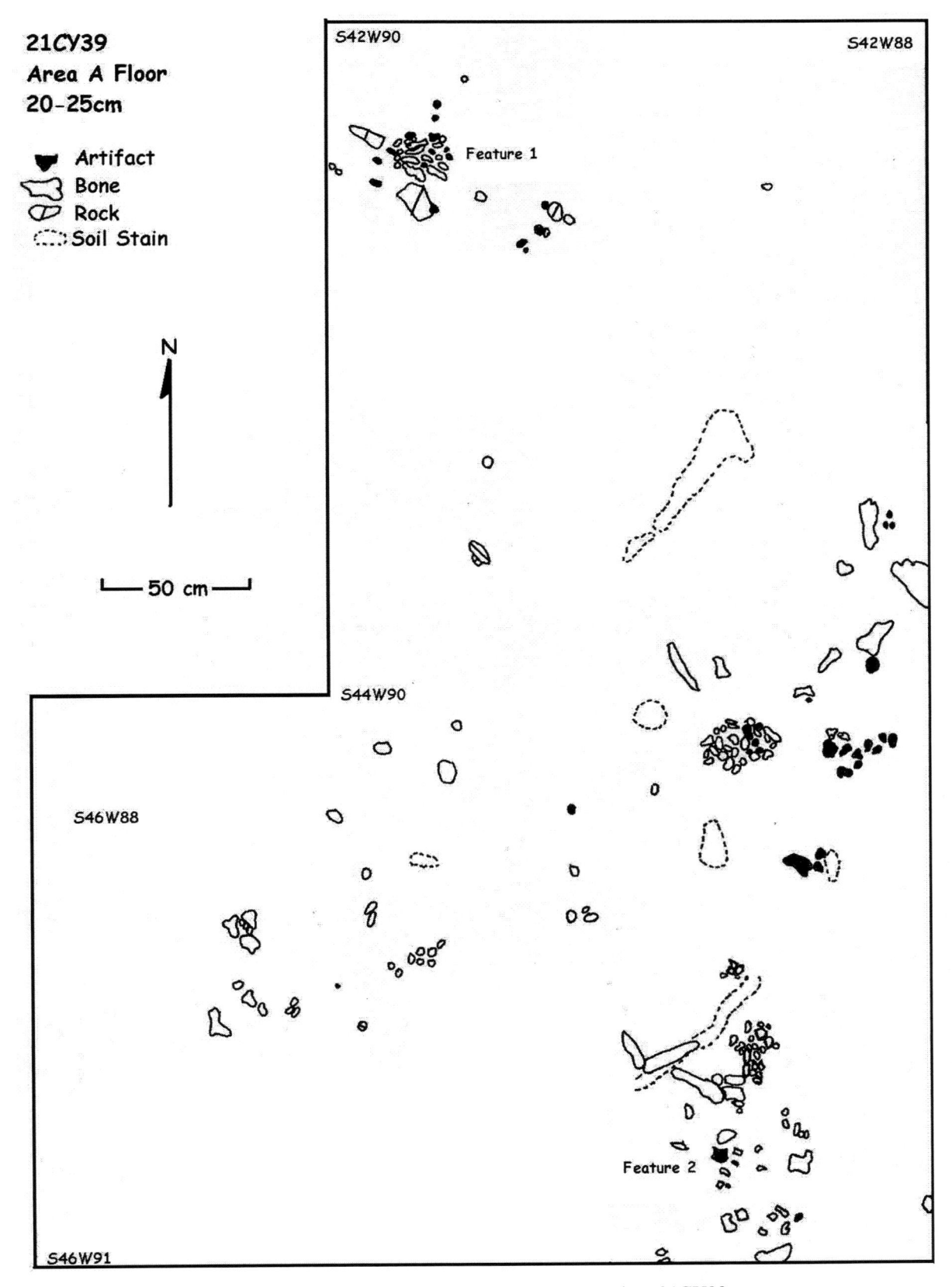

Figure 10. Living floor in main block excavation, 21CY39.

Figure 11. Feature 2 at 35 cm, 21CY39.

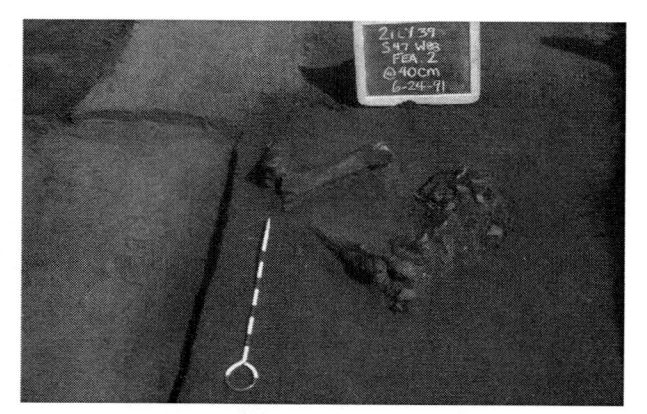

Figure 12. Feature 2 at 45 cm, 21CY39.

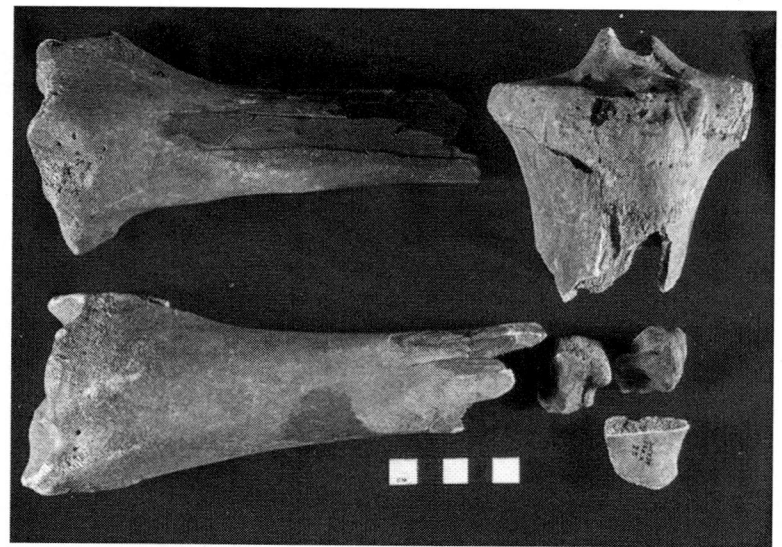

Figure 13. Bison bone from feature 2, 21CY39.

tion of the 1991 excavations where features 1 and 2 were located. Figures 11 and 12 show feature 2 as it became visible at about 30 cm, a point in the profile where the lighter-colored B-horizon soils at this location allow feature definition. It is shown again at 45 cm as the pit contents were being exposed.

The presence of cracked rock, bone fragments, and charcoal flecks in features at CY39 is no surprise. Almost anywhere people settle will have evidence of fire. Somewhat more surprising is the pit feature (no. 2). This pit extended from about 30 cm below the surface to about 70 cm. There is no good reason to suppose that disposing of trash in pits would be a priority in a hunters' camp. In fact, refuse pits might have originally been dug for food or material storage and used for refuse only after their original purpose was exhausted. If pits for storage were actually dug, it would indicate a more sustained use of this site than might otherwise be assumed.

Feature 1. S43W89, 22-25 cm below surface (see Figs. 9-10)

This feature consisted of a concentration of bone, burnt bone, cracked and burnt rock, potsherds, lithic debris (scant), and a few flecks of charcoal. It appears to be a disturbed hearth, probably burrowed through by rodents. The matrix was floated, but almost no organic material other than bone was recovered.

Feature 2. S47W88, 32-72 cm below surface (see Figs. 11-12)

This was a pit with a large quantity of bone, including hundreds of fragments and many larger fragments that were identifiable. All the identifiable elements were bison. Ceramics were also present, including many sherds from probably three Blackduck vessels. A few items of lithic debris were also recovered. Flotation did not provide any additional material except for

Table 3. 10 and 5 cm Arbitrary Level Recovery, 21CY39

	1985 10 cm Recovery					1991/2002 5 cm Recovery			
	Lithic	Ceram	Bone	Total		Lithic	Ceram	Bone	Total
0-10	84	23	72	179	0-5	11	35	59	105
10-20	130	68	422	620	5-10	49	85	136	270
20-30	174	70	755	999	10-15	84	188	249	521
30-40	62	16	327	405	15-20	97	245	551	893
40-50	43	12	96	151	20-25	149	484	1381	2014
50-60	21	2	101	124	25-30	156	261	511	928
60-70	28	1	62	91	30-35	86	108	414	608
70-80	21	0	29	50	35-40	99	62	398	559
					40-45	58	30	178	266
	Total			2619	45-50	38	15	109	162
					50-55	0	0	11	11
					55-60	3	0	20	23
					60-65	2	1	13	16
					65-70	0	0	8	8
					Total				**6384**

small bone fragments. Feature 2 in profile is more or less bowl-shaped.

Feature 4. S52W100, 37 cm below surface

This is a very light scatter of cultural material on the same surface. It consisted of a large fire-cracked rock, several potsherds, and two animals bones in close association. No evidence of rodent disturbance was noted. This was probably nothing more that a cluster of living debris discarded from an activity area nearby.

C-14 Date

After the 2002 field season, a sample of more than 500 g of bone from feature 2 was submitted for C-14 analysis. These were all unidentifiable fragments. The identifiable bone found in this feature, however, was entirely bison, and the pieces submitted for the date were probably the same. The sample required collagen extraction, and it was analyzed using standard techniques with a scintillation spectrometer. The results provide a date for the living floor on which the features rest and from which most of the cultural material was recovered. The age of the site is based on this single C-14 assay, which is consistent with the diagnostic artifacts found here. The date is listed below with lab data.

Beta 169772
Bone collagen date: collagen extraction with alkali
Date: 920 $\pm$ 40
13C/12C= -15.6 $^{0/00}$
2sigma calibrated date: A.D. 890-1020 (1060-930 B.P.)

This date situates the site in the earlier part of the Late Woodland period in the Upper Midwest and northeastern plains. The date is consistent with dates for diagnostic materials found at the site, including ceramics and projectile points. Archaeologists who have studied Blackduck pottery seem to be of two opinions. One is that Blackduck has an early and late phase, the earlier being more widespread, and the late phase being restricted to the Rainy River area (Lugenbeal 1979:23). Others (e.g., Lenius and Olinyk 1990:78) move late Blackduck ceramics to the Rainy River composite, presumably dating to about A.D. 1100 to 1400. The date for 21CY39 fits into the middle of the range for Blackduck as defined by Lenius and Olinyk. The date is clearly consistent with the diagnostic ceramics found at the

Table 4. Bison Remains, 21CY39

Element	#	Part	Side	Age	Modification
femur	1	distal	left	subadult	spiral fracture
femur	1	prox	-	-	-
tibia	1	prox	left	subadult	spiral
tibia	1	distal	right	-	spiral
radius	1	prox	left	adult	spiral
radius	1	distal	right	adult	spiral
scapula	1	-	right	adult	cutmarks
scapula	1	-	right	adult	cutmarks
humerus	1	distal	left	adult	spiral
metapodial	3	distal	-	-	-
metapodial	1	prox	-	-	-
metacarpal	2	prox	left (1)	-	spiral
metacarpal	1	distal	right	-	spiral
calcaneum	1	-	right	-	cutmarks
carpal/tarsal	8	-	-	-	-
phalanx 1	5	-	-	-	spiral (1)
phalanx 2	6	-	-	-	spiral (1)
phalanx 3	2	-	-	-	-
vertebrae	2	-	-	fetal	-
vertebrae	1	-	-	-	-
rib	1	-	left	adult	cutmarks
rib	8	-	-	-	cutmarks, spiral (2)
unknown limb	3	-	-	-	spiral (2) cutmark (1)
skull frag	1	-	-	-	-

site, and conforms with the presence of small side-notched points, which are common on the plains after about A.D. 700 (Greiser 1994:43).

Phytoliths

Robert Thompson, University of Minnesota, examined a sample of 15 sherds for the presence of phytoliths in residues on the pottery from 21CY39. The extraction and identification of phytoliths from cooking residues on pottery has been reported in several previous studies involving assemblages in both North and South America (e.g., Hart, Thompson and Brumback 2003).

Phytoliths are abundant in the residues from CY39 and were removed from two sherds, both from Area A, the open area excavation around feature 2 (see Fig. 10). One of these sherds was found in feature 2, the other in an adjacent unit. These phytoliths were compared to residues of maize, *Hordeum*, *Setaria*, and *Zizania*. A detrended correspondence analysis shows that the phytolith samples from CY39 are maize. A second detrended correspondence analysis compared residues with only the maize comparative samples and focused on morphology alone (leaving out the size data). This shows that both residue samples are like midcontinental (flint) corn samples from prehistoric sites, and unlike both the northeast and dent types of maize. The phytoliths from this site most resemble those described today as "Mandan corn."

Fauna

Animal remains were the most abundant material at 21CY39. A substantial sample of the 1985 and 1991 collection, much of it from feature 2, was submitted for identification. These were examined for species and body part representation, evidence for modification, and overall condition of the bone. Of the 2,989 pieces of bone reviewed for further examination, species identification proved possible for only 32 (Haury 1991). Thirty of these are bison (*Bison bison*) elements. The remaining two were ugual phalanges (claws) of genus *Buteo* (hawk). Sixty-five additional elements were presumed to be from some sort of large mammal/ungulate. Since all the identifiable ungulate bone is bison, the remainder of large mammal remains is most likely also bison (Fig. 13).

During the 2002 excavations, several additional bison bones were recovered. These include one radius/ulna fragment, three phalanges, one metapodial fragment, and several fragments of bovid teeth. A few clamshell fragments and two turtle carapace or plastron fragments were also found.

Using standard procedures, Haury calculated from scapulae that the people at 21CY39 used at least two adult bison. Unfused portions of at least four elements represent a juvenile bison. Fetal bison remains are also present, evidenced by three elements. At least four bison of varying ages were therefore used.

Some of the elements show signs of processing. Among the 97 elements submitted for examination, 16 have green stick or spiral fractures, a possible indication of marrow extraction activities. One of these exhibits impact marks from the fracturing blow. Two bones with spiral fractures also show butchering marks, and five others have cutmarks but exhibit no spiral fractures.

Almost all of the 30 identified bison elements that were recovered from 21CY39 are leg bones. Most of these are carpals/tarsals and phalanges. There is one bison skull fragment and many of the rib and longbone fragments are presumed to be bison as well (Table 4).

This distribution is interpreted to be the result of cultural activity. Hunters are often unable to retrieve all the useful portions of a kill back to their main camp, due to the distance and labor involved (especially if the animal is a large one). In these cases, they select for transport those portions of the animal that yield the highest amount of meat to the least amount of unusable weight. Limbs are usually selected in such situations for this reason. Though the excavations exposed only a limited area of the site, it appears from bone throughout the deposit that the inhabitants of 21CY39 were practicing this form of selection. It is a pattern consistent with other Blackduck sites where bison is heavily exploited. The Stott site (D1Ma-1) in southwestern Manitoba has a similar distribution, although overall bone frequencies are much higher. The investigators of D1Ma-1 note that the "proportional recovery figures can be explained if some bones were smashed beyond recognition, or if the bison were processed initially at the kill site, leaving behind certain elements" (Badertscher, Roberts and Zoltai 1987:132). Obviously, many bones at CY39 were smashed beyond recognition. However, transport selection is regarded as the primary reason for the representation of bison body parts at this site.

Much of the bone analyzed also reflects the depositional and post-depositional conditions at the site. Twelve bones were rodent gnawed, and 16 had other signs of weathering, such as exfoliation of the bone cortex or pitting and erosion of the bone surface. Root etching is found on nine. Eleven others show damage described only as post-depositional.

The collection of bone provides a picture of some of the activities that must have occurred at 21CY39. At least some of the activity at the site was in late winter/early spring, prior to calving. The bison fetal bone indicates this. The turtle fragments and clamshell suggest that some of the activity took place during a time when people would have had access to aquatic and semi-aquatic foods. This is not inconsistent with a hypothesized use of the site during the spring; however, a later time in the year, late spring or summer, would be a more likely time for use of mussels and turtle.

The faunal remains obviously indicate big game hunting as the focus of activity at this site. However, animals were not killed at, or probably even very near, this site. The representation of elements is heavily biased toward limb fragments. Much of the bone from the bison did not make it from the kill to this site. Presumably, this is because distance was a factor. In addition, a small number of bison could account for the bones from the site. It is possible that these people were not involved in massive drives and kills. Animals were, perhaps, culled from the great herds as they were needed.

The condition of the bone, particularly the exfoliated surfaces, pitting and surface erosion, suggest

Table 5. Ceramics, 21CY39

Type	Cordmarked	Smooth	Other	Indeterminate	Total
Number	616	27	4	1376	2023
Weight in g.	740	38	14	384	1176

that the bone was exposed on the ground surface for some time prior to burial. On this elevated position, burial of the site materials would have been slow. Extended exposure to the elements would allow time for the erosion of the bone collection, and perhaps also partially account for the deteriorated condition of the living floor in general.

Ceramics

The ceramic collection from the site consists of 2,023 sherds weighing 1.176 kg. The average sherd weighs about 0.58 g, indicating the small size of most of the pottery. This small size may be related to breakage due to rough handling or high-temperature cooking, or to trampling of the sample after it had been abandoned on the ground. Breakage might also be due to post-depositional processes such as animal burrowing. The condition of the bone and potsherds, most of which were broken into small pieces, may be a result of people trampling over surface litter during repeated uses of the site.

Basic quantitative data on the ceramics may be seen in Table 5. All of this pottery is tempered with crushed rock or sand in all cases where temper is visible in the sherd breaks. Crushed rock was by far the most common temper type. Since variability in temper was not observed, this trait was not used in the ceramic study. Although "indeterminate" is the largest category, my impression is that most of these very small sherds were grit tempered and cordmarked. In the pottery analysis, most sherds smaller than about 1 cm diameter were placed in the indeterminate category.

The ceramic collection was divided into 13 identifiable vessels, some well represented with rims and body fragments, others represented by only a couple sherds that were distinguished from other vessels on the basis of some distinctive surface feature. Vessel counts were made by laying the collection of all sherds larger than 1 cm on a table and comparing them for similar features. Occasionally, somewhat similar sherds from very distant units were defined as separate vessels.

Vessel 1 (Fig. 14)

6 rims and 13 sherds, S47W88, S45W89, feature 2, 20 to 60 cm below surface. Crushed rock temper, angular quartz and feldspar up to 3.5 mm diameter. Body is cordmarked, section is blocky to slightly laminar. 6.5 to 9.5 mm thick (body and lip). Yellowish brown color (10YR 5/4). Everted rim, thickened lip, flat. Cordwrapped-object decorations on lip and rim (exterior and interior), punctates made with same implement, coarse combing extends down entire rim. Estimated vessel diameter at orifice is 20 cm.

Vessel 2 (Fig. 15)

1 rim and 70 sherds. S47W88, S46W90, S45W88, S47W89, feature 2, 5 to 45 cm below surface
Crushed rock temper. Body is vertical cordmarking, section is blocky to laminar. 4 to 6 mm thick. Dark brown (7.5YR 4/2). Rim everted, lip beveled out. Punctates at 3.5 cm intervals immediately below lip. Many of the small sherds from feature 2 probably belong to this vessel. Estimated diameter 20 cm.

Vessel 3 (Fig. 16)

2 rims, 5 near rims with decoration, several neck fragments. S20E4, S18E5, 5 to 35 cm below surface. Crushed rock temper, sparse. Surface cordmarked and decorated near rim, section is laminar to slightly blocky. Rim is 1 cm thick, neck 6.2 mm. Dark yellowish brown to dark grayish brown (10YR 4/4 to 10YR 4/2). Wedge shaped rim, everted, lip beveled out. Decoration is cordwrapped object, punctuates, at 8 mm intervals. This is a classic Blackduck vessel with the typical pattern of oblique cordwrapped-object impressions extending down from the lip and horizontal cordwrapped-object im-

pressions with punctuates. Residue is thick on the sherd interiors. Estimated diameter is 22 cm at vessel orifice.

Vessel 4 (Fig. 17)

1 rim, 2 body sherds. S20E0, S10W5, 10 to 70 cm below surface. No visible temper. Smooth surface, section is laminar to blocky. Thickness 5 mm. Light brownish gray (10 YR 6/2). Rim straight with flat lip. Very short oblique cordwrapped-object impression on the rim interior. The paste is different from all other pottery at the site, with a chalky feel to it.

Vessel 5 (Fig. 17)

1 decorated body sherd, 3 undecorated sherds. S53W99, 20 to 25 cm below surface. Crushed-rock temper, up to 2.5 mm diameter. Smooth surface, blocky to laminar section. 5.5 to 6.5 mm thick. Dark grayish brown (10YR 4/2). One sherd has an exterior boss. Body sherds are large enough to allow an estimate of 14 cm for a vessel diameter; however, it is not known which dimension is measured.

Vessel 6 (Fig. 18)

5 rims, 1 body sherd. S53W98, S53W99, S52W99, 10 to 30 cm below surface. Crushed rock temper. Cordmarked surface, blocky section. 5 to 6 mm thick. Dark grayish brown (10YR 4/2). Residue on the exterior of the rim. Too small for diameter estimate.

Vessel 7 (Fig. 19)

1 rim. S53W100, 40 to 45 cm below surface. Temper is fine crushed rock (grit) with a few larger temper fragments. Surface is cordmarked, section is blocky to laminar. 4.5 mm thickness. Dark grayish brown-yellow colors (10YR 4/2 to 7/6). Rim is slightly everted with a flat to slightly beveled lip.

Figure 14. Vessel 1, 21CY39.

Figure 15. Vessel 2, 21CY39.

There are very shallow cordwrapped-object impressions on the lip, and combing begins about 1 cm below the lip. Some residue below the lip on the exterior rim.

Vessel 8 (Fig. 20)

2 rims and numerous small sherds. S43W89, S45W88, S47W88, S46W90, S43,W88, S45W89, 10 to 35 cm. below surface. Crushed-rock temper with many shiny micaceous fragments. Surface is cordmarked, section is laminar to slightly blocky.

Figure 16. Vessel 3, 21CY39.

Figure 17. Vessel 4 (upper two sherds), Vessel 5 below, 21CY39.

3.5 to 6.0 mm thick. Light yellowish brown, brown, dark grayish brown (10YR 6/4 to 4/2). Rim probably everted (based on neck fragment), lip flattened on small rim fragment. Decoration is cordwrapped-object impressions on lip only. This is the third vessel identified from the vicinity of feature 2. This vessel is most like vessel number 2. Some of the body sherds assigned to this vessel may belong to vessel 2 and vice versa, but the rims are different. Diameter estimate is 20 cm.

Vessel 9

11 body sherds, no rims or decorated pieces. S20W10, S10W5, 10 to 50 cm. below surface. Crushed-rock temper. Cordmarked, section is blocky to laminar. 4.5 to 5.5 mm thick. Brown to very dark brown (10YR 4/3 to 3/2). These sherds are all from a dark colored, cordmarked vessel. Most of the cordmarkings are distinct, but smoothed over in some spots.

Vessel 10 (Fig. 21)

2 small sherds, 1 near-rim. S10W5, 10 to 20 cm below surface. Crushed-rock temper with many black mineral inclusions. Very fine cording on the surface, blocky in section. 4.1 to 5.8 mm thick. Brown (7.5YR 5/4). One sherd has a single row of shallow cordwrapped-object impressions. These two small sherds have a distinctive color and fine cordmarking that serve to define them as a separate vessel. No diameter estimate possible.

Vessel 11

About 30 sherds, all from a vessel body, no rims. S20E4, S18E5, 5 to 50 cm below surface. Crushed-rock temper (granite?). Cordmarked surface and blocky section. 5.5 to 6.0 mm thick. Grayish brown to very dark brown (10YR 5/2 to 2/2). Some sherds

Figure 18. Vessel 6, 21CY39.

Figure 19. Vessel 7, 21CY39.

Figure 20. Vessel 8, 21CY39.

Figure 21. Vessel 10, 21CY39.

Figure 22. Vessel 13, 21CY39.

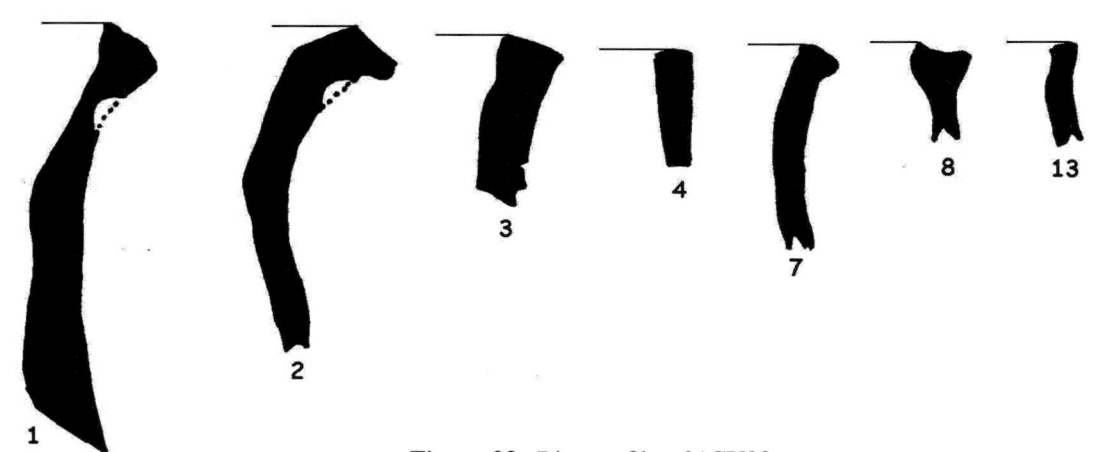

Figure 23. Rim profiles, 21CY39.

from this vessel have been refitted. Diameter estimate based on refit sherds is 12 to 16 cm.

Vessel 12

12 body sherds. S30W100, S10W140, S20W120, 5 to 20 cm below surface. Very small crushed-rock temper. Cordmarked surface, laminar section. 2.5 to 4.5 mm thick. Dark gray to yellowish brown in color (10YR 4/1 to 5/4). Possibly more than one vessel is represented here, since the sherds come from units somewhat distant from each other. No diameter estimate is possible.

Vessel 13 (Fig. 22)

1 rim. S6E6 10 to 20 cm below surface. Crushed rock temper, small sized, sparse. Smooth surface, laminar in section. 4.3 mm thick. Light yellowish brown (10YR 6/4). Slightly everted rim, flat lip. One interior rim/lip tool impression, oblique from the lip. No diameter estimate possible.

If we consider only the identifiable sherd sample, about 95 percent are cordmarked and less than 5 percent are smoothed. This is one reason the site is regarded as only Late Woodland, since cordmarking is so common on Late Woodland, as against Middle Woodland or Plains Village ceramics. Furthermore,

Figure 24. Small unidirectional cores, 21CY39.

Figure 25. Projectile points and fragments, 21CY39.

Figure 26. Bifaces and fragments, 21CY39.

Figure 27. Scrapers, 21CY39.

Figure 28. Above, 2 gravers, awl, denticulate; below, utilized flake, spokeshave; 21CY39.

cordmarking is typical of Blackduck pottery, which is easily the best represented ware in the rim and decorated sherd sample at the site. At least three of the 13 identified vessels have smooth surfaces (nos. 4, 5, and 13); however, the three are represented by a total of only seven sherds. One of these vessels (no. 5) features a single boss. Bossing is found as a minor decorative element on Blackduck pottery (Lugenbeal 1979:27).

The smooth surface on vessel 5 might dictate classification as Laurel or Malmo, both of which are Middle Woodland wares in Minnesota. The other smooth-surfaced vessel fragments are too small to classify. In fact, vessels 4 and 13 may be from cordmarked vessels on which the upper portion of the vessels were smoothed over. The only identified vessel for which we may be certain that the body was smoothed is vessel 5.

Given this information, 21CY39 could be classified as either multicomponent or single component. If the smooth-surfaced ceramics are accepted as a different ware from the Blackduck at the site, defining at least two components is warranted. However, the only properly identified ceramic ware at the site is Blackduck; all of the smooth-surfaced vessels are too fragmentary to classify. It is possible that the smoothed vessels are nothing more than anomalous vessels within the Blackduck assemblage. The site exhibits only a single stratigraphic peak in materials frequency, which suggests a single component. Spatial data from the site shows Blackduck pottery in the main excavation near S47W88, and at S53W100, and also in the eastern site area around S20E5. Cordmarked body sherds that are consistent with Blackduck are also found commonly in the test units extending across the northern part of the site to W120. If there is more than one component to this site, it is difficult to find sufficient diagnostic pottery to characterize it, and it cannot be located spatially or stratigraphically in the site matrix. For these reasons it seems safest to regard the site as simply a

Table 6. Lithic Debris Raw Materials, 21CY39

Material	SRC	RRC	KRF	TRS	Qx	Qzite	Chalced	Other	Total
#	498	294	172	62	49	17	30	170	1292
%	39	23	13	5	4	1	2	13	100

Size Grade   G1 = 5%   G2 = 23%   G3 = 65%   G4 = 7%

Table 7. Lithic Manufacturing Categories, 21CY39

		#	# with Cortex
Cores	Unidirectional	3	2
	Multidirectional	2	1
	Bipolar	3	0
	Fragments	33	18
Flaking Debris	Core Reduction	44	23
	Thinning	876	138
	Pressure	68	3
	Blades	5	2
	Bipolar	1	1
Shatter		206	52

Blackduck site. The definition of another component at the site must depend on future discoveries.

Of those vessels with enough of a rim (Fig. 23) present to estimate orifice diameter, the measured values average 18.33 cm on six vessels. Mean orifice diameter on a large sample of vessels from the Smith site is 21.2 cm, but the mode is 30 cm (Lugenbeal 1979:26). At 21CY39, on the other hand, the mode is 20 cm. From this limited collection, it appears that the vessels at CY39 are smaller than those found at some of the major Blackduck sites in the lake-forest area. This might indicate smaller social groups cooking meals in more modest sized vessels.

Another aspect of the ceramic collection is vessel wall thickness. Lugenbeal (1979:26) reports average vessel wall thickness on Blackduck ceramics of about 4.0 mm. The vessels at CY39 are somewhat thicker on average. Vessels 1 through 3, all good Blackduck, have body sherds of 6.5, 4.0, and 6.2 mm thickness if the rim measurements are left out. Vessel 7, also Blackduck, is 4.5 mm. Other vessels range from 3.5 mm to 5.75 mm in thickness. Thick-walled vessels are normally regarded as more resistant to mechanical stress, while thin-walled vessels are believed to be more resistant to thermal stress (Rice 1987:227-228). In other words, thick-walled vessels are more resistant to breakage when struck or struck against something, while thin-walled vessels are more likely to break when struck, but less likely to crack when heated to high temperatures. Perhaps the relatively thick-walled vessels at CY39 were meant for efficient transport rather than for heat efficiency. It is also possible that thickness figures are simply normal variation and not different enough from averages to have functional significance. The vessels are globular, although this is known from only a few cases where refits made body shapes apparent. Rim shapes (Fig. 23) are everted to straight. This is consistent with Late Woodland pottery in general, and Blackduck in particular.

Lithics

The lithic collection from 21CY39 is somewhat smaller than the ceramic sample in quantity. It consists of 1,333 pieces of lithic debris and cores, in addition to 29 tools, tool fragments and utilized or worked pieces. Various raw materials are represented in this collection, including Swan River Chert, Red River Chert, Tongue River Silica, Knife River Flint, quartz, quartzite, chalcedony, Grand Meadow Chert, jasper, several other minor lithic raw material types, and a single piece of copper.

Many of these material types are found in local glacial till, exposed a few miles east of the site, and in Lake Agassiz beach deposits on which the site is situated. These include Swan River Chert, Red River Chert, jasper, quartz, quartzite, occasionally Tongue River Silica, and even small pieces of Knife River Flint (Table 6). Undoubtedly, most or even all of the Knife River Flint at site 21CY39 is exotic and derives from the Knife River quarries in western North Dakota. It is true that occasional pieces of Knife River flint are found in glacial till in the eastern Dakotas, but these are normally very small cobbles and pebbles (Gregg 1987). It is difficult to imagine making tools the size of those found at this site from such small cores. Two other clearly exotic materials are Grand Meadow Chert, which probably has its origin in the Grand Meadow Chert quarry in southeast Minnesota, and copper from the Lake Superior basin or some immediately adjacent area. Copper and Grand Meadow Chert were represented by only debris. Tongue River Silica is found locally, although pieces I have found in the Lake Agassiz region are not of very high quality. The imported raw materials at 21CY39 comprise about 15 percent of the lithic sample. The exotic materials were derived from a catchment area extending from west of the Missouri River to Lake Superior.

Analysis of the lithic debris from the site included size-grading flakes in screens of one inch, one-half inch, and one-quarter inch. Since quarter-inch screening was used to recover material during all three seasons, the size grade smaller than quarter inch could not be used, as is typically the case in size grading studies (cf. Andrefsky 1998:128 ff). In spite of this shortcoming, it is clear from the frequencies of debris in size grade-classes that the larger size grade is relatively abundant at the site. Size grading suggests that all of the major raw materials at the site were processed in roughly the same way. Overall, 5 percent of the lithics are in category G-1 (larger than 1 inch). This, taken along with the presence of core fragments and large primary core reduction flakes in the sample, indicate that some early-stage reduction occurred at the site. On the other hand, most of the debris would be classified as one or another type of thinning flake, and some are probably pressure flakes from carefully controlled edge finishing. Most of the core fragments are Swan River Chert or other local materials. Only about a dozen very thin, small flakes, however, represent the imported Grand Meadow Chert, possibly from a single episode of tool finishing or refurbishing.

Lithic flaking debris was divided into various categories under the major headings of cores, flakes and shatter. Each of these categories was subdivided, and cortex flakes in each category were also counted. This data is presented in Table 7. About 18 percent of the total contains cortex, reflecting a stage of reduction involving the original surface of the cobble. About 3 percent of the total are cores (Fig. 24) or core fragments, and another 16 percent are shatter, that is, lithic debris lacking striking platforms, dorsal/ventral features, or bulbar features. The remaining 81 percent are flakes. The relatively large representation of cores, core reduction flakes (relatively large, thick flakes that appear to come from an early stage of working the core) and shatter suggests that lithic procurement and tool manufacturing probably took place at this site. The large representation of thinning flakes (ordinary flakes, flake fragments, non-blades and pressure flakes) indicates various stages of reduction and tool preparation. The pressure flakes (about 5% of the total sample) may indicate tool finishing, controlled edging of tools and tool maintenance.

Artifacts

The lithic collection includes 29 tools and broken tools. This includes one hammer, nine projectile points and point fragments, seven bifaces and fragments, eight scraper and scraper fragments, one spokeshave, two gravers, one awl, and one utilized flake. These are described below (see Figs. 25-28).

Artifact 1. Projectile point

Swan River Chert, S53W101, 20 to 25 cm bs. 20.5 x 14.2 x 4.2 mm, edge angles 25 to 30°. This is a complete artifact. Notches and blade are symmetrical. No basal grinding, bifacially flaked. No observable wear at 10x. Notches are wide and the side below the notch is rounded. Classified as Prairie Side-notched.

Artifact 2. Projectile point

Knife River Flint, S53W99, 20 to 25 cm bs. 19.3 x 14.4 x 3.8 mm. Edge angles 25 to 30°. This artifact was found with part of the base missing. Refitting attached the base to the blade, although a part of the base below one notch is still missing. No observable wear at 10x. Notches are narrow, and the side is straight below the notch on the undamaged portion of the point. Classified as Plains Side-notched.

Artifact 3. Projectile point, broken

Swan River Chert, S52W100, 15 to 20 cm bs. 16.7 x 14.1 x 3.2 mm. Edge angles 25 to 30°. This is a triangular point with one corner and part of the base missing. The break is a simple fracture with no bending or hinge. Presumably it broke in use. The extreme tip of the point seems to have two flakes removed, perhaps through use. No wear is visible on the edges.

Artifact 4. Projectile point, blade

Knife River Flint, S32W99, 30 to 35 cm bs. ? x 15.9 x 4.5 mm. Edge angles about 25°. This is a very well made point blade with a symmetrical section, shallow, invasive pressure flaking that meets at a central ridge on one side. The base is missing, and rounding wear is observable on the blade edge. The tip is intact. It is possible this point broke in manufacture since the fracture is hinged and probably broke as pressure was applied to a nearby edge.

Artifact 5. Projectile point, tip

Knife River Flint, S53W98, 10 to 15 cm bs. ? x 6.x 2.5mm. Edge angle about 40°. The fracture is hinged and may have broken during manufacture or repair. One side of this tip seems to be particularly worn and rounded.

Artifact 6. Projectile point, tip

Swan River Chert, S52W99, 25 to 30 cm bs. ? x 17.6 x 3.8 mm. Edge angle 25 to 35°. This broken tip displays a simple snap fracture on the bottom. Potlidding suggests it was burned after being broken since one potlid is visible on the snapped surface. No wear is visible on the edges, nor any damage to the tip. Perhaps broken during use given the nature of the fracture. This may have been used in a kill and returned to the site in a meat package.

Artifact 7. Projectile point, tip

Red River Chert, S43W89, 35 to 40 cm bs. ? x 6.2 x 3.7 mm. Edge angle 25°. This point tip has a hinge fracture at the break. Possibly this artifact was broken during reworking of the point. No wear is evident.

Artifact 8. Projectile point, blade fragment

Red River Chert, S32W99, 30 to 35 cm bs. 16.3 x ? x 3.7 mm. Edge angle 60°. This item is the entire length of a projectile point fractured longitudinally. Very expert bifacial flaking with thin, parallel pressure flakes removed. Break is spiral, no wear is evident on the edge.

Artifact 9. Projectile point, base

Swan River Chert, S53W97, 10 to 15 cm bs. ? x 15.7 x 3.5 mm. Edge angle 60°. Rounding is visible along the edge of this item. The break is a straight snap fracture. Possibly this point broke during use and was returned to the site attached to a shaft.

Artifact 10. Biface, hafted

Dark gray chert, surface, 57.5 x 39.4 x 9.9 mm. Edge angle 30 to 60°. The blade is oriented at an angle from the base at about 25°. A patina is developed over both sides of the lower portion of the artifact. Flaked bifacially over its entire surface. The blade is convex on one edge, concave on the other.

The notches are wide, the tip is broken. There is grinding on the base of the blade above the notches. Rounding and some polish are apparent at 10x on the convex side of the artifact. The slightly concave side of this tool is probably a spokeshave.

Artifact 11. Biface

Swan River Chert, no provenience, 34.9 x 26.6 x 6.8 mm. Edge angle 30 to 60°. This is a triangular shaped biface with dorsal-ventral curvature from the flake on which it is made, although it is worked on both faces. One edge is straight, the other convex. Chipping is apparent on the edges, but not much rounding. The tip is intact. Possibly this was used for cutting or scraping.

Artifact 12. Biface

Swan River Chert, no provenience, ? x 36.3 x 8.7. Edge angle 30 to 60°. This biface is broken transversely. It has a lenticular section, and rounding is observable on both edges. The fracture is hinged in the middle portion of the break.

Artifact 13. Biface, fragment

Knife River Flint, S6E5, 50 to 60 cm bs. ? x ? x 4.8 mm. Edge angle 25°. This is the medial section of a biface. Rounding and chipping wear is quite evident along most of the remnant edge.

Artifact 14. Biface, fragment

Tongue River Silica, S46W90, 45 to 50 cm bs. ? x 31.3 x 7.7 mm. Edge angle is 45°. This is the base of a well made biface. The piece is deep red and may have been fired. The entire perimeter is rounded from use. The break is transverse and a slight hinge is evident.

Artifact 15. End scraper, multipurpose tool

Knife River Flint, S50W100, 45 to 50 cm bs. 40.9 x 19.7 x 5.5 mm. This is a complete end scraper. Edge angle 30 to 60°. This tool is made on a fair-sized piece of flint. The dorsal side of the scraper is the ventral side of the flake. The distal end is fashioned into an end scraper; however, both of the long sides are prepared bifacially with careful pressure flaking. Most flaking is parallel and very well executed. The narrow butt end is also flaked as a burin. Thus, this tool may be a scraper-knife-burin. Chipping is seen along the edges, especially at the juncture of the scraper-biface edge. Rounding and polish may be seen along the burin edge.

Artifact 16. End scraper

Red River Chert, no provenience, 24.2 x 19.6 x 7.1 mm. Edge angle 50°. This is a classic thumbnail scraper on a flake. There is rounding on the side and on the bit edge. The edge also shows chipping.

Artifact 17. End scraper, broken

Hudson Bay Lowland Chert, S33W100, 35 to 40 cm bs. 22.5 x 17.0 x 5.0 mm. Edge angle 65°. This tool is fractured longitudinally. It is worked on only the front end. The break is irregular and there is a stubby hinge in the middle of the break. The working edge exhibits fine chipping along the entire front and crushing on one end. There is a patina over much of the dorsal side.

Artifact 18. End scraper

Yellow jasper, S46W90, 5 to 10 cm bs. 13.6 x 18.7 x 5.4 mm. Edge angle 65°. There is minor chipping along the front edge, but little other evidence of use. The tool is so small it must have been hafted for use.

Artifact 19. End scraper

Red River Chert, S53W99, 10 to 15 cm bs. 16.1 x 13.8 x 5.4. Edge angle 75°. This item appears to be a complete tool, even though it is quite small. Probably used with a haft. Very heavy chipping and rounding is apparent along the edge of the bit.

Artifact 20. End scraper, broken

Gunflint Silica, S6E5, 50 to 60 cm bs. ? x 17.1 x 4.4 mm. Edge angle 60°. This is the working edge, or bit, of an end scraper. It is split on both sides of the working edge. Rounding and even polish are evident along the working edge. Snap fractures on both sides indicate possible breakage during use.

Artifact 21. End scraper, broken

Knife River Flint, S45W88, 22 cm bs. ? x ? x.7.7 mm. Edge angle 80°. This scraper is broken on the base and the side. There is a simple snap fracture on the side and a hinge fracture on the base. Chipping, crushing, and rounding are apparent on the edge.

Artifact 22. End scraper, broken

Red River Chert, S10W5, 10 to 20 cm bs. 28.0 x 23.7 x 7.7 mm. Edge angle is 85°. This is an almost complete end scraper, broken transversely toward the proximal end. Both sides of the tool display ripple marks from flaking. The break on the proximal end is a clean fracture. Heavy crushing and chipping are evident on the working edge. Breakage during use is most likely.

Artifact 23. Graver, multipurpose tool

Knife River Flint, S46W90, 15 to 20 cm bs. 24.5 x 18.8 x 4.7 mm. Edge angles 25 to 55°. This is a complex tool on a flake, with the form of a graver. One side has a wide-angled, unifacially-trimmed scraper edge, another has a narrow area of utilization, a third edge has a transverse trimmed knifelike edge. One corner of the square shaped tool has a burin flake removed, and the opposite corner has a protruding, rounded end with heavy rounding and polish, similar to that of an engraving tool. Other used edges show chipping.

Artifact 24. Graver

Knife River Flint, S432W90, 0 to 5 cm bs. 19.8 x 23.6 x 4.7 mm. Edge angle 40°. This tool is made on a flake, and is broken opposite the graver bit. Rounding and polish are apparent on both sides of this implement. It feels abraded to the touch. The tip is worn and is blunted by loss of a flake.

Artifact 25. Awl

Knife River Flint, S43W88, 30 to 35 cm bs. ? x 11.7 x 5.0 mm. Edge angle 50° and 25° on tip. The tip of this elongate flake tool is clearly worked and looks well worn. The base is a clean snap fracture. There is chipping wear along the two edges of the tool away from the tip.

Artifact 26. Denticulate or possible point fragment

Knife River Flint, burnt, S52W100 25 to 30 cm bs. 15.6 x 10.0 x 3.7 mm. Edge angle is 30°. This bifacially flaked fragment is split longitudinally and looks about the size of a point blade. The edge is deeply serrated, however, and it was probably used as something other than a projectile tip. No wear is evident.

Artifact 27. Utilized flake

Knife River Flint, S48W90 30 to 35 cm bs. 21.4 x 12.7 x 4.4 mm. Edge angle 30°. This broken flake shows rounding and polish on the distal edge and chipping on the lateral part of the flake. A projecting corner of the flake is rounded and polished.

Artifact 28. Spokeshave and biface fragment

Swan River Chert, S32W99, 10 to 15 cm bs. 25.5 x 28.4 x 12.3 mm. Edge angle 45° for biface, 50° for spokeshave. This looks like the medial portion of a biface that was made into a spokeshave after being broken. Both working edges look used and are rounded, but the spokeshave edge is also chipped heavily from use.

Artifact 29. Hammerstone

Basalt, S20W10 40 to 50 cm bs. 75.4 x 45.6 mm. Weight 270 g. This is a moderate sized hammerstone. There is pitting on both ends of the somewhat elongate rock. On one end the pitting is in two different spots. Also, the rim on the wider side of the stone is pitted on one end. Pitting is light to moderate.

Eleven of these tools are Knife River Flint, seven are Swan River Chert, four are Red River Chert, and the others are made from a variety of materials. This is typical of sites in the Red River region. Knife River Flint, which comprises 13 percent of the flaking debris, makes up about 38 percent of the actual tools. Swan River Chert, which is the most abundant single raw material in the lithic debris sample, consisting of 39 percent, makes up about 24 percent of the tools.

Typologically the complete projectile points are Prairie Side-notched and Plains Side-notched types. These points are typical of the types found at a site of Blackduck affiliation. Lugenbeal (1976:346-348) reports roughly similar points from Blackduck levels at the Smith site on the Rainy River, although at Smith the majority of points associated with Blackduck levels were unnotched triangular. At the Stott site, however, small notched points were the rule (Hamilton et al. 1981:132).

The relatively large number of points, bifaces and scrapers is expected at a site related to large game hunting. As the faunal remains indicate, bison hunting is the major activity represented here. Over 80 percent of the tools are points, bifaces, and scrapers, and most of these are broken.

Edge angles span a range of values from 25 to 85° and may reflect the many tasks performed at the site. These values, along with the variety of tools present, show that many more tasks than simple butchery were conducted at this site. This is reinforced by the relatively substantial ceramic sample. Only one utilized flake was identified at the site (although several tools were made on flakes). This tool kit seems to be a well prepared one in which labor was invested in creating a range of implements for the efficient completion of tasks. Hunter-gatherers involved in big game hunting commonly require well-made, dependable tools that can be used, repaired, and re-used. The assemblage at 21CY39 resembles such a technology, sometimes referred to by archaeologists as a curated assemblage. The multipurpose tools at the site reinforce this notion of an intensive labor investment in tool preparation, which is typical of a curated tool assemblage.

Discussion

21CY39 is significant for several reasons. It represents one of the more westerly excavated stations of the Blackduck complex. Normally, Blackduck is found in the Minnesota lake-forest country (Lugenbeal 1978:49). Also, because it is dominated by Blackduck pottery, the site provides an opportunity to obtain a detailed description of Blackduck site content without the complication of other major components, a problem common to many Blackduck sites. This site is not stratified, and there is no intrusion of materials from another component into the Blackduck component. Also, through a study of the encrustations of ceramic interiors, it is possible to arrive at an understanding of some of the plant foods cooked by these peoples. The lithic assemblage provides insights about Blackduck raw material usage and relationships with plains cultures. The overall artifact collection allows us to understand more fully the way in which Late Woodland groups made use of the northeastern plains area. Some aspects of the cultural assemblage are unexpected in a hunting camp on the prairie.

21CY39 is an extensive scatter of cultural material, extending east-west along an axis of about 140 m on the edge of a terrace. There are "hot spots" within this distribution; however, the impression created by the scatter of materials is that people used this place over some period of time. Presumably, Blackduck peoples came to this terrace on more than one occasion, using a slightly different location during their repeated visits. Since the scatter is so light it seems unlikely that a large group of people lived here simultaneously. There was probably a sequential series of camps, each being of modest size and of limited duration. The eroded bison bone and the shattered pottery suggest long-term exposure and possible trampling.

Blackduck was primarily a woodland oriented culture. These people practiced hunting and gathering, were skilled in exploiting resources of their forested surroundings, probably used wild rice, and were successful in utilizing a region that spanned the entire northwestern portion of the Great Lakes area. Nevertheless, Blackduck is found consistently on the northeastern portion of the Great Plains. At the Stott site, Blackduck peoples participated in the typical pattern of large-scale bison hunts, with a driveline and mass kill (Badertscher, Roberts and Zoltai 1987:315). The people of 21CY39 were obviously at this site to make use of large game. The faunal remains associated with the cultural deposits at the site are almost exclusively bison. It is certain that these animals provided sustenance for their hunters; the cutmarks indicate that the remains were butchered for meat and the green bone fractures demonstrate that marrow was also utilized. The evidence strongly argues that it was a bison processing station.

The bison bone indicates at least four animals were partially butchered here, and the presence of fetal bone suggests a late winter/early spring use. Turtle and clamshell indicate some camps were probably used in the warm season, perhaps summer. The site may not have been used in the same season every year. Except for feature 2, there are no concentrations of bison bone debris. This site is decidedly unlike the Stott site in Manitoba, where large deposits of bison bone are found in several cultural layers (Hamilton et al. 1981). 21CY39 may have been visited on several occasions by relatively small groups, perhaps several families, who made use of a few bison prior to moving on. The relatively small ceramic vessels (15-20 cm diameter) would indicate small task groups, perhaps the size of nuclear families, rather than large, cooperative social groups using large vessels for group meals. There is nothing at this site to indicate a massive communal drive and kill. This finding is, at least in part, contrary to the views of some archaeologists (e.g., Walde, Meyer and Unfreed 1995:56), that Blackduck people conducted only communal bison hunts on the plains.

Several conclusions may be drawn from the examination of the lithic collection. Raw materials were obtained mostly from local sources, but a significant amount was exotic, most of this being from the Knife River quarries of North Dakota, about 250 miles west of the site. Knife River Flint is more common at archaeological sites to the west, and there is a linear fall-off in its popularity at sites as one moves eastward from the quarries. This is typical of "down-the-line" trade, but it does indicate that the people at 21CY39 were interacting with people to the west who had access to KRF and who were susceptible to inducements to give some of it away. Other exotics at the site, such as Grand Meadow Chert and copper, are present in such small quantities that any statements about cultural processes related to them are inappropriate here, except to say that the site inhabitants had access to eastern Minnesota resources.

The variety of lithic debris categories, including cores and shatter, core reduction flakes, thinning flakes, pressure flakes, blades and bipolar flakes, make it clear that various stages in stone reduction and tool preparation occurred at the site. It is mildly surprising to find this degree of heterogeneity in the collection. The expected lithic collection for a short-term hunting camp might include some broken tools and the by-products from repair and refurbishing tools. At this site, however, almost the entire gamut of stone reduction products is represented. The number of core fragments shows clearly that lithic procurement and the initial phases of reduction are represented. The presence of unidirectional and multidirectional cores indicates more than one method of tool making, something made even more obvious by the presence of several small blades at the site, presumably struck from unidirectional cores. Most of the flaking debris consists of ordinary thinning flakes of one sort or another (e.g., complete, broken or fragmented flakes).

The tools themselves include items for piercing, cutting, scraping, boring, incising and hammering. The tool sample from the site includes seven categories defined on the basis of artifact form. These are point, scraper, biface, graver, spokeshave, awl, and hammer. This collection is consistent with activities that would be expected at a bison-processing site; however, it is likely that they reflect other activities as well. Projectile points and scrapers dominate the collection. Together these account for about 60 percent of the tools. They are almost certainly related to the procurement and processing of bison. Other activities probably undertaken at the site include woodworking (spokeshave, graver), lithic reduction (hammer, as well as cores), and hide finishing (awl). If we couple this with the range of debris types, the variety of lithic reduction activities, and the relative abundance of ceramics, which are more common at the site than lithics, it seems that the occupation of this location involved a variety of procurement, processing, manufacturing, and domestic activities.

Many of the tools were fashioned for a specific task. Even though every flake from the site was examined more than once, only a single utilized and worked flake was identified. The almost complete lack of such expedient tools is unusual in any site, and part of this might be explained by the presence of a great deal of Swan River Chert. This is a very tough stone that does not readily show wear. Some lightly worked or used pieces of this material may have been missed. Also, some of the formal tools at the site are made on flakes, and other observers might classify these (for example, the two gravers) as worked flakes. Even so, there are a high proportion of formal tool types represented in the assemblage.

This collection would best be described as a curated assemblage. In curated assemblages there is a separation in time and/or space between the manufacture of a tool and its use and discard (Towner and Warburton 1990:311). More effort is devoted to creating such an assemblage than would be invested in an expedient tool kit. Curated tools are designed to work without fail, so to speak. Curated tools are often used for many different tasks, and they may be reshaped for other uses. They are typically found in situations where there is a high return rate on food-procurement efforts (Bousman 1993:64, 73). All of this points to 21CY39 being a logistical camp where a specialized technology was being put to use for collection of a highly valued resource -- that is, bison. However, from lithics alone it is obvious that lithic procurement and initial reduction were also occurring here. Naturally, these activities are not mutually exclusive, but it is clear that there is some variability in behavior that is masked by labels such as logistical camp or bison-processing station. Not only is a range of activities represented in the artifact collection, but also the sample of animal bone from the site suggests use in more than one season. Blackduck use of the prairie may have been multi-seasonal and not restricted to a single foray. Furthermore, these forays may have involved a range of domestic activities beyond bison procurement.

The two complete projectile points from the site are well made and are within the range of points described in Kehoe's (1966) "The Small Notched Point System of the Northern Plains." One of these is Prairie Side-notched and the other is Plains Side-notched. These points are well flaked, quite thin, and unlike some of the less-refined points described for Blackduck sites in the lake-forest area where most Blackduck sites are found. For example, at White Oak Point in Itasca County, Minnesota, only five of 23 points are notched, and one of these is notched with wide indentations creating a stem. Another is almost as wide as it is long, and one other is over 40 mm long. Points from Blackduck levels at the Smith site are clearly not as well executed as those from 21CY39 (Lugenbeal 1976:348-49).

Prairie and Plains Side-notched point types overlap in time on the Northern Plains and were found together in the same levels at the Stott site (Hamilton et al. 1981:132). Small side-notched points tend to be the dominant projectile point in archaeological assemblages over much of the Northern Plains around A.D. 1000 (Dyck and Morlan 2001:127-8), although the dynamic processes that brought this form to so many disparate assemblages is not worked out. I have suggested that artifact styles are transmitted between people in face-to-face contact when social tension is high and conforming behavior is likely (Michlovic 1981). At any rate, when Blackduck people used the prairie environment, they do appear to have adopted the technological styles commonly found throughout the Northern Plains. The basic side-notched style is related to bow and arrow use and, undoubtedly, Blackduck hunters used the bow, although many eastern woodland peoples preferred use of the Eastern Triangular un-notched point. These un-notched forms are found in many Blackduck sites in Minnesota. The preference for the side-notched form at this site is probably related to the popularity of this type among many prairie groups.

The ceramic collection represents perhaps 13 vessels. It is not highly variable in terms of vessel form. Almost all vessels with measurable diameters provide values of about 20 cm. These would comprise modest-sized cooking pots large enough to prepare a meal for a nuclear family-sized group, but certainly not for a large social gathering. Many of the rimsherds are encrusted with burnt food residue and so the vessels must have been employed in food preparation. These were probably not for storage or other special uses. One of the surprising aspects of the CY39 collection is the slight predominance of ceramic over lithic material. This was noted after the 1991 season, and appeared true again in the 2002 excavation sample. One might expect that big game hunting camps would contain more butchery material than cooking vessels. This, along with the variety of lithic reduction phases and the variety of tools, might be regarded as unusual in a specialized hunting camp.

Of the 13 vessels identified in the site collection, no two are identical, or even very similar. This probably does not reflect many different ethnic or cultural groups using the site. Blackduck pottery

Table 8. Activity Indicators at 21CY39

Indicators of Small, Special Purpose Collector Camps at 21CY39	Indicators of Multi-Purpose Forager Camp at 21CY39
Small vessels	Range of lithic reduction phases
Light material scatter, small groups	Variety of domestic debris
Only four bison represented	Possible presence of maize
Curate tool assemblage	Range of pottery, lithic forms and edge angles represented

is often variable at single sites. At the Stott site in western Manitoba, Blackduck ceramics were so variable that the commonly used classification systems applied to their analysis broke down. There were 17 variations on six major decorative modes. This calls to mind an incident recorded by Frances Densmore (1979:162-163). She mentions a Chippewa cemetery on Lake Winnepegosis, Minnesota, that was exposed by erosion in 1918. The graves were only a few decades old. Over 200 pot fragments were found, decorated with twisted cord roulettes, and stick and fingernail impressions. The pottery description sounds like Blackduck or perhaps Rainy River Composite. However, even though the pottery came from the same community cemetery and the vessels were roughly the same age, there was great variety. Densmore reports that hardly three or four duplicates could be found in the entire collection. This suggests that the variability in Historic period ceramic production among northern Minnesota Chippewa might have revolved around family decorative traditions rather than ethnic affiliation.

Much of the ceramic collection is broken into small pieces, possibly the result of trampling. This scatter indicates primary discard throughout the site area. There is only a single instance of secondary debris accumulation, feature 2, which was a refuse pit. However, the refuse pit was probably originally created for storage of food or materials, not to discard the garbage people generated.

Almost all of the activity indicators at this site offer mixed messages (Table 8). The ecofacts are mostly animal bone, and the vast majority of those are bison. 21CY39 was a processing camp. It was probably not very near a kill, since there are few skull elements, vertebrae or pelvic bones. On the other hand, the phytoliths recovered from ceramic vessels' interiors tells us that people here were using maize. Was this a small amount of corn transported from elsewhere? Or were these Blackduck peoples involved in a kind of life-style here that does not fit our current notion of hunter-gatherer seasonal rounds? It is possible that the people at CY39 could have obtained maize from farmers or gardeners in the Missouri Valley (near the Knife River quarries) or from southern Minnesota or northern Iowa (in the vicinity of the Grand Meadow Chert quarries). It is even possible they were growing maize themselves. If nothing else is assumed, it is important to recognize that the evidence from this site raises the possibility that Blackduck populations not only utilized the large game resources of the grasslands, but that they had access to domesticated plant foods as well. The question of whether they themselves may have produced domestic plants is very important but, unfortunately, cannot be answered with data from this site alone.

Meyer and Hamilton (1994:122) suggest that Blackduck groups penetrated more deeply onto the plains than their Laurel predecessors. Reeves (1989:173) argues that one of the important features of the successful use of the Northern Plains was the communal hunt. If these two claims are correct, it may be that the social organization of Blackduck peoples allowed their success on the prairie, where they had the organizational skills to make full use of the bison herds. Furthermore, the enormous forage production of the northeastern plains would have encouraged large, stable bison herds (Bamforth 1988:185, Gordon 1979:43). This dependable resource would have been a major attraction for properly equipped and organized hunters able to take advantage of a highly desirable resource such as bison. However, it is not necessary to assume bison use was everywhere the same. Communal hunts were clearly used in some areas. In others, perhaps smaller groups may have culled herds for a few animals at a time. 21CY39 may be one of those locations. The behavioral variability reflected in the lithic and ceramic collection, the maize phytoliths, and even the presence of a small storage facility (feature 2) indicate that there was more to the activities of Blackduck peoples at these camps than bison processing.

Site Management

The excavations at 21CY39 bring several site excavation and management issues into focus, and deserve comment here. The digging at this site was performed using two slightly different recovery procedures. During the first season, excavations were in 10 cm arbitrary levels, and in the following two seasons 5 cm arbitrary levels were used. There was no difference in the results of these two protocols at the site, except that use of 5 cm levels required far more labor. However, the 5 cm level has become standard in CRM work throughout the region and it is currently used in both Minnesota and North Dakota. In a stratified site, of course, digging should be done by natural layers and not by arbitrary levels. In unstratified "solum" sites such as CY39, where the site is contained in the A and B horizons, the 5 cm level now in use does not seem to hold any advantage over the 10 cm level. Since the 5 cm level involves about double the paperwork as 10 cm levels, both on site and in the lab, it would be a more efficient use of time to employ the 10 cm level unless finer-scale recovery was clearly needed.

21CY39 is a protected site. It is on State of Minnesota property and is managed by a state university. If you visit the site today, you may see an exhibit with some of the artifacts on display at the Regional Science Center facility. The site itself is the occasional destination of grade school groups who visit the Science Center and tour the grounds to learn more about science in the outdoors. There is a single interpretive panel erected under plexiglass at the western boundary of the site explaining what was learned from the archaeological study. The obvious management recommendation would be to leave the site alone. Any further excavation will only destroy more of the site.

This plan for management makes sense insofar as any excavation is thought of as the destruction of a site. Archaeologists seem to enjoy describing excavations as "destruction." Perhaps this is for shock value. But it is hardly the whole story. Archaeologists do not destroy the site in the way a bulldozer would, or in the way a site would be destroyed if it slumped into an artificial lake eroding the sides of the bluff it sat on. It might be more appropriate to explain that archaeology is the transformation of an unknown, intact site, to a disassembled, organized laboratory collection of site data. Besides this, during an excavation, archaeologists almost never disassemble an entire site, but take only a sample, even when the site is actually going to be really destroyed by other means.

Unfortunately, some preservationists seem not to have ever given much thought to this complication. For them, excavation is destruction and the only appropriate course for the archaeologist is to refrain from digging (for them, destroying) unless the site is in imminent danger. Site 21CY39, no longer in imminent danger from golf course development, should be left alone under the preservationist program. The problem is that this site exists in a real world of natural processes, not in an ideal world of pristine integrity. The ground squirrel and the pocket gopher, earthworms and ants, badgers and foxes and tree falls constantly modify the "pristine" site. Features are obliterated, cultural strata are mixed, context is compromised, and sites are destroyed. If you were to walk over this site during the middle of the summer, you might "see" a field of prairie grasses and imagine a landscape that has been here since Lake Agassiz emptied. Look closer in the tall grass, however, and you will notice mounds of fresh earth in uneven piles, sometimes single mounds, more often clustered together. There are hundreds covering the site surface, and each one represents a small excavation by a ground squirrel or a pocket gopher into the site itself. Often, after a light rain, bone fragments and artifacts may be observed in these rodent spoil piles.

We can see the archaeological results of this at 21CY39. Feature 1 is hardly recognizable, and feature 2 exists only because it was such a deep, densely packed refuse pit. Feature 4 is barely visible. The artifact densities themselves must be characterized statistically or graphically to discover "where" in the soil profile the occupation actually rested. Yet this field was never plowed or disturbed in any significant way by people except for a golf cart road on the eastern perimeter. Without any appreciable human impact, with no major natural threats such as erosion or slumping, this site is slowly slipping into oblivion. What is left of this site now will continue to degrade, to disaggregate, and to lose its integrity. It is already partway to being little more than a buried "surface collection." 21CY39 and sites like it need to be sampled and understood. They need not be wiped clean by total excavation, but they must be tapped for their stories before the land takes back from us what it has preserved until now for us to see and know.

Acknowledgements. Excavations at 21CY39 were sponsored and funded by Minnesota State University Moorhead. I would like to thank Dr. George Davis, director of the MSUM Regional Science Center, along with Tony Bormann and Joe Gartner, who assisted with the project in its various stages. The faculty research grants program at MSUM provided special funding for radiocarbon dating, faunal analysis, and for phytolith identification. Over 30 MSUM students volunteered to work at 21CY39 over the years. Their efforts are largely responsible for the results presented here.

References Cited

Andrefsky, W. Jr.
1998 *Lithics.* Cambridge University Press, Cambridge.

Badertscher, P.M., L.J. Roberts and S.L. Zoltai
1987 *Hill of the Buffalo Chase: 1982 Excavations at the Stott Site, D1Ma-1.* Papers in Manitoba Archaeology. Final Report No. 18. Department of Cultural Affairs and Historical Resources, Historic Resources Branch, Winnipeg.

Bamforth, D.B.
1988 *Ecology and Human Organization on the Great Plains.* Plenum Press, New York.

Bluemle, J.P.
1977 *The Face of North Dakota: The Geologic Story.* Washburn Printing Center, Washburn.

Borchert, J. R.
1950 The climate of the central North American grassland. *Annals of the Association of American Geographers* 40:1-39.

Bousman, C.B.
1993 Hunter-Gatherer Adaptations, Economic Risk and Tool Design. *Lithic Technology* 18(1-2):59-86.

Coues, E.
1897 *Manuscript Journals of Alexander Henry and of David Thompson: 1799-1814, v. 1. The Red River of the North.* Ross and Haines Publishers, Minneapolis.

Densmore, F.
1979 *Chippewa Customs.* Reprint of 1929 edition. Minnesota Historical Society, St. Paul.

Dyck, I. and R.E. Morlan
2001 Hunting and Gathering Tradition: Canadian Plains. In *Handbook of North American Indians,* ed. by R.J. DeMallie, vol 13, part 1, pp. 115-130. Smithsonian Institution, Washington, D.C.

Gordon, B.H.C.
1979 *Of Men and Herds in Canadian Plains Prehistory.* Archaeological Survey of Canada, Paper No. 84. National Museums of Canada, Ottawa.

Gregg, M.L.
1987 Knife River Flint in the Northeastern Plains. *Plains Anthropologist* 32(118):367-388.

Greiser, S.T.
1994 Late Prehistoric Cultures of the Montana Plains. In *Plains Indians AD 500-1500,* ed. by K. Schlesier, pp. 34-55. University of Oklahoma Press, Norman.

Hamilton, S., W. Ferris, S. Hallgrimson, G. McNeely, K. Sammons, E. Simonds, and K. Topinka
1981 1979 Excavations at the Stott Site (D1Ma-1). *Misc. Paper #12, Papers in Manitoba Archaeology.* Department of Cultural Affairs and Historical Resources, Historic Resources Branch, Winnipeg.

Hart, J.P., R.G. Thompson, and J. Brumbach
2003 Phytolith Evidence for Early Maize (Zea mays) in the Northern Finger Lakes Region of New York. *American Antiquity* 68(4):619-640.

Haury, C.E.
1991 *Identification and Notes on Bone Elements from the Ponderosa Site (21CY39).* Report submitted to the Moorhead State University Archaeological Laboratory.

Hazard, E.B.
1982 *The Mammals of Minnesota.* University of Minnesota Press, Minneapolis.

Jacobson, M.N.
  1982 *Soil Survey of Clay County, Minnesota.* National Cooperative Soil Survey, Washington, D.C.

Kehoe, T.
  1966 The Small Side-Notched Point System of the Northern Plains. *American Antiquity* 31:827-841.

Lenius, B. and D.M. Olinyk
  1990 The Rainy River Composite: Revisions to Late Woodland Taxonomy. In *The Woodland Tradition in the Western Great Lakes: Papers presented to Elden Johnson*, ed. by G.E. Gibbon, pp. 77-112. Department of Anthropology, University of Minnesota, Minneapolis.

Lugenbeal, E.N.
  1976 *The Archaeology of the Smith Site: A Study of the Ceramic and Culture History of Minnesota Laurel and Blackduck.* Ph.D. dissertation, Department of Anthropology, University of Wisconsin. University Microfilms International, Ann Arbor.
  1978 Blackduck Ceramics of the Smith Site (21KC3) and Their Implications for the History of Blackduck Ceramics and Culture in Northern Minnesota. *Midcontinental Journal of Archaeology* 3 (1):45-68.
  1979 Blackduck. In *A Handbook of Minnesota Prehistoric Ceramics*, ed. by S.F. Anfinson, pp. 23-37. Minnesota Archaeological Society, St. Paul.

Meyer, D. and S. Hamilton
  1994 Neighbors to the North: Peoples of the Boreal Forest. In *Plains Indians A.D. 500-1500*, ed. by K. Schlesier, pp. 96-127. University of Oklahoma, Norman.

Michlovic, M.G.
  1981 Patterns of Social Interaction and the Dynamics of Artifact Style. In *Current Directions in Midwestern Archaeology: Selected Papers from the Mankato Conference*, ed. by S.F. Anfinson, pp. 41-48. Occasional Publications in Minnesota Anthropology No. 9, Minnesota Archaeological Society, St. Paul.
  1982 *Archaeological Resources on the Moorhead State Foundation Ponderosa Center.* Department of Sociology and Anthropology, Moorhead State University, Moorhead.

National Oceanic and Atmospheric Administration [NOAA]
  2003 The Fargo Climate Summary for the Year 2003. NOAA, Fargo-Grand Forks. <http://www.crh.noaa.gov/fgf/data/climate/farclmyer>

Reeves, B.O.K.
  1989 Communal Bison Hunters of the Northern Plains. In *Hunters of the Recent Past*, ed. by L.B. Davis and B.O.K. Reeves, pp. 168-194. Unwin Hyman, London.

Rice, P.
  1987 *Pottery Analysis: A Sourcebook.* University of Chicago Press, Chicago/London.

Towner, R.H. and M. Warburton
  1990 Projectile Point Rejuvenation: A Technological Analysis. *Journal of Field Archaeology* 17(3):311-321.

Walde, D., D. Meyer and W. Unfreed
  1995 The Late Period on the Canadian and Adjacent Plains. *Revista Arqueologia Americana.* 9:7-66.

Williams, R.L.
  1982 *Region Science Center Biological Resource Inventory.* Final Report Submitted to the Moorhead State University Foundation.

Elliot Park Neighborhood Archaeology Project
July 27th to 31st, 2005

The Elliot Park Neighborhood Archaeology Project is a five-day community event centered on excavation of a historic archaeological site in this downtown Minneapolis neighborhood. For those five days, the site is a focus of community attention as archaeologist, students and community members work together exploring city history. These photos are from the July 27th to 31st, 2005 excavations of the nineteenth century Eustis and Peck households at 631 and 633 East 14th Street.

Left: Shovel testing at the back of the Peck household lot. *Below*: View from the back corner of the site toward the central business district and Minneapolis skyline.

Upper left: Archaeologist Chuck Diesen maps the site using a plane table.
Center Right: Wash basin recovered from a trash midden associated with the old stable at the back of the Peck household lot.
Below: Archaeology students and middle-school students cleaning, sorting and bagging artifacts in the field lab.

Upper right: Volunteers in a little portable shade waiting to welcome visitors, and helping to sort and inventory artifacts. The group in the background, center right, is excavating an ash bin discovered in the cellar of the Peck house.

Center left: A turn-of-the century moustache cup found in the ash bin. The ceramic band along the lip, visible on the fragment to the right, helped keep a gentleman's moustache dry as he sipped from the cup. *Below*: Participants, standing within the footprint of the Peck house, prepare to excavate an informal test trench across the site from east to west. The trench showed that most of the foundation of the Peck House had been removed and the hole filled with sandy fill; that the Eustis driveway remained intact in the narrow stretch of land between the houses; and that the footprint of the Eustis house was filled with jumbled demolition fill, suggesting that at least some parts of the cellar could remain intact beneath the surface.

Upper left: Birds-eye view of the excavated, brick-walled ash bin in the cellar of the Peck house. Note the modern cement-block repairs to the old limestone foundation, near the top of the photo, and the angular paving blocks placed along the outer foundation wall in the back yard.

Center left: Excavation unit at the top of the ash bin. *Lower left, lower right*: Excavation of the ash bin in progress, showing layers of ash.

Left: Archaeologists and students draw maps and profiles diagrams of the excavation units containing the ash bin, as other volunteers and visitors look on.

Center right: Details of the ash bin after excavation. Note the ash bin's dirt floor, visible in the lower photo.

Lower right: Excavation of the ash bin in progress, showing some of the noncombustible household trash discarded in the ash bin. Note the shoe partly visible just below the center of the picture. The artifacts suggest that the ash bin was abandoned some time around the turn of the century.

Upper right: A mid-nineteenth century chamber pot discarded in the ash bin around the turn of the century. *Center left*: The chamber pot in situ.

Lower left: Bottom of a broken plate from the ash bin, showing a British maker's mark indicating that this design was registered with the Patent Office in January of 1876. *Bottom right*: In situ view of a small bowl made in Maastricht, Netherlands. The blue spot is a finely detail rendering of a cricket.

Photos: Patricia Emerson, Minnesota Historical Society
Layout: Deborah Schoenholz
Text: Kent Bakken

Triangular Cross Section Adzes from the Upper Mississippi River Valley: The Liska Cache

Robert "Ernie" Boszhardt
Mississippi Valley Archaeology Center, University of Wisconsin–La Crosse

Chipped and ground stone adzes have been reported from the Great Lakes region for over a century. In the Upper Great Lakes, two cross-section varieties are most common: triangular (three faceted) and lenticular (four- faceted), both of which have been referred to as "trihedral adzes." The age of both forms has been suggested to correlate with Late Paleoindian cultures in Wisconsin, Minnesota, southwestern Ontario and southeastern Manitoba, but rarely have they been found in datable contexts. A cache of five triangular cross section adzes was excavated at the Liska site along the Upper Mississippi River, and this cache is described and discussed.

Introduction

In March of 2001, Terry and Connie Liska brought a set of large basalt tools to the laboratory of the Mississippi Valley Archaeology Center (MVAC) at the University of Wisconsin–La Crosse for identification. The artifacts were recognized as examples of "trihedral adzes," a rare and little-known artifact form from the Driftless Area of southwestern Wisconsin. When asked where the adzes were obtained, the Liskas reported that one was kicked up by a ditch-witch while they were installing a buried power cable to their new home on a terrace overlooking the Mississippi River. The second one was found by Mr. Liska who reached arms-length into the trench and felt another, which he pulled out. In addition, the ditch-witch had brought up two sections of a large silicified sandstone biface. Furthermore, he had marked the spot with a stake and invited the archaeologists to excavate before their grass took hold. The excavations encountered a pit feature containing three additional adzes and burned limestone. The pit was not discerned until a depth of 55 cm below the modern surface, suggesting substantial age; however, absolute dating has not been undertaken because of a relative lack of associated carbon and funding. This find is discussed, along with a brief summary of adzes from the Upper Midwest, in terms of distribution, age, and function.

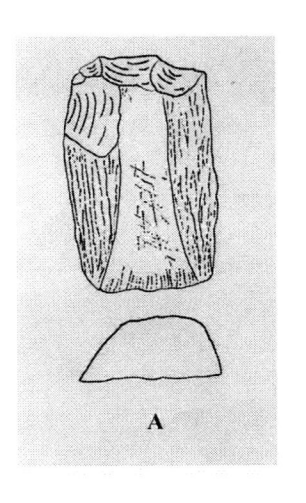

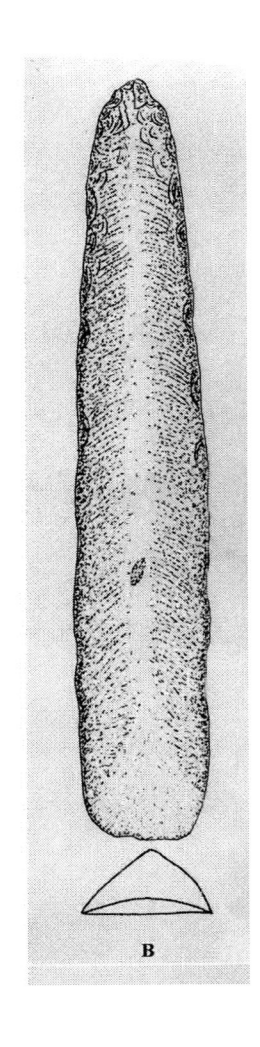

Figure 1. Drawings of two basic forms of trihedral adzes. A: rectangular cross-section variety (adapted from McLeod 1981). B: triangular cross-section variety from Liska Cache (47Cr637).

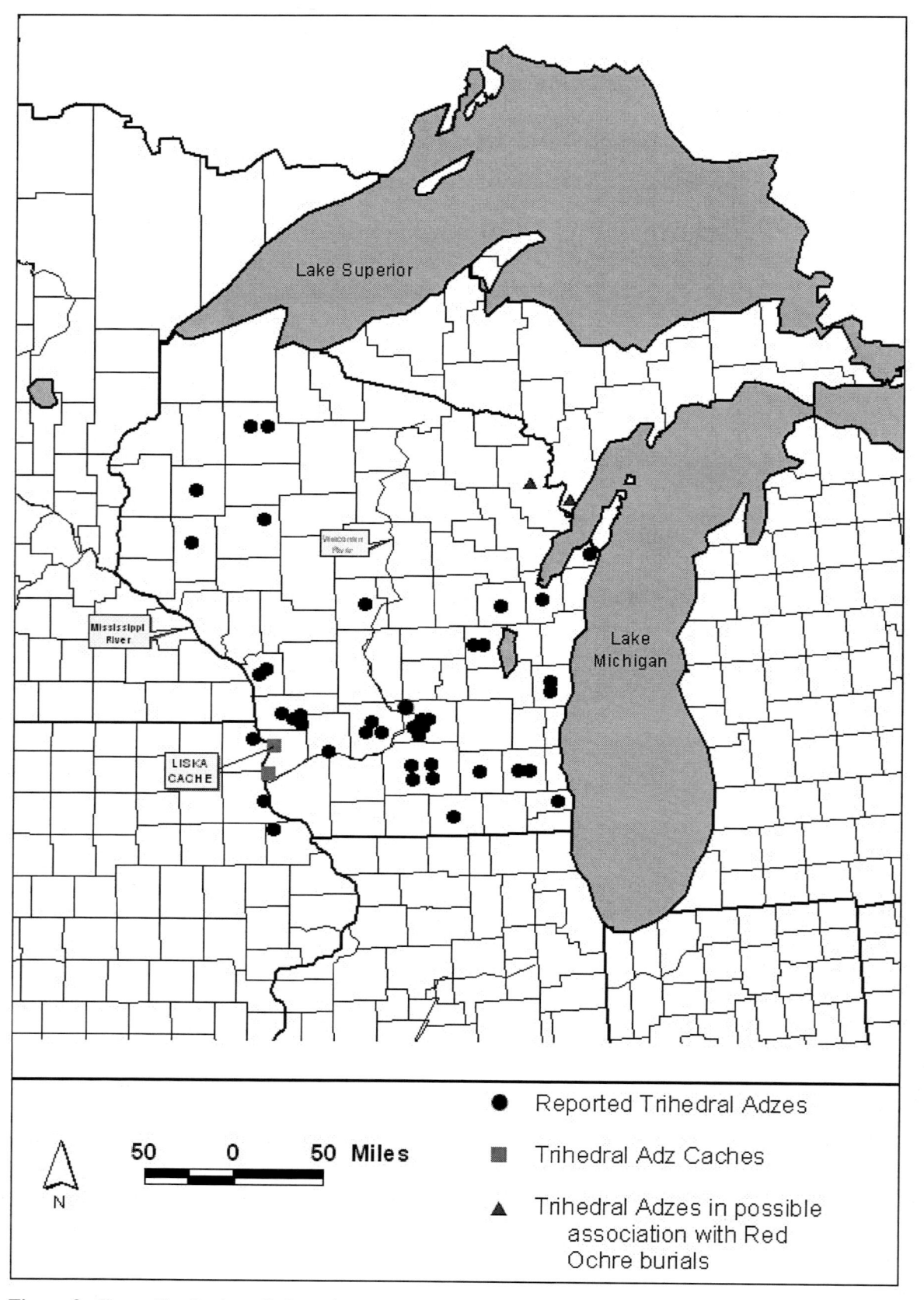

Figure 2. Know distribution of triangular cross-section adzes in Wisconsin and adjacent portions of the upper Mississippi Valley, including location of Liska Cache (47Cr637).

Table 1. Metric (mm) Data for Triangular Cross-Section Trihedral Adzes from Wisconsin

Specimen	Max Length	Max Width	Max Height	Length of bit end wear (Basal Surface)	Comments
Liska 1	310	52	46.2	50.5	Heavy wear
Liska 2	320	49.6	47.5	150	Heavy wear
Liska 3	317	54.4	41.8	79.7	Heavy wear
Liska 4	204*	50.2	39.2	77.2	Pole end missing
Liska 5	189*	55.6	36.8	NA	Pole end missing, surface exfoliated
Liska Averages	*315.6*	*52.36*	*42.3*	*89.35*	
Crawford Co MPM	329	59.9	51.1	60	Heavy wear. From the Prairie du Chien cache.
Portage Co WHS	231	50.5	35.5	66.5	Heavy wear
Portage Co WHS	267	54	41.2	44	
Marquette Co WHS	252	47.5	38	50	Heavy wear
Jefferson Co WHS	430	51.2	42.5	78.2	Minimal use
Rock Co WHS	155	41.6	38.6	33.8	Crude, slight wear
Sauk Co WHS	120	40.5	29.5	25	Re-chipped bit end?
Sauk Co WHS	159	41.8	33.2	NA	Unused preform?
Sauk Co WHS	185	58	26	NA	Unused?
Dane Co WHS	135	46	31	54	Broken, but reused
? WHS	318	75	43.7	NA	Flat-topped, no bit wear-but edge wear
? WHS	140	46	30	NA	Preform, Base also chipped-not natural fracture plane.
? WHS	102	54	24	39.5	Base heavily ground. Bit wear us not "U-Shaped"
Dane Co UW-Madison	179	51.5	27	33	Heavy wear
Dell, Vernon Co. Private	252	60	57	60.5	Medium wear

MPM = Milwaukee Public Museum   WHS = Wisconsin Historical Society

Trihedral Adzes

There is some confusion over the term "trihedral adze." In the northern Great Lakes region (including northern Minnesota, northern Wisconsin, western Ontario, and Manitoba) the term trihedral adze has been used to refer to relatively short tools that are rectangular in plan view, have a flat base and three dorsal surface planes (Fig. 1a). Often the central dorsal plane is flat and parallel to the base, while the two side planes on the dorsal surface are chipped and taper upward from the base to the central dorsal plane. McLeod (1981:24) refers to this form as a "Type 2" trihedral adze in his analysis of nearly 50 specimens from Dog Lake in western Ontario. This form is comparable to Lamoka-type adzes in the eastern Great Lakes (Mason 1981), and "lenticular-shaped" adzes in eastern Wisconsin (Behm 1987).

The term trihedral adzes has also been applied to a generally longer form with a rounded or pointed pole end and triangular cross section (Fig. 1b). These are somewhat comparable with gouges from the eastern Great Lakes, but are somewhat distinctive in having a central dorsal ridge and a shallower ventral surface groove. McLeod (1981:24) recognized a similar form as a "Type 1" trihedral adze from the Dog Lake assemblage, but those had a characteristic pointed and polished bit end. The Liska adzes, and others analyzed for this paper, are all of the triangular cross section variety, but the highly polished bit ends represent the widest part of the tool.

Attributes of Triangular Cross Section Trihedral Adzes from Southern Wisconsin

Triangular cross section trihedral adzes from southern Wisconsin

- are nearly always manufactured from basalt, which originates in pre-Cambrian bedrock near Lake Superior;
- are characteristically triangular in cross section, with a flat base that usually retains indication of a natural fault plane;
- have tops that were chipped from the base, forming the triangular cross section;
- have flake scars that are often readily apparent at the pointed "pole" end, while use-wear polish has often obscured the flaking at the wider bit end;
- have bits that are curved, often slightly asymmetrically, and finely honed to a sharp cutting edge; and
- probably functioned as woodworking tools, but it is not clear if or how they were hafted.

This distinctive triangular cross section adze form has been recognized since the early 1900s, with brief reports in *The Wisconsin Archeologist* (Brown 1934; Crosby 1903) that suggested their use as woodworking tools and recognized a generalized clustering along the central Wisconsin River (Fig. 2). There has been very little study of this variety of trihedral adzes since that time, and they have only rarely been found in formal archaeological studies (e.g., Overstreet 1979, 1989:332-333). None of these produced datable contexts and, while these have been inferred as representing Late Paleoindian artifacts (Mason 1997; Overstreet 1988), their age and cultural affiliation remains uncertain.

One early report is of a cache of three or four triangular cross section adzes from the Prairie du Chien Terrace at the confluence of the Wisconsin and Mississippi Rivers, less than 20 miles from the Liska Cache. These were found in 1928 and 1929, eroding from a hog pen (Brown 1934:93), and tracings of two are preserved in the Charles E. Brown manuscripts for Crawford County, Wisconsin. The largest of this set was obtained by the Milwaukee Public Museum in 1930 (Miller 1930). The size of these specimens approximates those of the Liska Cache (see Table 1).

Environmental Setting

The Liska site (47Cr637) is located on a 20-meter high Pleistocene outwash terrace at the mouth of Buck Creek, a minor tributary of the Upper Mississippi River. This setting is within the unglaciated Driftless Area (Martin 1965), a rugged topographic region with deeply dissected stream systems between upland interfluves. The major river system in this region is that of the Upper Mississippi, the main channel of which flows within a dissected trench that is bounded by steep, 500 foot tall bluffs, and which is partially filled with sand and gravel outwash terraces. The Liska site is situated on a high outwash terrace that corresponds to the Savanna Terrace system (Flock 1983). This system was deposited between 20,000 and 12,500 B.P. (Bettis and Hallberg 1985).

The original vegetation of the Driftless Area as recorded in the mid-nineteenth century was largely oak savanna with prairie on uplands, sandy terraces along the Upper Mississippi River, as well as south- and west-facing bluff slopes. The northeast slopes, interior valleys, and the floodplain of major rivers such as the Mississippi would have supported deciduous forests, but remnant pine stands were situated along sandy locales. This vegetative pattern likely extended back for approximately 4,000 years, but it was preceded by the much drier Altithermal, which peaked around 7000 B.P. At the end of the Pleistocene around 10,000 years ago, the area witnessed a succession from permafrost and tundra conditions to boreal forests to conifers and then oak and prairie (Theler and Boszhardt 2003).

The associated animal communities began with a variety of megafauna including mastodon and mammoth, which became extinct by 10,000 B.P. Subsequently, an early form of bison (*Bison occidentalis*) inhabited the western portion of the Driftless Area until ca. 8000 to 6000 B.P. By 4,000 years ago, white-tailed deer and elk had become the dominant large-game species. In addition, a variety of wetland animals such as beaver, muskrat, waterfowl, fish and shellfish were hunted by Native cultures (Theler and Boszhardt 2003).

Cultural Context

The Driftless Area contains a wealth of archaeological resources. These range from Early Paleoindian (fluted points) through Archaic hunter-gather cultures, Woodland (Hopewell and Effigy Mound) mound-builder societies, and Mississippian (Middle and Upper [Oneota]) cultures (Theler and Boszhardt 2003). Site types include camps, villages, quarries and workshops, mounds, cemeteries, rockshelters and deep caves with both habitation deposits and rock art. Local lithic sources include Prairie du Chien and Galena cherts from Ordovician limestone deposits and silicified sandstone from Cambrian sandstone formations. With the exception of gravel deposits along the Mississippi River, igneous rock is not locally available, and finds of basalt tools such as hammer stones, grooved axes, and celts very

Figure 3. Three adzes and burned limestone at base of pit feature, 55-65 cm below scraped surface, Liska Cache (47Cr637).

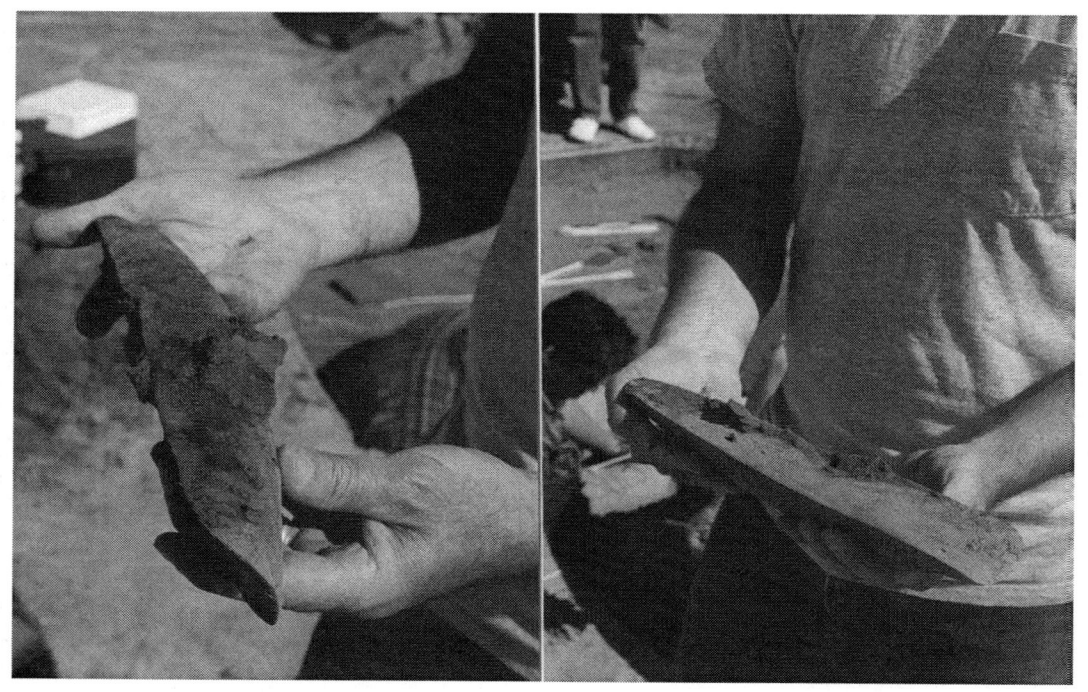

Figure 4. Top and bottom of adze immediately after removal from feature, Liska Cache (47Cr637).

Excavations

In April of 2001, MVAC excavated two 1 x 2 m units on either side of the ditch-witch trench at the find location that had been marked by Mr. Liska. The topsoil had been scraped, removing the natural A-horizon. Excavations proceeded through a 15 cm thick E-horizon, encountering a heavily iron-mottled B-horizon. Both of these zones were composed of fine sands (representing Pleistocene outwash deposition), and both were sterile of cultural materials until a depth of 55 cm below surface. At that point, a slightly pink stain appeared in the floor on the east side of the ditch-witch trench. Continued excavation revealed this to be a basin-shaped pit feature, containing another three adzes (Figs. 3, 4). These adzes were in undisturbed contexts, associated with a disintegrating piece of burned limestone (the source of the pink staining). The profile above the cache pit did not reveal an intrusive stain (Fig. 5), suggesting either that the surface at the time the pit was created was approximately 55 cm below the modern (scraped) surface or that the age of the pit was such that pedogenesis had blurred the upper portion to the degree that it was no longer apparent.

Excavation to the west, on the opposite side of the 20 cm wide ditch-witch trench, did not encounter the feature. Excavation of both units was extended below the base of the pit in order to ascertain if a buried cultural or natural surface was present at about 55 cm below the modern surface. The corresponding levels produced no artifacts or evidence of a buried natural surface, indicating that the pit probably did originate at or near the modern surface of this Pleistocene deposit, and that substantial age and pedogenesis had obscured the pit above the cache deposit. Slumped soil from the ditch-witch trench produced several crushed fragments of silicified sandstone from the ditch-witch breaking the biface, but no other large sections of the biface were recovered. A few small charcoal fragments were recovered from the pit fill through flotation of collected matrix samples. These have not yet been analyzed for species identification nor submitted for radiocarbon dating.

Discussion

The Liska Cache consists of five triangular cross section trihedral adzes, a large silicified sandstone

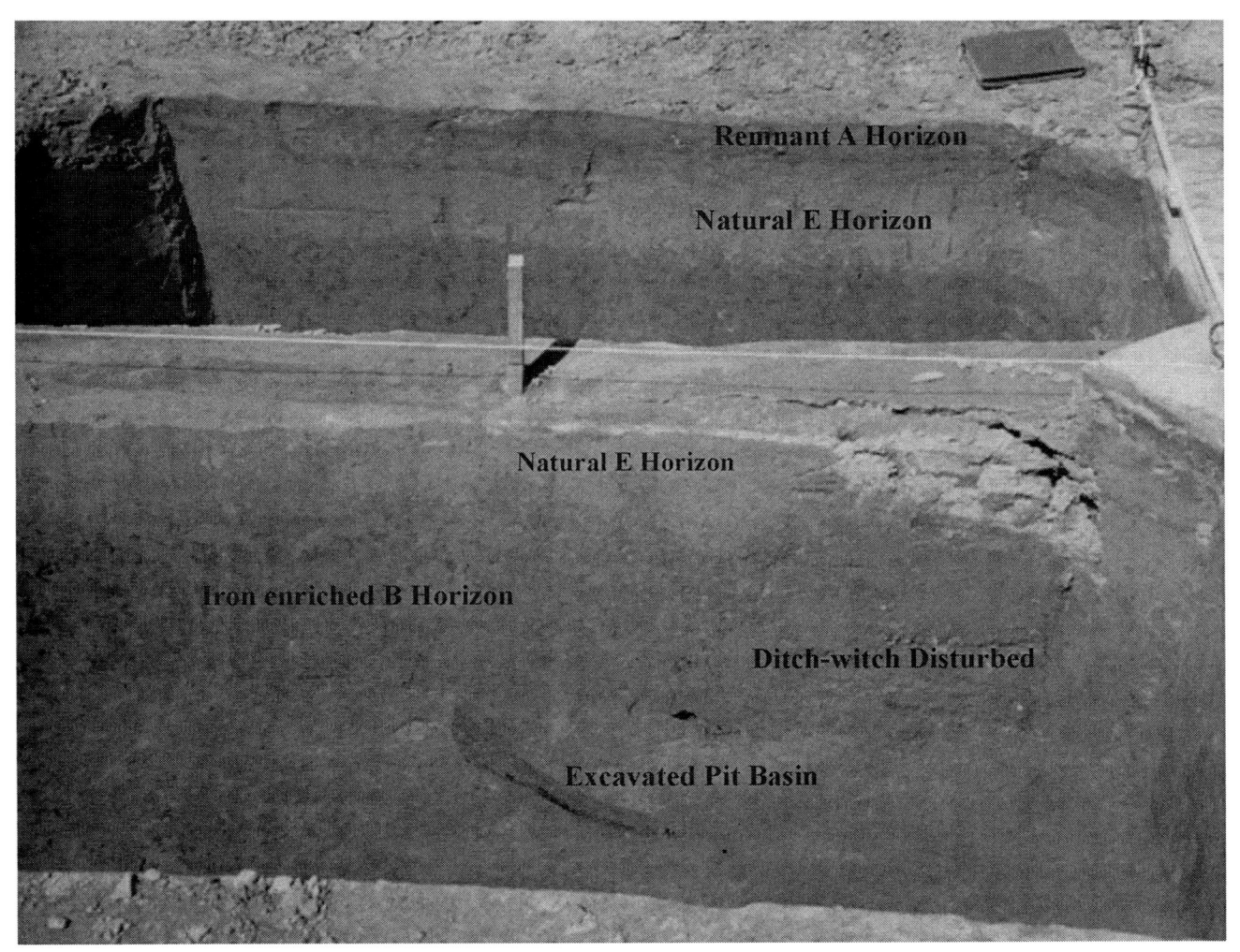

Figure 5. West profiles of test units showing lack of discernable intrusive pit stain due to lengthy pedogenesis, Liska Cache (47Cr637). Note stake marks the spot along the ditch-witch trench where the Liska's found two adzes and large biface fragments.

biface (Fig. 6), and a burned fragment of limestone, all of which were deposited in a pit feature. The feature was not recognized in plan view or profile until a depth of 55 cm, but the pit must have originated at or near the modern surface. The absence of a clear pit stain between the surface and 55 cm suggests substantial age in this well-developed soil. Unfortunately, only tiny fragments of organic material were associated with the cache, and radiocarbon dating has not yet been attempted. All of the five adzes in the Liska Cache exhibit evidence of wear, and two were broken before deposition. The three complete specimens are nearly identical in size, although differing degrees of wear are evident based on measurement of polish on the basal surface. For comparison, measurements of 15 additional triangular cross section adzes from Wisconsin reveal some variation in size and use wear (Table 1).

The silicified sandstone biface from the Liska Cache was broken by the ditch-witch, and any missing portions were not recovered during the excavation. Silicified sandstone outcrops and quarry/workshops occur in west-central Wisconsin, approximately 50 to 100 miles north of the Liska Cache (Boszhardt 1996, 1998). The most well known source is Silver Mound where Hixton Silicified Sandstone (HSS) outcrops (Behm 1984; Brown 1984; Carr and Boszhardt 2005). The Liska biface does not appear to be manufactured from HSS, but rather a lower-quality orthoquartzite.

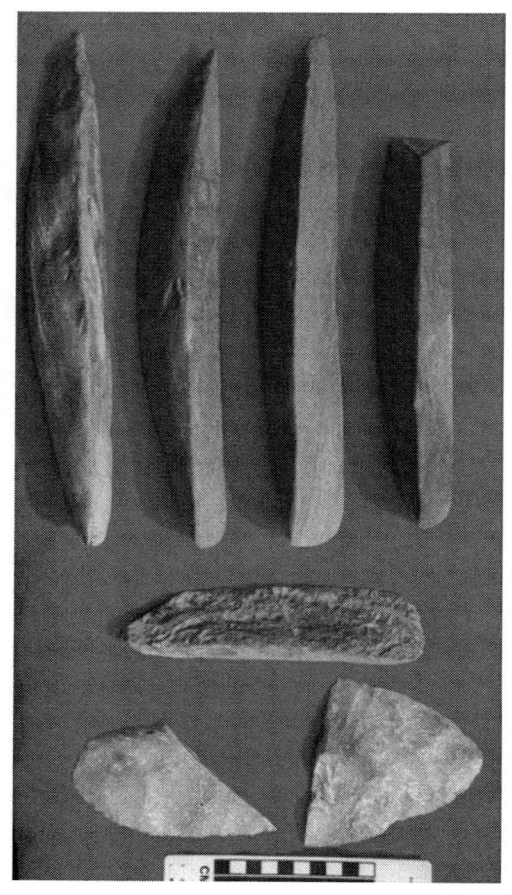

Figure 6. Top and side views of Liska adzes and obverse/reverse of biface fragments, Liska Cache (47Cr637).

Age

The age of the triangular cross section trihedral adzes is currently unknown. Chipped-stone chert adzes have been affiliated with the Late Paleoindian/Early Archaic Dalton Complex in the southeastern United States (Goodyear 1973), and some researchers have suggested Late Paleoindian affiliation for basalt and rhyolite adzes from the upper Mississippi Valley and northern Great Lakes (Behm 1988; Dudzik 1991; Malik and Bakken 1993; Mason 1997:98; McLeod 1981; Overstreet 1988). The suggested affiliation for the latter is based on apparent association with diagnostic Late Paleoindian projectile points, but those adzes are generally rectangular in plan shape and lenticular in cross section.

For example, Behm (1987) reported on a series of 36 chipped and ground stone adzes from the Rush Lake area of Winnebago County, Wisconsin, which were attributed to Late Paleoindian/Early Archaic cultures based on surface association with diagnostic projectile points. Behm also summarized several other probable Late Paleoindian adze associations in Wisconsin, including the Delmer Blank site in Chippewa County (Behm 1984), the Bass site in Grant County (Stoltman, Behm and Palmer 1984), the Metzig Garden site in Winnebago County (Behm 1986), the Bloyer site in Crawford County (Stoltman and Behm 1982) and others. At Bloyer, two crude adzes were found at the base of Holocene prairie soils, resting atop Pleistocene outwash gravels of the Bagley or Kingston Terrace System, which was deposited around 9850 B.P. (Bettis 1988; Hajic 1991; Knox 1996). At Metzig Garden, adzes were found in test excavations in likely association with Late Paleoindian projectile points. In addition, in his summary of Paleoindian complexes in northwestern Wisconsin, Dudzik (1991:145) illustrates a trihedral adze from Douglas County that appears to be of the lenticular form.

Numerous examples of the lenticular cross section variety trihedral adze have been attributed to

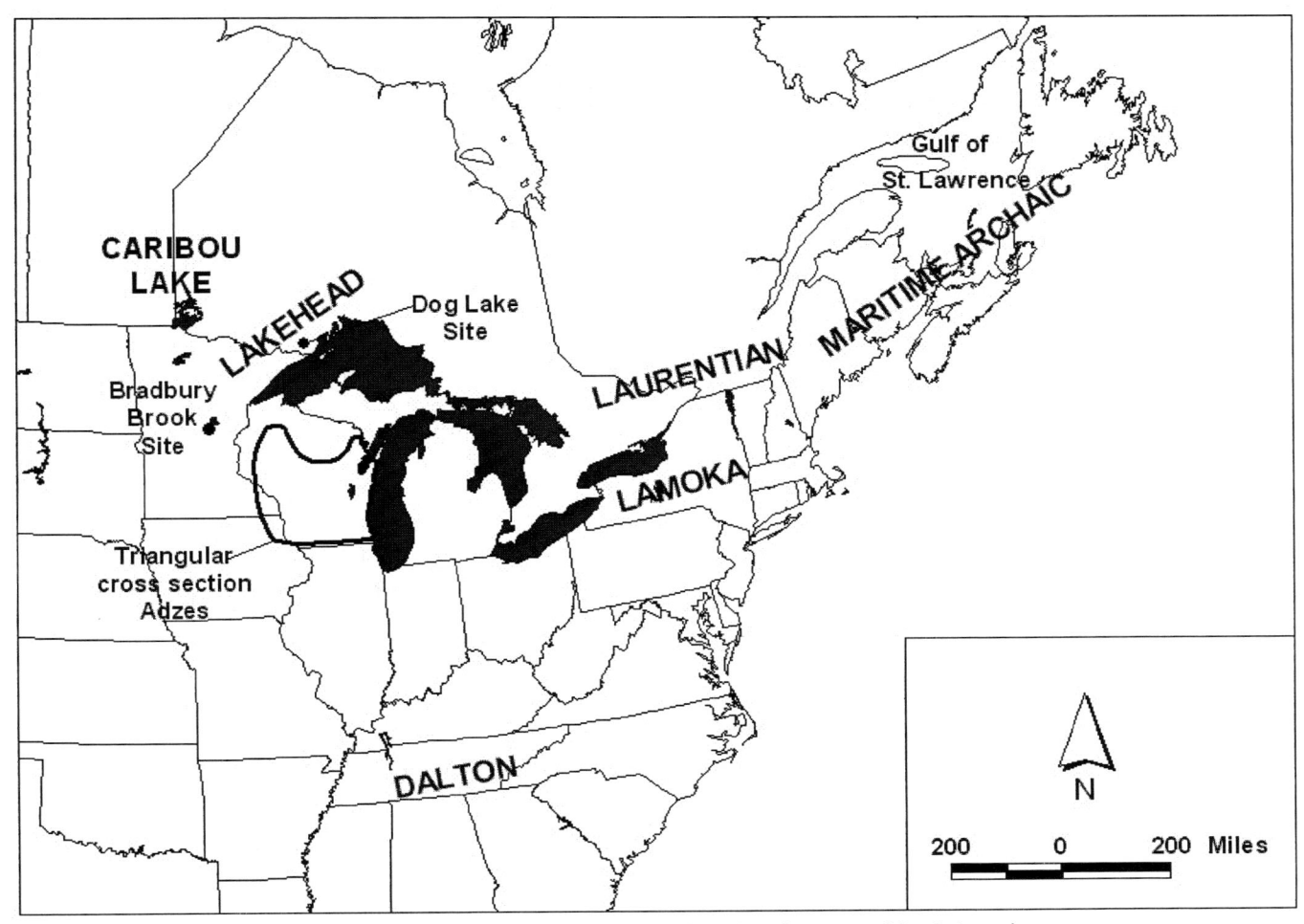

Figure 7. Distribution of cultural complexes with adzes in eastern North America.

the Late Paleoindian Caribou Lakes and Lakehead complexes of Manitoba and northwestern Ontario, respectively (Fig. 7). McLeod (1981) reports on a number of trihedral adzes from the Dog Lake site near Thunder Bay, Ontario and attributes these to the Caribou Lakes Complex, which is inferred to date after 8500 B.P. and before 5500 B.P. A cruder version of a triangular cross section trihedral adze was recovered during excavations of the Bradbury Brook site in Mille Lacs County, Minnesota (Malik and Bakken 1993:44-45) in association with a "keeled scraper." An AMS radiocarbon date of 9220 ± 75 B.P. was obtained from samples collected during these excavations (Malik and Bakken 1993:24). Based on the absence of adzes at later Archaic sites such as Petaga Point near Mille Lacs (Bleed 1969), it appears that these tools were no longer used to the west of Lake Superior following the "pine maximum" (ca. 8500-5500 B.P.), when birch became more common and offered an alternative technology to canoe building.

Beveled (lenticular) adzes and polished gouges have been found in Middle to Late Archaic contexts throughout the eastern Great Lakes and Gulf of St. Lawrence, including such cultures as Lamoka, Laurentian, and Maritime Archaic (Mason 1981:141-180; Tuck 1978; see Fig. 7). Tuck (1978) has recognized affinities among the Archaic cultures throughout the Great Lakes and St. Lawrence region in what he termed the Lake Forest region, including the presence of adzes, gouges, and copper spuds. Gouges were sometimes included as grave offerings in the Maritime Archaic cultures along the Atlantic seaboard. Old Copper "spuds" (Wittry 1957) may represent a material variation of these and it is possible that the triangular cross section adzes of the Upper Mississippi Valley represent a distinct variant of these Archaic woodworking tools. Private reports suggest that triangular cross section adzes were associated with terminal Archaic Red Ocher burials in northeastern Wisconsin, but one of these may have been associated with a Late Paleoindian eared Eden point (Neil Ostberg, pers. comm. 2002).

The depth of the Liska Cache, and lack of an apparent intrusive pit in the well-developed overlying soils, suggests substantial age, but it is not yet possible to make an accurate chronological interpretation. However, pedogenic iron enrichment of the 40 cm-thick B-horizon above the recognized adze cache feature may reflect an age of 4,000 to 8,000 years (Ed Hajic and Michael Kolb, pers. comm. 2005).

Finally, across much of the Upper Midwest, grooved and ungrooved (celt) axes first appear during the Middle Archaic stage (Stoltman 1997) and persist through both Woodland and Mississippian Traditions before being replaced with iron tools during the Historic era. It appears that ground stone axes replaced adze technology in much of the Midwest during the Archaic Tradition.

Function

There is little doubt that triangular cross section adzes were utilized for woodworking purposes, although replica studies and use wear analyses are not known to have been undertaken in the Great Lakes region. As early as the first report of this artifact type, it was suggested that they were used to make dugout canoes (Brown 1934), and this assumption has prevailed over time (Buchner 1984:36). Indeed, comparable adzes are common during the Mesolithic period (8500-7500 B.P.) of Norway, and are interpreted as having been used to manufacture dugout canoes (Lotte Eigeland, pers. comm. 2005). McLeod (pers. comm. 2001) has suggested that these adzes were used for working pine and conform to the "pine maximum" period of 8500 to 5500 B.P. The pine maximum occurred between the post-glacial retreat of tundra and before the succession of birch, which offered an alternative material for canoes. The known distribution of the triangular cross section variety tends to cluster south of the northern deciduous forest and large birch trees as recorded in the mid-nineteenth century (Curtis 1959). This boundary would have been further north during the Altithermal (ca. 9000-6000 B.P.), and this geographic segregation corresponds with a boundary between bark canoes across the Sub-Arctic and dugout canoes in Eastern North America (Driver and Massey 1957:288-290). The general association with major waterways such as the Central and Lower Wisconsin and Upper Mississippi River valleys also suggests dugout canoe construction. The central Wisconsin River valley cuts through a sandy region, which includes relic stands of large white pine that would have been suitable for dugout canoes owing to the relative ease of working this "soft wood," and the fact that pine is highly buoyant.

However, some trihedral adzes have been found well up secondary drainages where canoes were probably not efficient. For example, at least three of these adzes have been reported in private collections from the town of Dell in Vernon County, which is situated on Weister Creek, a small tributary of the Kickapoo River nearly 40 miles from its confluence with the Wisconsin River. Likewise at least two trihedral adzes are reported from small tributaries of the La Crosse River, over 15 miles from the confluence with the Mississippi. These streams are generally too narrow for canoe travel. Consequently, these adzes probably served as multifunctional woodworking tools such as for making frames for shelters, weapon and tool handles, and wooden bowls as Tuck (1978) has suggested for adzes in the eastern Great Lakes.

It has also been suggested that some of these adzes may also have been used as digging tools (Buchner 1984:39). Based on battered and dull use wear on the working end of the Bradbury Brook trihedral adze, Malik and Bakken (1993:45) interpreted that tool as having possibly been originally used for woodworking, but its final use was for digging.

The replacement of adzes by grooved axes and celts during the Archaic, Woodland and Mississippian traditions indicates a technological shift. Both adzes and axes were undoubtedly used for woodworking, but the resulting cuts differ. Adzes, with their curved bits, are specialty tools that perform better for scouring and appear ideal for carving out dugout canoes. Ground stone axes of the Upper Midwest have straight bits, often taper to thick bodies, and have battered pole ends. Among the many woodworking functions these axes may have been employed for, it is clear that one use was as a splitting wedge. Celts, in particular, may have served this purpose and become ubiquitous after the introduction of the bow and arrow, when splitting wood for bow staves would have become essential.

Summary and Conclusion

The Liska Cache is a rare example of an in situ discovery of chipped and ground stone adzes from the Upper Midwest, and offers an opportunity to examine these tools in the context of form, distribution, age, and function. The term "trihedral adze" has been applied to two basic forms that differ in cross section. One form, which is represented by the five adzes in the Liska Cache, is typically triangular in cross section with a tapered or pointed pole end. Another, more common, form is lenticular in cross section, with four facets. Examples of the triangular cross section variety tend to be longer than those of the lenticular form. In addition, the triangular cross section variety tends to cluster across southern Wisconsin, while the lenticular form is more common to the north, although there is overlap. The lenticular cross section form is also comparable to the Lamoka Adze type, which occurs throughout the eastern Great Lakes, while gouges in that area are more comparable to the longer triangular cross section variety adze.

It has been inferred that the lenticular varieties of trihedral adzes from the western Great Lakes represent Late Paleoindian activities, although in situ finds and absolute dating have been very rare. The Late Paleoindian association is generally based on repeated surface association of trihedral adzes with diagnostic Late Paleoindian projectile point forms, and this pattern has been recognized from Manitoba and Ontario to eastern Wisconsin. Lamoka adzes and related gouges, however, are affiliated with Archaic cultures to the east. The Liska cache provided one of the first opportunities to evaluate the age of the triangular trihedral adze variety because they were found in a pit feature, well below the modern surface. Unfortunately, although minuscule amounts of carbon were found within the pit fill, funds are not yet available for radiocarbon dating. However, the feature profile revealed extensive iron enrichment of a well-developed B-Horizon, which suggests substantial age. Soil scientists who observed the profile record suggest that the pedogenesis required perhaps 4,000 to 8,000 years to develop over the adzes. Consequently, these adzes may represent Early to Middle Archaic tools.

Adzes by definition are classified as woodworking tools, and most interpretations of chipped and ground stone adzes from the Upper Great Lakes region have suggested that their primary function was in the hollowing of dugout canoes. A general association with pine forests supports this interpretation in that large pine trees would have been suitable for carving and floating. However, some adzes have been found along minor streams where dugout canoes were likely unfeasible, implying that these tools served multiple woodworking functions. Others have suggested that some adzes with battered working ends may have also been used as digging implements. Experimental studies and use wear pattern analyses would provide information to evaluate such interpretations.

The fact that five adzes were cached in a pit feature along the Mississippi River raises questions of purpose. One possibility is that these were stored for future use but never reclaimed. However, the presence of two broken adzes in the set raises doubts about such an interpretation. Similarly, it is difficult to imagine discarding the three unbroken specimens, which appear to have extensive potential use life remaining. It is also possible that the deposition represents ritual activity. Ground stone adzes and gouges have been found in Archaic burial association in the eastern Great Lakes. No evidence of a burial was detected in the Liska cache feature, but bone preservation capabilities of the encompassing sandy soil are poor and, given the apparent substantial age of the feature, it is possible that any associated bone may have disintegrated. Nonetheless, the presence of this find, coupled with the cache found at Prairie du Chien in the late 1920s, indicates that other comparable finds may exist. Discovery of relatively deep feature deposits with no near surface indications, however, will be difficult through traditional methods of surface and shovel test survey. We are fortunate that the Liska's recognized the importance of their accidental find and contacted and collaborated with professional archaeologists to pursue the discovery.

Acknowledgements. This research would not have been possible without the interest and cooperation of Terrance and Connie Liska, who brought the find to our attention. Once the project was initiated numerous individuals aided in the research, including Jeff Behm, Mark Dudzik, Bill Green, Ed Hajic, Robert Hruska, Mike Kolb, Ron Mason, Mike McLeod, Neil Ostberg, Tom Pleger, Bill Ross, Jim Theler, Dawn Shere-Tomae, Dan Wendt, Dennis Wiggens, Dean Wilder, and Lotte Eigeland from Norway. Graphic production was assisted by Jean Dowiasch and Lindsey Mass of MVAC.

References Cited

Behm, Jeffery A.
1984 Comments on Brown's Research at Silver Mound. *The Wisconsin Archeologist* 56(2):169-173.
1986 Preliminary report on the Metzig Garden site (47-Wn-283), Winnebago County, Wisconsin. *Fox Valley Archaeology* 8:1-9.
1987 Rhyolite Adzes from the Rush Lake Area, Winnebago County, Wisconsin. *Fox Valley Archaeology* 12:23-73.

Bettis, E.A.
1988 Quaternary History, Stratigraphy, Geomorphology, and Pedology. In *Archaeology and Geomorphology in Pools 17 and 18, Upper Mississippi River*, pp. 18-91. Center for Archaeological Research, Southwest Missouri State University, Springfield

Bettis, E.A. and G.R. Hallberg
1985 The Savanna (Zwingle) Terrace and Red Clays in the Upper Mississippi River Valley: Stratigraphy and Chronology. In *Pleistocene Geology and Evolution of the Upper Mississippi Valley*, ed. by R.S. Lively, pp. 41-44. Minnesota Geological Survey.

Bleed, Peter
1969 *The Archaeology of Petaga Point: The Preceramic Component.* Minnesota Historical Society, St. Paul.

Boszhardt, Robert F.
1996 Newly Discovered Lithic Resources in Western Wisconsin. *The Minnesota Archaeologist* 57:85-96.
1998 *An Archaeological Survey of an Orthoquartzite District in West Central Wisconsin.* Reports of Investigations No. 306. Mississippi Valley Archaeology Center, University of Wisconsin-La Crosse.

Brown, Charles E.
1934 Stone Adzes. *The Wisconsin Archeologist* 13(4):91-93.
1984 Notes on Silver Mound. *The Wisconsin Archeologist* 65(2):159-168.

Buchner, Anthony P.
1984 *Investigations at the Sinnock Site, 1980 and 1982.* Papers in Manitoba Archaeology, Final Report No. 17. Historic Resources Branch, Department of Culture, Heritage and Recreation, Winnipeg.

Carr, Dillon and Robert F. Boszhardt
2005 National Historic Landmark Nomination for the Silver Mound Archaeological District. Copy on file, Mississippi Valley Archaeology Center, University of Wisconsin-La Crosse.

Crosby, Henry A.
1903 The Triangular Stone Adze. *The Wisconsin Archeologist* (OS) 2(4):91-92.

Curtis, John A.
1959 *The Vegetation of Wisconsin.* University of Wisconsin Press, Madison.

Driver, Harold E., and William C. Massey
1957 Comparative Studies of North American Indians. *Transactions of the American Philosophical Society* 47(2). Philadelphia, Pennsylvania.

Dudzik, Mark J.
1991 First People: The Paleoindian Tradition in Northwestern, Wisconsin. *The Wisconsin Archeologist* 72 (3-4):137-154.

Flock, M.A.
1983 The Late Wisconsinan Savanna Terrace in Tributaries to the Upper Mississippi River. *Quaternary Research* 20:165-176.

Goodyear, Albert C. III
1973 The Significance of the Dalton Adze in Northeast Arkansas. *Plains Anthropologist* 18 (62):316-322.

Hajic, E.R.
1991 Terraces in the central Mississippi Valley. In Hajic, E.R., Johnson, W.H., and Follmer, L.R., trip Leaders. *Quaternary Deposits and Landforms, Confluence Region of the Mississippi, Missouri, and Illinois Rivers, Missouri and Illinois: Terraces and terrace Problems.* Midwest Friends of the Pleistocene, 38th Field Conference, May 1991, pp. 1-32.

Knox, James C.
1996 Late Quaternary Upper Mississippi River Alluvial Episodes and their Significance to the

Lower Mississippi River System. *Engineering Geology* 45:263-285.

Malik, Riaz and Kent Bakken
1993 *Archaeological Data Recovery at the Bradbury Brook Site, 21 ML 42, Mille Lacs County, Minnesota.* Report prepared for the Minnesota Department of Transportation, Archaeology Department, Minnesota Historical Society, St. Paul, Minnesota.

Martin, Lawrence
1965 The Physical Geography of Wisconsin. University of Wisconsin Press, Madison.

Mason, Ronald J.
1981 *Great Lakes Archaeology.* Academic Press, New York.
1997 The Paleoindian Tradition. In *Wisconsin Archaeology*, ed. by Robert A. Birmingham, Carol I Mason, and James B. Stoltman. *The Wisconsin Archeologist* 78(1/2):78-111.

McLeod, Mike
1981 The Early Prehistory of the Dog Lake Area, Thunder Bay. *Manitoba Archaeological Quarterly* 5(2):12-37.

Miller, Towne L.
1930 Diary entry for July 1, 1930. Copy on file, Mississippi Valley Archaeology Center, La Crosse, Wisconsin.

Overstreet, David F.
1979 *Cultural Resources Overview of the Chequamegon National Forest Vol. IV--Cultural Resources Inventory Forms (47BA-48).* Reports of Investigation No. 50. Great Lakes Archaeological Research Center. Waukesha, Wisconsin.
1988 Tri-Hedral Adze. In *Historical Dictionary of North American Archaeology*, ed. by E.B. Jelks and J.C. Jelks, pp 494. Greenwood press, New York and London.
1989 *Oneota Tradition Culture History--New Data from the Old Spring Site (47Wn350).* Reports of Investigation No. 219. Great Lakes Archaeological Research Center, Milwaukee.

Stoltman, James B.
1997 The Archaic Tradition in *Wisconsin Archaeology*, ed. by Robert A. Birmingham, Carol I Mason, and James B. Stoltman. *The Wisconsin Archeologist* 78(1/2):112-139.

Stoltman, James B. and Jeffery A. Behm
1982 Excavations at the Bloyer Site (47 CR 339). In *Archaeological Survey and Testing in the Prairie du Chien Region: the 1980 Season*, by James B. Stoltman, Constance Arzigian, Jeffery A. Behm, Robert Boszhardt, and James L. Theler. Department of Anthropology, University of Wisconsin-Madison.

Stoltman, James B., Jeffery A. Behm, and Harris A. Palmer
1984 The Bass Site: A Hardin Quarry/Workshop in Southwestern Wisconsin. In *Prehistoric Chert Exploitation-Studies from the Midcontinent*, ed. by Brian M. Butler and Ernest E. May, pp. 197-224. Occasional Paper 2, Center for American Archaeological Investigations, Southern Illinois University, Carbondale.

Theler, James L. and Robert F. Boszhardt
2003 *Twelve Millennia: Archaeology of the Upper Mississippi River Valley.* University of Iowa Press, Iowa City, Iowa.

Tuck, James A.
1978 Regional Cultural Development 3000-300 B.C. In *Handbook of North American Indians Vol. 15 Northeast*, ed. by Bruce G. Trigger, pp 28-43. Smithsonian Institution, Washington D.C.

Wittry, Warren L.
1957 A Preliminary Study of the Old Copper Complex. *The Wisconsin Archeologist* 38(4):204-221.

Animal Remains from the Midway Site (21BL37), Beltrami County, Minnesota

Jonathan D. Baker
Department of Anthropology
The University of Tennessee, Knoxville, TN 37996
jbaker18@utk.edu

James L. Theler
Department of Sociology and Archaeology
University of Wisconsin–La Crosse, La Crosse, WI 54601
theler.jame@uwlax.edu

Excavations at the Midway Site, located in the city of Bemidji, Minnesota produced an extensive vertebrate faunal assemblage, with over 23,000 remains representing a minimum of 116 individual animals from 55 different taxa. Despite the lack of a detailed analysis of the cultural remains, the faunal data provide important information on Woodland subsistence strategies in northern Minnesota. Although fish are numerically most abundant, large mammals, including moose, white-tailed deer, elk, black bear, and caribou, likely provided the bulk of the animal protein in the local diet. Evidence indicates a multi-season use of the site, with a fall-winter deer harvest, use of moose (probably along with wild rice) during the winter, and spring harvest of riparian animals, spawning fish, and turtles. The representation of large mammal skeletal elements suggests an off-site processing of the animal carcasses, with the retention of only specific elements. Overall, the species represented at the Midway Site indicate that the Bemidji area, with its lakes, marshes, and deciduous forest margin located at the southern margin of Beltrami County, may have furnished an optimal ecotonal niche to be exploited by prehistoric peoples.

Introduction

The Midway Site (21BL37) is multi-component prehistoric occupation located in the city of Bemidji in Beltrami County, Minnesota. The site is situated on a narrow isthmus between Lake Bemidji and Lake Irving, both flowages of the upper Mississippi River (Fig. 1). The area surrounding the site has been heavily developed, and construction associated with the expansion of Minnesota Trunk Highway 197 provided a substantial threat to the archaeological deposits.

In order to evaluate the site's integrity and archaeological potential, Phase II excavations were conducted during the fall of 1999 by the Leech Lake Heritage Sites Program (LLHSP) of the Leech Lake Band of Ojibwe (Kluth and Kluth 2000). These investigations revealed substantial archaeological deposits, including evidence of seven culturally distinct groups: Late Archaic, Brainerd, Laurel, St. Croix, Blackduck, Sandy Lake, and Oneota-like components (Kluth and Kluth 2000). Given the extent and integrity of the cultural deposits, the site was recommended as eligible for listing on the National Register of Historic Places.

The parameters of the proposed construction activities made avoidance of the site infeasible. Accordingly, an extensive Phase III data recovery plan was implemented to mitigate impacts to the archaeological deposits (Kluth and Kluth 2000; LLHSP 2002). This involved the excavation of 48 one-meter units in three discrete portions of the site. Phase III excavations commenced in the fall of 2000 and were completed in the summer of 2001. A final report was produced on these investigations (LLHSP 2002), and a version of this paper was included as part of that report (Theler and Baker 2002). Unfortunately, the analysis of the cultural material from the site has remained preliminary. Certainly, this faunal analysis will be much more meaningful if a detailed study of the cultural data is conducted at some point in the future. However, by itself this analysis does provide some important information on Woodland subsistence strategies in the Headwater Lakes region and adds to the limited, yet growing, database

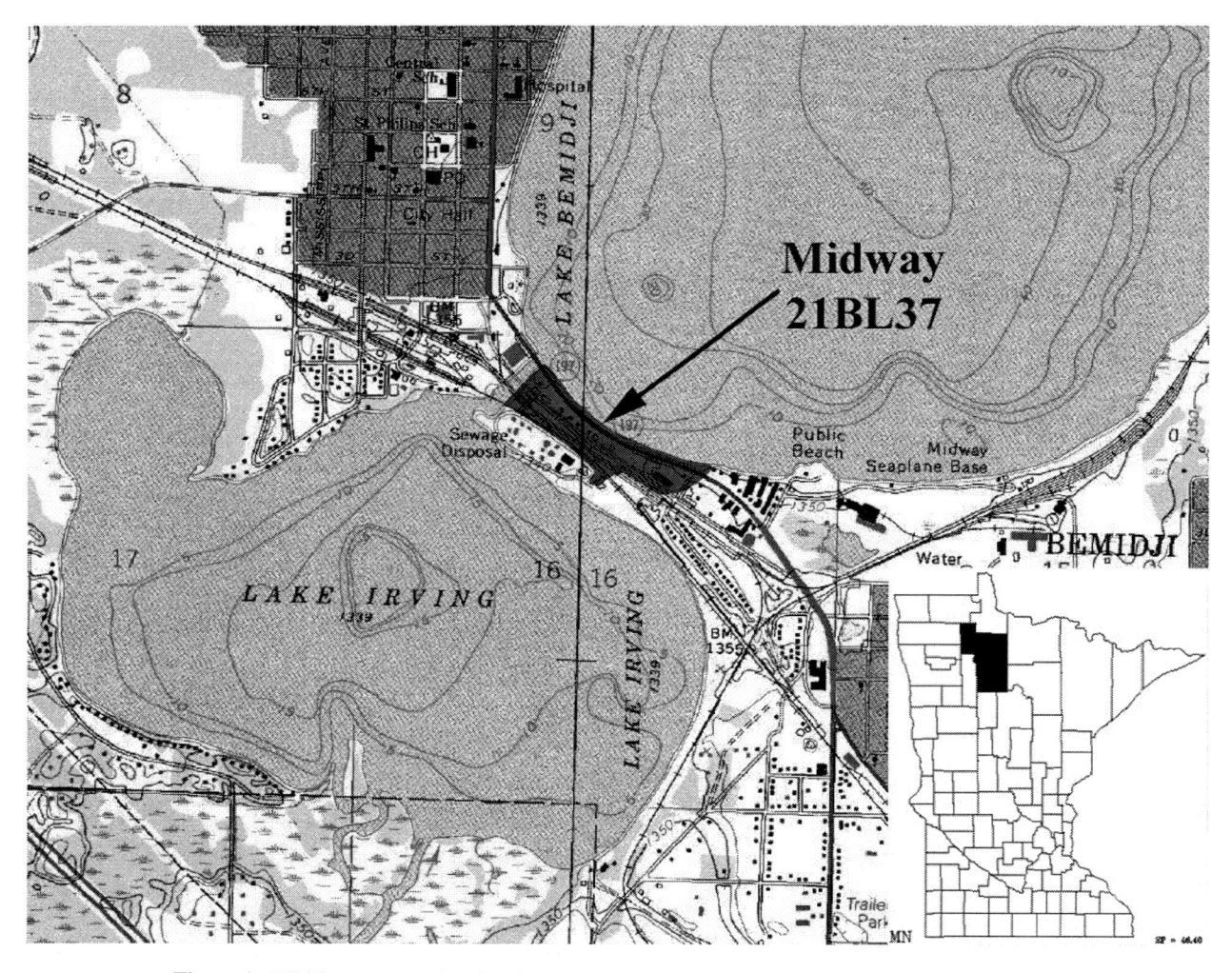

Figure 1. USGS quad map showing the location of the Midway site (21BL37).

of prehistoric faunal remains from northern Minnesota.

Methods

Most of the analyzed faunal materials were from the Phase III excavation. A total of 22,983 fragments of animal bone were recovered from the 48 one-meter units. The units were excavated in arbitrary 3-cm levels, with each level divided horizontally into four 50-cm quadrants and each quadrant excavated separately. Soil from the northeast, southeast, and southwest quadrants was screened through 1/4-inch mesh, and soil from the northwest quadrant was screened through 1/8-inch mesh. Many units contained an upper level of redeposited A horizon material excavated as a single level, processed through 1/4-inch screen, and analyzed separately. Heavy fractions from 19 flotation samples also were analyzed. The flotation material came from a variety of contexts and was processed through 1/16-inch screen.

Faunal materials from the 1999 Phase II excavations had been inventoried earlier by personnel from the LLHSP (Kluth and Kluth 2000). For the current analysis, they were reexamined only to find any identifiable elements. Excavation and initial processing methods for the Phase II materials were similar to those for Phase III, although all of the Phase II soil was screened through 1/4-inch mesh.

The animal remains were identified through comparison to modern skeletal collections housed at the University of Wisconsin–La Crosse. Several bird elements were sent for identification to Dr. Paul W. Parmalee at the McClung Museum of the University of Tennessee. Dr. Holmes A. Semken, Jr. at the University of Iowa identified the vole and shrew remains.

Prior to analysis, all of the bone fragments were screened again through 1/4-inch mesh. Fragments smaller than 1/4 inch were scanned for identifiable material and counted, but not identified to class. Fragments larger than 1/4 inch were sorted by class and identified to the most specific taxonomic designation possible, with element, portion, and side recorded as appropriate. Each fragment larger than 1/4 inch was also examined for burning, rodent/carnivore gnawing, ingestion, fracturing, cut marks, and other signs of human or natural modification. Provenience, taxonomic, and attribute information was recorded on a paper datasheet and entered into a Microsoft Access database (Stevenson et al. n.d.).

Taxonomic names for mammals follow Hazard (1982), with the exception of the American elk (*Cervus canadensis*), which is after Thomas and Toweill (1982). Bird terminology comes from Green and Janssen (1975), with the "true duck" subfamily (Anatinae) after Kaufman (1996). Terminology for fish comes from Becker (1983), reptiles and amphibians are from Oldfield and Moriarty (1994), and the single freshwater mussel follows Turgeon et al. (1998).

To understand the dietary significance of the species and classes of animals, usable meat weights were estimated for animals identified to the genus or species level. Mammals the size of a Plains pocket gopher (*Geomys bursarius*) or smaller, as well as toads (*Bufo* sp.), were excluded from the meat weight estimates because their occurrence at the site was probably natural. Variation in animal size was accommodated through the use of conservative estimates for usable meat: for mammals, 50 percent of the live weight; for birds, 70 percent of the live weight, following White (1953:398); and for fish and reptiles, 50 percent of the live weight.

Live weights for ungulates come from Banfield (1974), and those for other mammals come from Theler (1987), with the exception of the porcupine (*Erethizon dorsatum*) and the snowshoe hare (*Lepus americanus*), which are derived from Hazard (1982). Live weight estimates for fishes and turtles are based on individual comparisons to modern specimens of known size. Live weights for birds come from several different sources, listed for each species as appropriate.

After identification, the animal remains were placed in polyethylene bags, with a tag on white acid-free paper identifying the acquisition numbers and the appropriate provenience and taxonomic information. With completion of the analysis, the remains were returned to LLHSP for curation at the Minnesota History Center through a repository agreement with the Minnesota Historical Society.

Results

Of the 22,983 tabulated fragments from the Phase III excavations, 11,158 were identified to class, and 892 were further identified to the family, genus, or species level. The Phase II materials contributed another 328 specimens identified to family, genus, or species. The following sections summarize the analyzed remains by taxonomic category. Elements from the redeposited A horizon or other contexts labeled as disturbed are noted as appropriate.

Mammals

Mammal bones dominate the faunal assemblage. In all, 8,869 mammal bones/fragments were tabulated, with 826 (9.3%) identified to the species, genus, or family level, representing at least 46 individuals of 28 native and 2 introduced mammal species. As a class, mammals contributed 1,096 kg (95%) of the usable meat (Table 1).

Even-Toed Ungulates (Artiodactyla)

Deer Family (Cervidae)

In terms of both usable meat and hides, the most important mammals were four members of the Cervidae or deer family: deer, moose, elk, and woodland caribou. A fifth large mammal species, black bear, will be discussed below with other carnivores.

*Deer (*Odocoileus *sp.):* Deer elements were by far the most numerous of the large mammal remains, with 354 elements positively identified and another 38 identified as probable deer. Two deer species occur in Minnesota, the mule deer (*Odocoileus hemionus*) and the white-tailed deer (*O. virginianus*). The Midway deer remains could not be separated by species based on their osteological characteristics. Range information is somewhat more helpful. The

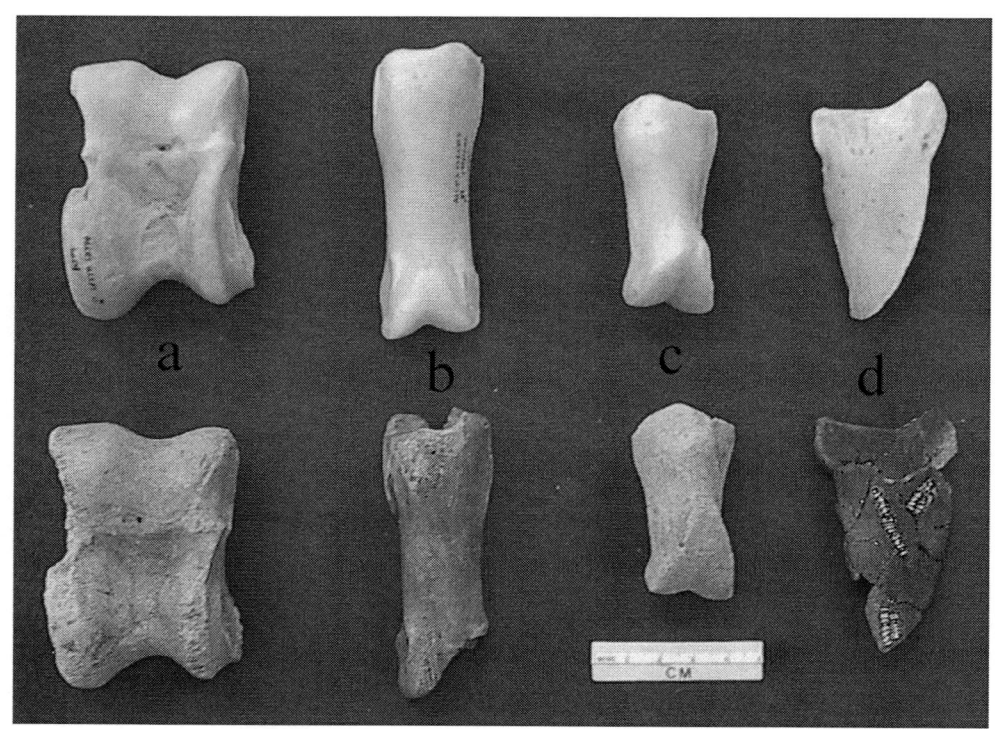

Figure 2. Upper row: modern moose (*Alces alces*) elements. Lower row: moose elements from the Midway site (21BL37); (a) left astragalus, (b) first phalanx, (c) second phalanx, (d) third phalanx.

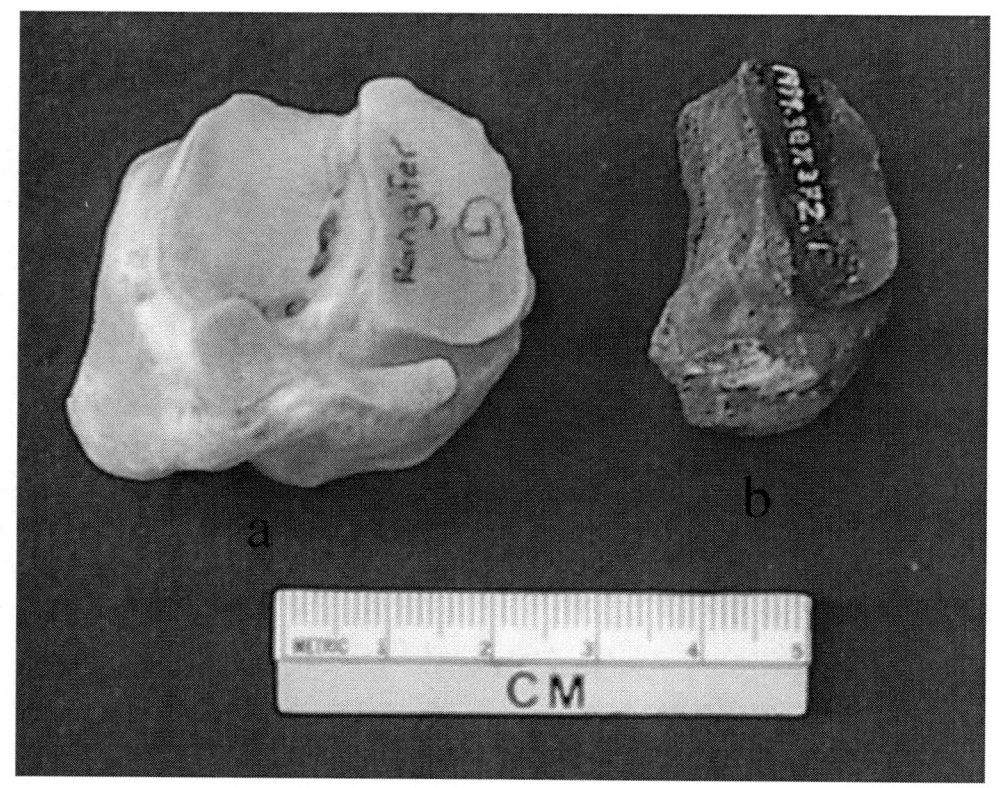

Figure 3. Left naviculo-cuboid (a) from a modern caribou (*Rangifer tarandus*), and (b) that of one from the Midway site (21BL37).

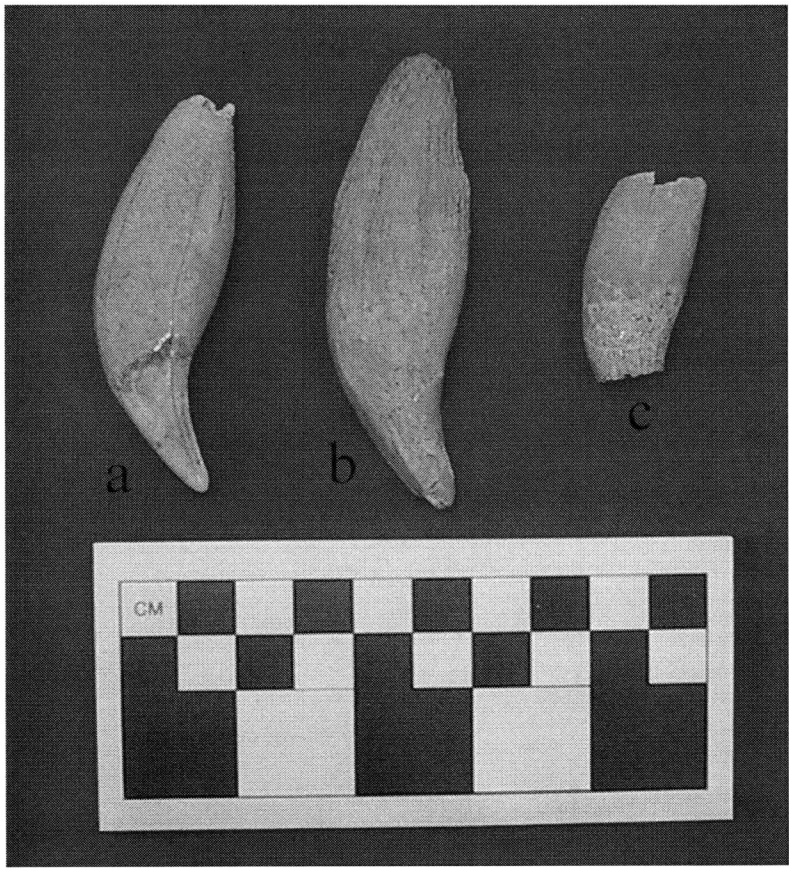

Figure 4. Black bear (*Ursus americanus*) canines (a, b), and cf. black bear canine (c) from the Midway site (21BL37).

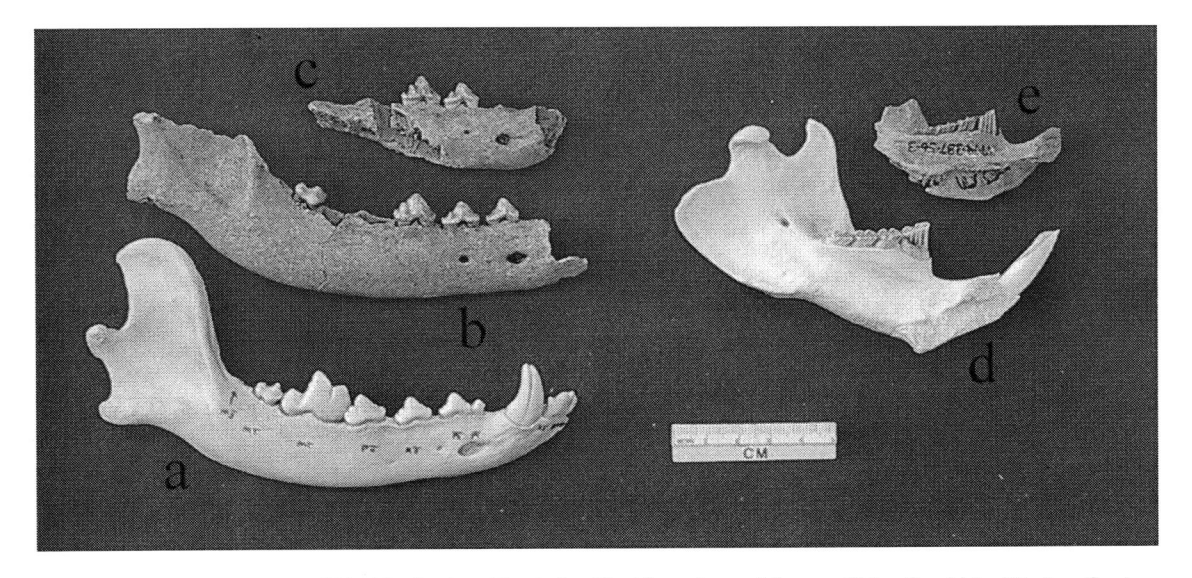

Figure 5. Modern right mandible (a) of a dog (*Canis familiaris*), and two right mandibles (b, c) identified as *Canis* sp. from the Midway site (21BL37). Modern left mandible (d) of a beaver (*Castor canadensis*), and (e) one recovered from Midway.

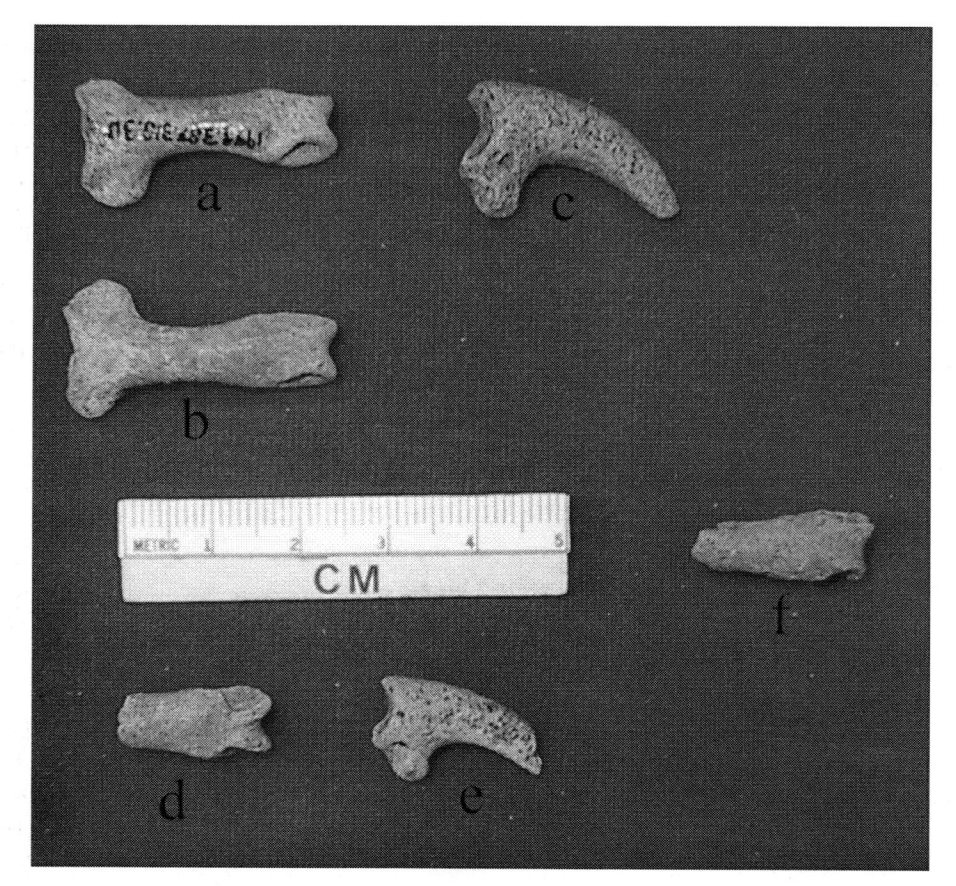

Figure 6. Eagle remains from the Midway site (21BL37): (a-c) bald eagle, (d-e) cf. bald eagle, and (f) cf. eagle. Unpositioned foot phalanges (a, b, d, f) and terminal foot phalanges/talons (c, e).

Figure 7. Worked bone from the Midway site (21BL37): (a) harpoon head, (b) awl fragment?, (c) mammal bone with grooves on edge, (d) polished mammal bone, (e) mammal bone with groove, and (f) drilled turtle carapace.

mule deer is a western species, and the eastern margin of its range is marked with rare, sporadic occurrences in Minnesota, including in counties adjacent to Beltrami (Hall and Kelson 1959:1006, Map 490; Hazard 1982:Map 71). Mule deer might have been native to northwestern Minnesota in Kittson, Roseau, and Wilkin Counties, but there is no resident population known in the state today (Hazard 1982:158; Swanson et al. 1945:15).

White-tailed deer, in contrast, are common and widespread in north-central Minnesota today, including Beltrami County (Hazard 1982:159-162, Map 72). They were not always so widespread. Before logging and fires reshaped vegetation regimes after A.D. 1860, deer were rare in the region's closed coniferous forests (Pike 1966 appendix I:54-56; Swanson et al. 1945:26; Schoolcraft 1966:223-4, 244-252). Higher densities, however, occurred in vegetational edge habitats such as those found at Bemidji. Most of the deer elements from Midway can probably be attributed to white-tailed deer, based on records of historic distributions.

Table 2 shows the numbers of different deer elements in the Midway assemblage. Of the 354 positively identified elements, 327 (92%) are either limb extremities ($n = 220$, or 62%) or cranial fragments or teeth ($n = 107$, 30%) (Table 3). This element distribution might reflect deboning of deer at kill locations, with only selected elements returned to the site.

The minimum number of individuals (MNI) for deer, as determined from unique element counts, is five, as indicated by five lower right third premolars and five lower right third molars (Table 4). Tooth wear analysis (Table 5) provides another means for evaluating MNI. Tooth wear in the Midway sample shows evidence of deer up to at least seven years of age. Dividing the dentition into age classes raises the MNI from five to six: one fawn, two yearlings, two deer 2.5 to 5.0 years old, and one deer seven years or older at death.

The season of deer harvest is indicated by tooth eruption patterns and a male frontal bone (Table 5). Based on dentition, at least one fawn and two yearlings were killed during the period October through December. A left frontal bone with the antler base attached to the skull also reflects a fall to early winter kill.

The 38 elements identified as probable deer (Table 6) show patterns similar to those of the positively identified remains: 15 (40%) are limb extremities, and 22 (58%) are tooth and cranial fragments. Disturbed/redeposited contexts contributed 11 additional deer elements and 4 other probable deer fragments.

*Moose (*Alces alces*):* The Midway excavations produced 23 positively identified moose bones and six probable moose bones. An additional two moose remains and one probable came from disturbed/redeposited contexts. Moose would have been relatively abundant in the deciduous-coniferous forests of north-central Minnesota. During the summer, moose browse on aquatic vegetation, particularly the leaves and tubers of the water lily and the early successional stages of deciduous vegetation. In winter, moose often seek cover in dense stands of hardwoods or conifers (Banfield 1974:396; Hazard 1982:163).

In 1806, Zebulon Pike reported that moose were present in the Leech Lake area and above there in the Mississippi Headwaters, but there were very few deer or bear (Pike 1966:Appendix I:54). In the historic period, moose were present in the Bemidji area (Hazard 1982:Map 73), a region that could be considered ecotonal in terms of the distributions of white-tailed deer and moose. Moose have a competitive advantage in deep snow, while deer are more resistant to the endemic flatworm *Parelophostrongylus tenus,* which is fatal to moose (Hazard 1982:164; see also Discussion, below). There are at least five records of moose at Late Holocene archaeological sites in north-central Minnesota (Faunmap 1994:445). Moose bones also have been reported recently from mound burial contexts at the Gull Lake Dam site in Cass County; they were originally identified as bison until reexamined by David Mather, as reported by Blue (2000).

The identified moose elements from Midway (Table 7, Fig. 2), except for one molar, are all from the limb extremities. At least two moose are represented, as indicated by left distal tibia and right proximal metatarsals. Interestingly, of the elements that could be identified as coming from the front or hindquarters, all were from the meat-rich hindquarters (excluding a distal humerus from the redeposited A horizon). As suggested for deer, moose were probably deboned at the kill location, with only a few elements from the limb extremities returned to the site. Moose elements from the McKinstry Mound in northern Minnesota showed a similar high proportion of extremities; of the 191 moose elements from McKinstry, 54 percent were phalanges (Lukens 1973:40-41). Among the seven Midway bones identified as probable moose (Table 8) was one ulna, representing a front quarter. The other six were from hindquarters or undetermined positions. Two of the moose elements from Midway (a distal tibia and a first phalanx) had cut marks produced by a metal implement, indicating they were associated with a historic occupation of the site.

A moose provides a substantial package of meat. Adult males range from 385 to 545 kg and females from 330 to 385 kg (Banfield 1974; Hazard 1982; Jackson 1961). On average, a moose offers roughly 135 to 225 kg of usable meat. The two moose represented in the Midway assemblage might have provided as much meat as the six deer.

*American Elk (*Cervus canadensis*)*: The four elk bones identified from Midway, including one from the redeposited A horizon, are all from limb extremities and represent an MNI of one (Table 9). Two additional bones were classified as probable elk. In earlier historic times, elk were widespread in Minnesota, particularly at the prairie-hardwood forest ecotone, and were present in the Beltrami County region (Hazard 1982:156; Swanson et al. 1945:13-14). An adult male elk can weigh as much as 320 kg and provide 160 kg of usable meat (Banfield 1974; Jackson 1961). Elk remains also have been reported at archaeological sites near Mille Lacs, 160 km southeast of the Midway site (Whelan 1990:64, 70).

*Woodland Caribou (*Rangifer tarandus*)*: A caribou is represented by one element, a naviculo-cuboid from the distal portion of the rear leg (Fig. 3), found in the uppermost level of a unit. In the historic period, caribou were reported from the northern portion of the state, including Beltrami County, east of the prairie biome (Hall and Kelson 1959:1021; Hazard 1982:165; Surber 1932:16; Swanson et al. 1945:100). Two late Holocene occurrences are recorded in north-central Minnesota for the McKinstry Mound and the White Oak Mound (Faunmap 1994:455; Lukens 1973). Because the caribou element in the Midway assemblage was found in a surface level, its association with the pre-European occupation of the site is difficult to confirm.

Other Artiodactyla Remains

The 92 remaining elements from ungulates included 1 eroded third molar of a cervid and 91 elements assigned to the order Artiodactyla (Table 1). Of the 91 specimens from good context (not from the redeposited A horizon or other contexts labeled as disturbed), 9 were metatarsal or metacarpal fragments, and the remaining 82 were teeth. All of the tooth fragments were from molars or premolars, and most were probably from deer (*Odocoileus* sp.); however, they were too fragmented to permit positive identification.

Carnivores (Carnivora)

The Midway assemblage includes elements from 11 carnivores: timber wolf, probable domestic dog, red fox, black bear, raccoon, pine marten, probable mink, badger, striped skunk, river otter, and domestic house cat (discussed separately with other domestic species). In terms of usable meat, fat, and hides, black bear would have been the most important of these species.

*Black Bear (*Ursus americanus*)*: The nine bear bones found at Midway (Table 10) are consistent with those of a black bear. They are a left maxilla, a right and a left canine, an incisor, four metatarsals, and an astragalus. An MNI of two individuals is based upon two upper canines. Although one is a right and one is a left, the two teeth differ significantly in size and obviously came from two individuals (Fig. 4). Another damaged canine from the redeposited A horizon was identified as probable bear. An additional cranial fragment, an occipital condyle, also came from the redeposited A horizon material.

The black bear is a widespread, low-density species in northern Minnesota and a characteristic species of the Mississippi Headwaters region. The presence of canines and a maxillary portion might reflect an interest in securing canines for ornamental or ritual purposes, and the metatarsals might indicate use of the bear skin, transport of the hindquarters, or removal of the terminal (third) phalanx or claw for ornamental or ritual uses.

It is unlikely that the grizzly bear (*Ursus arctos*) occurred as a resident in north-central Minnesota during the later prehistoric period. Euro-American sightings of these bears were reported around the year 1800 as close as the Red River of North (Hazard 1982:126), where grizzlies were coterminous with bison herds near what is now the Minnesota-North Dakota border. Grizzly bear terminal phalanges were found in mortuary context at the McKinstry Mound (Stoltman 1973), and they were probably items acquired to the west.

Dog Family (domestic dog, coyote, or wolf) (Canis sp.): The assemblage contains 16 elements identified as *Canis* species and 2 additional bones classified as probable *Canis* species (Table 11). The MNI of three is based on the number of lower right fourth premolars. Of the 16 positively identified elements, 13 are teeth or related cranial fragments (Fig. 5), and the others are an atlas vertebra, a distal metapodial, and a distal femur. The two elements classified as probable *Canis* sp. are atlas vertebra fragments from the same provenience (Unit 17, Level 7). All of the recovered elements are consistent in size and form to the domestic dog, *Canis familiaris*. The overwhelming predominance of cranial elements might be attributable to disposal practices for animals used as food (Synder 1991; Theler 2000:127, 129).

Timber Wolf (Canis lupus): A timber wolf was represented at the Midway site by two bone fragments, a right proximal metapodial and a proximal second phalanx. Another left metapodial is probably that of a timber wolf. The timber wolf is widespread across North America and preys on a range of vertebrate species, especially deer, elk, and moose in the Minnesota Headwaters region. Its presence in the Midway assemblage is not surprising.

Other Carnivores: Eight other carnivore species are present in the Midway assemblage, each identified by a small number of fragments. At least two river otters (*Lutra canadensis*) are represented by two left proximal ulnae and one lower first molar. Other carnivore elements are a fourth premolar of a red fox (*Vulpes vulpes*), a second phalanx of a badger (*Taxidea taxus*), a distal right fibula of a striped skunk (*Mephitis mephitis*), and a left horizontal ramus of a raccoon (*Procyon lotor*). Additional materials from the redeposited A horizon include a left horizontal ramus (with the first molar) from a pine marten (*Martes americana*), and an axis vertebra fragment identified as probable mink (*Mustela vison*).

Rodents (Rodentia)

Bones from at least eight species of rodents were recovered at the Midway site (Table 1). Some species (porcupine, beaver, muskrat, and perhaps the woodchuck) were probably subsistence related, but others (Plains pocket gopher, chipmunk, meadow vole and red-backed vole) would have occurred naturally at the site.

*Beaver (*Castor canadensis*)*: The assemblage includes 101 elements positively identified as beaver and 9 others classified as possible beaver. Three of the positively identified elements are from the redeposited A horizon material, but of the remaining 98 specimens, 56 (57%) are cranial or tooth fragments. The MNI of four individuals was based on lower right fourth premolars (Table 12). The proportions of different elements seem to indicate that the beaver were processed at the site. An emphasis on cranial-mandibular bones (Fig. 5) might reflect a desire to procure the sturdy incisors to use as woodworking tools (Lukens 1973:39-40; Theler 2000:127); however, none of the 6 incisors or 17 incisor fragments found show signs of such wear or modification.

Historically, beaver were widespread in northern Minnesota. They live in colonies of 4 to 10 individuals, and their primary warm-season foods are aquatic vegetation and tree bark. During cold weather, they subsist on bark-covered deciduous limbs they cache near their lodge. Stable winter water levels controlled by log dams are essential to their existence (Hazard 1982:80). Several early travelers in the Mississippi Headwaters region mentioned beaver as important dietary resources (Pike 1966 appendix I:54,56; Schoolcraft 1966:223-224, 244-245). Minnesota archaeological sites, including McKinstry Mound (Lukens 1973; Morey et al. 1996) and Woodland sites near Mille Lacs (Whelan 1990), have produced abundant beaver remains.

*Muskrat (*Ondatra zibethicus*)*: The Midway remains include 59 elements positively identified as muskrat (two of them from disturbed context), and an additional six classified as probable muskrat (Table 13). The 57 definite muskrat bones not from disturbed contexts represent at least five individuals, based on right first molars. At least three individuals are represented by the postcranial bones (from proximal ulnas and proximal femurs). Twenty-seven (48.0%) of the bones are cranial-dentary and the rest are postcranial; the distribution shows representation of all major bones but also some apparent selection for cranial elements. The bones holding the muskrat incisors might have been selected for potential use of the incisors as tools, like those of beaver.

Muskrats require stable water levels and depend primarily on aquatic vegetation as a food source (Hazard 1982:98). Muskrats were and are widespread across northern Minnesota, including the Mississippi Headwaters region.

Other Rodent Taxa: Two other rodent species that might have been part of the aboriginal diet are porcupine (*Erethizon dorsatum*), with an MNI of one based on an upper left first or second molar, and woodchuck (*Marmota monax*), with an MNI of one from a horizontal ramus with a fourth premolar and first molar.

One species that is not treated here as part of the human diet, but might have been consumed, is the Plains pocket gopher (*Geomys bursarius*). This species is represented by 24 positively identified elements and 7 probable identifications (Table 14). The 24 definite gopher bones have an MNI of 4, from left mandibles with dentition. Of the 24, 11 (46.0%) are cranial or dentary. The MNI from the postcranial remains is 2 (from left humeri and left innominates), a pattern similar to that for muskrats.

Other small rodent species interpreted as naturally occurring at the site are the eastern chipmunk (*Tamias striatus*), the red-backed vole (*Clethrionomys gapperi*), the meadow vole (*Microtus pennsylvanicus*), and a white-footed mouse (*Peromyscus* sp.), with one individual each (Table 1).

Rabbits and Hares (Leporidae)

The only remains from this family recovered at Midway are those of the snowshoe hare (*Lepus americanus*). One element was positively identified, and another was classified as probable (Table 1). The scarcity of snowshoe hare remains at prehistoric Woodland sites in the heart of this species' range has been commented on by others (Lukens 1973:42). Some societies consider this species a starvation food, and perhaps they were rarely selected in premodern times.

Insectivores (Insectivora)

This family is represented by one mandible from a masked shrew (*Sorex cinerus*), a species common to the Mississippi Headwaters region, including Beltrami County (Hazard 1982:21, Map 5). This species is part of the natural "rain" of fauna that could be expected at the site.

Birds

At least 14 individual birds, of 10 different taxa, are represented at the site (Table 15). The most common bird remains are those of ducks, with three individuals identified to the genus or species level and three others to the subfamily level. The second most common bird is the double-crested cormorant, with an MNI of three. Other species with an MNI of one are the bald eagle, common loon, great blue heron, and ruffed grouse. The identified birds do not appear to have been an overly important component of the diet, ranking third in both NISP and MNI, behind both mammals and fish. In terms of weight, the birds would have provided 10.2 kg of usable meat, ranking fourth behind mammals, fish, and reptiles and contributing only 0.9 percent of the usable meat.

Ducks (Anatidae)

The most common bird family in the assemblage is Anatidae (ducks, geese, and swans). A total of 36 bones could be confidently assigned to the family and an additional three compared favorably (Table 15). All of these elements are believed to be from the subfamily Anatinae (the true ducks), based upon size. Five elements could be placed in the genus *Anas* (dabbling/puddle ducks). Two other Anatidae elements were assigned to the genus *Aythya* (diving ducks).

Within the genus *Anas*, three bones were identified to definite or probable species. A single gadwall (*Anas strepa*) was represented by a left coracoid. This species is a regular inhabitant of Minnesota, but in modern times it has been rare in the north-central portion of the state, including the Bemidji area (Green and Janssen 1975:46). Observations of migration patterns indicate that the earliest gadwalls arrive at the very end of March and the latest leave by mid-December. No winter stragglers are known north of the Twin Cities area.

A distal right coracoid compares favorably to mallard (*Anas* cf. *A. platyrhynchos*), but this species is too similar osteologically to the black duck (*Anas rubripes*) to permit a positive identification. Although the two species are similar in both their physiology and their behavior, mallards are far more common in the region, with the black duck being a rare traveler of the Upper Mississippi flyway (Bellrose 1976:254-257). The two species are most common in northern Minnesota from March through November, with some individuals remaining through the winter. In prehistoric times, wintering individuals would have been unlikely, since most of today's winter residents are drawn to open water near power plants (Green and Janssen 1975:45-46).

A final member of the genus *Anas* was identified from a complete right coracoid. This element compared well to both green-winged teal (*Anas crecca*) and blue-winged teal (*Anas discors*), and the two species could not be separated osteologically. Both species are common throughout Minnesota during the warmer months; they are usually among the earliest to leave during the fall and the latest to return during the spring. In the north, most of these birds are usually gone by the middle of October and do not return until April, and in the historic period, few have been observed to winter in the northern half of the state (Green and Janssen 1975:47-48).

Based on distal right scapulas, an MNI of six is calculated for the family Anatidae. This includes the three individuals identified more specifically, even though these individuals were not identified from their right scapulas; they are included in this total count because one or more of the six scapulas may belong to them. Variation in body weights among ducks precludes calculating meat weights for the three individuals not identified to genus or species.

Overall, the ducks at the site were most likely taken during the spring through fall, since few if any would have remained in northern Minnesota during the winter. This seasonal information corresponds well with that derived from the deer and fish remains and from the other birds.

*Double-Crested Cormorant (*Phalacrocorax auritus*)*: Four bones from Midway were identified as those of the double-crested cormorant. The presence of three anterior sternums (with the coracoid facets) indicates an MNI of three. Cormorants are a regular summer inhabitant of Minnesota, although their numbers have dropped dramatically since the 1950s. They were once abundant in flocks of 1,000 to 5,000 individuals (Green and Janssen 1975:34) and were probably common in prehistoric times. They inhabit the shores of lakes and rivers, subsisting on fish and other small aquatic animals as well as some plants (Kaufman 1996:423-43). Cormorants are migratory, arriving in northern Minnesota during mid-March and leaving by late October (Green and Janssen 1975:34).

*Bald Eagle (*Haliaeetus leucocephalus*)*: Three elements were positively identified as bald eagle, two others compared favorably to bald eagle, and one compared favorably to either bald or golden eagle (*Haliaeetus leucocephalus/ Aquila chrysaetos*). In total, these elements may only represent a single individual, but they are significant in that they seem to be the only eagle remains from a non-mortuary archaeological assemblage in north-central Minnesota. They are also interesting in terms of the elements represented (Fig. 6): all six bones are phalanges from the foot, including two terminal phalanges or talons. The dominance of these elements, together with the general scarcity of eagle remains, suggests ritual significance. On the other hand, these elements are also the most likely to be preserved from a carnivore-scavenged animal, since they come from the part of the leg with no meat. In fact, two of the phalanges do show evidence of carnivore gnawing or pitting, which would not be expected if humans were reserving these elements for special use. Because of their possible ritual significance, the eagle elements are not interpreted as a dietary item and are not included in the estimates of usable meat weights.

Bald eagles are regular summer inhabitants of northern Minnesota. They typically live on large lakes and rivers and are most often seen within 200 m of such water bodies (Grim and Kallemeyn 1995:16). The eagle's diet consists mainly of fish, small mammals, other birds, and carrion. Like ducks, bald eagles are migratory birds that leave the area as the lakes become ice covered in the late fall, and return in mid- to late March (Green and Janssen 1975:66-67). Occasionally, eagles remain for the winter in areas with sufficient open water.

*Great Blue Heron (*Ardea herodias*):* A heron is represented by three elements (a coracoid, a proximal humerus, and a dentary). Great blue herons are common summer residents of Minnesota. They are most abundant in non-wooded areas of southern Minnesota but are found throughout the state. They are a highly adaptable species that can live in several habitats, but they are common along lakes and rivers, where they eat a variety of foods, including fish, crayfish, amphibians, and small mammals and reptiles (Kauffman 1996:51-52). These migratory birds arrive in northern Minnesota beginning in late March, and most leave by November (Green and Janssen 1975:35). No wintering individuals are known north of the Twin Cities.

*Common Loon (*Gavia immer*):* Loons are a common summer inhabitant of northern Minnesota, with a stable population and breeding colonies as far south as the Twin Cities area (McIntyre 1988:153). Their range once extended as far south as Iowa (Green and Janssen 1975:30). At the Midway site, a loon is represented by two elements (a tarsometatarsus and a frontal). Although loons are common in the area, they are uncommon in prehistoric archaeological assemblages from northern Minnesota (see Mather 1998; Lukens 1973; Whelan 1990). Loon remains were abundant at the nearby Horseshoe Bay site (Hannes 1994), a 19th century fur-trading post, where they were perhaps taken more readily with firearms. In modern times, loons often get caught accidentally in gill nets. Although such netting practices were used prehistorically in the Great Lakes region (Cleland 1982), netting does not appear to have occurred at the Midway site (see discussion of fish, below) and probably does not account for the loon elements.

Loons are diving birds that subsist mainly on fish but are also known to eat insects, crayfish, mollusks, and some plants. They typically live on large lakes with ample room for take-off and plentiful small fish. Females usually nest along protected, vegetated shorelines, where they could have been taken during the summer months. Common loons arrive in northern Minnesota in late March, and most leave by mid-October (Green and Janssen 1975:30).

*Ruffed Grouse (*Bonasa umbellus*):* The ruffed grouse is the only bird identified in the assemblage that is consistently a year-round resident. A single carpometacarpus compared favorably to this species, and measurements (Hargrave 1972) separated it from the spruce grouse (*Canachites canadensis*), the sharp-tailed grouse (*Pedioecetes phasianellus*), and the greater prairie chicken (*Tympanuchus cupido*). All four species exist in the area, but ruffed grouse are the most common (Green and Janssen 1975:71-73). Although this element is identified as probable, a weight estimate of 0.6 kg (Johnsgard 1975) is still given, because at least one grouse is represented, and the other possible species are similar in size. The grouse would have provided 0.4 kg of usable meat.

Amphibians

In all, 23 elements were identified as *Bufo* and one as probable *Bufo*. Based on historic species distributions, these bones are probably those of the American toad, *Bufo americanus*. According to Oldfield and Moriarty (1994:68-69), the American toad is recorded for Beltrami County and is widespread in Minnesota. Other species that occur in Minnesota include the Great Plains toad (*Bufo cognatus*), found west of Beltrami County, and the Canadian toad (*Bufo hemiophrys*), which occurs in northwestern Minnesota but is not reported for Beltrami County (Oldfield and Moriarty 1994:72, 74).

At least three individual toads are represented, based on left ilia. Fifteen bones from one context (Unit 15, Level 10) are from one individual, and another six bones are from Unit 3, Levels 8 and 9. These clusters of bones probably represent individuals that died in place.

Reptiles

Spiny ? softshell turtle (Apalone cf. *A. spinifera):* One carapace fragment of a softshell turtle was recovered from redeposited A horizon material at the Midway site. There are two softshell species in Minnesota, the smooth softshell (*Apalone mutica*) and the spiny softshell (*Apalone spinifera*). The smooth softshell is known from the southeastern portion of the state, while the spiny softshell occurs as far north as Itasca County, which adjoins Beltrami County on the east (Oldfield and Moriarty 1994:112, 116). Based on distributional rather than osteological evidence, this specimen can be tentatively assigned to *A. spinifera*. The small size of this fragment precludes an accurate weight estimate.

*Snapping Turtle (*Chelydra serpentina*)*: The Midway excavations produced 16 specimens identified as snapping turtle and an additional phalanx probably assignable to this species. Carapace and plastron segments were identified to this species because of their distinct texture. Two right humeri shafts indicate at least two individuals in the Midway assemblage. One distinct cluster of eight bones was found in Unit 8, Level 6, and the other eight bones came from various contexts.

This aquatic species in widespread in Minnesota and is recorded for Beltrami County (Oldfield and Moriarty 1994:120). Native Americans throughout the Great Lakes region used snapping turtles in small numbers for food. Snappers are most vulnerable in the spring, when females venture on dry land to lay their eggs. Both individuals from the site were larger than our modern comparative specimens and together are estimated to have weighed 22.8 kg, yielding about 11.4 kg of useable meat.

*Painted Turtle (*Chrysemys picta*)*: Painted turtles are represented by three positively identified specimens and two additional elements probably assignable to this species. The presence of two carapace nuchal segments document an MNI of two. This common aquatic species has not been recorded in Beltrami County but is found in neighboring counties (Oldfield and Moriarty 1994:126). A combined meat weight estimate for the two individuals is 0.4 kg.

Fishes

The Midway excavations produced 1,762 fish bones from good contexts, 318 (18%) of which were assignable to the family, genus, or species level, with 10 taxa and 47 individuals represented (Table 16). These 47 fish had a total estimated live weight of 66.3 kg and contributed about 2 percent of the useable meat represented at the site. Two taxa in particular, pike and walleye, represented about 80 percent of the total. An additional 30 elements came from redeposited or disturbed material.

*Pike (*Esox *sp.)*: Two species of *Esox* occur in the Mississippi Headwaters region, the northern pike (*Esox lucius*), and the muskellunge or muskie (*Esox masquinongy*). Osteologically, these species are difficult to distinguish except that the dentary of a muskie has a larger number of pore openings on its inferior surface. The *Esox* dentary bones in Midway assemblage were fragmentary, so the species identification could not be confirmed.

Pike were the most important fish species at Midway, with 74 bones and three probable ones representing at least 15 individuals. Their live weights are estimated to total 32.6 kg, or 49.2 percent of the total for fish. The number of pike represented can be determined from unique elements as well as individual fish size. One small 50-gram fish is present, and 11 pike between 0.5 kg and 2.5 kg are indicated by left anterior dentary bones. Three additional fish each weighed between 4.0 and 6.0 kg.

The pike recovered at Midway could have been taken at any time of year; however, except for the smallest, they were all of breeding age when harvested, and northern pike are exceptionally vulnerable to human predation when they spawn in shallow water during the spring. Spawning takes place in flooded marshes or lake inlets and begins when the winter ice starts to break up during late March or April and water temperatures reach 1.1 to 4.4° C (Becker 1983:399).

*Walleye (*Stizostedion vitreum*)*: Walleye are the second most important fish species in the Midway assemblage, in terms of the amount of meat provided. Osteologically, walleye are hard to distinguish from the closely related sauger (*Stizostedion canadense*), but sauger are not native to the Mississippi Headwaters region (Hatch and Schmidt 2004), so the Midway specimens can be attributed to walleye. Here, a total of 118 elements were present, constituting at least 14 individuals, based on the anterior portion of the dentary. An additional 13 elements were assigned probable identifications. The 14 individual fish had estimated live weights ranging from 0.7 kg to 4.5 kg and totaled 21 kg, or 29.7 percent of all fish. This would have provided 10.5 kg of useable meat.

The sizes of the 14 fish indicate that they would have been sexually mature. Like pike, walleye are most vulnerable during spring when they spawn in shallow waters. Walleye spawning begins after ice-out, when water temperatures reach 3.3 to 6.7° C, and preferred locations are shallow waters of lake inlets on gravel substrates, wave-washed shores, or flooded marshes. Spawning peaks when waters warm to 5.6 to 10.0° C (Becker 1983:872-875).

Suckers (Catostomidae): Suckers are represented by one white sucker (*Catostomus commersoni*) with a live weight of 1.0 kg, a probable white sucker weighing 1.2 kg, and two redhorse suckers (*Moxostoma* sp.) weighing 2.3 and 3.4 kg. Although 17 sucker species are listed for Minnesota, only the white sucker and three species of redhorse are considered native in the Headwaters region (Hatch and Schmidt 2004). These four sucker species are spring spawners, with peak activity between 6.7 and 19.0° C, when they typically move into shallow-water streams or lake inlets (Becker 1983).

Bullhead Catfish (Ictalurus) (= Ameiurus): The Midway assemblage contained 53 *Ictalurus* elements representing at least three black bullheads (*Ictalurus melas*) and four brown bullheads (*Ictalurus nebulosus*). One additional *Ictalurus* bone was found in the redeposited A horizon. The individual bullheads were rather large, ranging in size from 0.3 to 0.5 kg.

*Yellow Perch (*Perca flavescens*)*: Yellow perch were represented by 20 positively identified elements from at least four individuals. Three of these fish were estimated to have live weights of 0.5 kg. Seven probable perch bones also were found. Yellow perch spawn shortly after ice-out, when water temperatures reach 7.2 to 11.1° C, closely following the spawning times for northern pike and walleye and coinciding with that of suckers (Becker 1983:886-887).

Other Fish Taxa: Three additional fish taxa were identified in the Midway assemblage, each from a single element: a pumpkinseed sunfish (*Lepomis gibbosus*), a probable rock bass (*Ambloplites rupestris*), and a probable smallmouth bass (*Micropterus dolomieui*). All three species would have occurred in the Lake Bemidji–Headwaters region.

Freshwater Mussels

The only identifiable shell in the Midway assemblage was a fatmucket (*Lampsilis siliquoidea*), a common freshwater mussel species found in relatively shallow waters of northern lakes and streams (Clarke 1981). This shell showed no indications of modification and might have been deposited by humans or by animals. A few other unidentifiable mussel shell fragments were recovered.

Domestic Animal Species

Bones of four different domestic animal species were identified. One of these, identified as probable domestic dog (*Canis familiaris*), is most likely of prehistoric origin and was described earlier with carnivores. The other three species are associated with Euro-American presence. The first is the domestic pig (*Sus scofa*), represented by a two first phalanges, one of which came from deposits classified as undisturbed. Its presence is clearly intrusive and might reflect bioturbation.

The second species is the domestic cat (*Felis cattus*), with probable identifications of an anterior mandible (with the third incisor) and a right astragalus. One of these elements is also from an apparently undisturbed context and must result from some form of disturbance. The other was recovered from the uppermost level of an excavation unit and could easily be associated with historic activities.

The final domestic species is the chicken (*Gallus gallus*), represented by a complete scapula and a proximal femur, both of them recovered from the uppermost excavation level. They, like the cat, are probably the result of historic activity. A complete chicken skeleton was discovered in the Phase II excavation (Kluth and Kluth 2000).

Overall, the recovery of historic species from the upper levels of some of excavation units is not unexpected. The occurrence of domestic cat and pig elements in apparently undisturbed contexts is less expected; however, these are only two bones out of thousands in the assemblage. They could have been incorporated into the prehistoric deposits through some form of small-scale disturbance, such as rodent burrowing.

Worked Bone

Six pieces of culturally-modified bone were identified in the Phase III material (Fig. 7). Three are mammal bone fragments with clear signs of modification. One has several small grooves carved along its edge, the second has a single groove carved into its surface, and the third has wear or polishing on the bone surface and the edges. Unfortunately, these fragments cannot be classified as any particular type of artifact.

The fourth bone artifact is a small piece of ground, polished mammal bone that might be an awl fragment. This specimen seems to have been made from a long-bone splinter of a medium-sized to large animal. The fifth artifact is a turtle carapace fragment with a small drilled hole, the exact purpose of which is unknown, but probably relates to use of the carapace for a bowl, container, rattle, or other item.

The final artifact is a piece of mammal bone that might be the tip of a harpoon. This long-bone shaft fragment from a medium-sized to large mammal was flattened through grinding and sharpened to a point on one end. Just behind the point is a small fracture along the shaft that appears to be where a barb broke off. This item seems to have been broken, discarded, and burned. A spear/harpoon point would fit well at the site, since this was probably the primary method for harvesting the fish represented (see above).

Bone artifacts recovered from the Phase II excavations were not reexamined for this analysis. Descriptions and photographs (Kluth and Kluth 2000) indicate nine probable bone tools, among them a 9.9-cm-long bone needle with an eyelet, a piece described as an awl fragment, and a small bone tube.

Taphonomic Modifications

All of the bones larger than 1/4 inch were examined for other human-induced alterations (burning, fracturing, and cut marks) and other types of modification not human-induced (rodent or carnivore gnawing, carnivore ingestion, and weathering). The Phase II materials were not included in this portion of the analysis, since only the identifiable elements were recorded. Excluding the Phase II materials and the Phase III fragments smaller than 1/4 inch left 11,158 fragments in the analyzed sample. The modifications are summarized by unit in Table 17.

Burned Bone

Burning documents human manipulation of the animal remains. Burned bone was assigned to three categories: scorched, burned/carbonized, and calcined. These categories represent different degrees of burning (Lyman 1994:384-391). Scorching or superficial burning darkens or blackens the surface or portions of the bone but leaves the rest unaltered. Longer exposure to heat carbonizes more of the collagen, causing burned or carbonized bone that is darkened or black throughout. If the heat exposure continues, the newly carbonized material begins to oxidize and change color from black to white or grayish blue. This white or gray, calcined bone also has a chalkier texture. Of the 11,158 analyzed fragments, 1,371 (12.3%) displayed signs of burning; 36 (0.3%) of them were scorched, 642 (5.6%) burned or carbonized, and 693 (6.2%) calcined (Table 17).

Occurrences of burned bone were also studied to look for differential distribution across the site. While the bones were still being identified, it was noted that the fragments from units 33 through 41 seemed different from the rest of the assemblage. These units were in Area F, the portion of the site interpreted from the Phase II investigation as containing possible Late Archaic deposits. The 9 Phase III units in Area F produced only 431 bone fragments, significantly less than other portions of the site. The fragments were small; in fact, only 56 were larger than 1/4 inch (Table 17). Of the 56 larger fragments, 42 (75%) were calcined. Despite the small sample size, this high proportion of calcined bone contrasts strongly to the proportion for the site as a whole (6.2%).

Burned and calcined bone does preserve better than nonburned bone, because carbonization of the organic material makes the bone less vulnerable to the action of microorganisms (Lyman 1994:391). The higher proportion of calcined bone in the Area F units could well result from its greater resistance to decay, which would fit the interpretation of this portion of the site as older. Only eight bones from units 33 to 41 were identifiable beyond class. One of them was an intrusive rodent, and five were large-mammal tooth enamel fragments, which are also resistant to decay. Fish bones, which decay more readily, were rare in these units (only three elements), although they were common throughout the rest of the site. Finally, the bone fragments from these units, particularly those that were unburned, were small, fragile, and poorly preserved. All of these factors suggest that the bone in this portion of the site was deposited earlier than in the other areas. Once again, this data would certainly be more useful in light of more detailed cultural information.

Fractured Bone

In addition to burning, humans modify bone by fracturing it. Fracture patterns on fresh (or "green") bone are different from those on dried bone (Lyman 1994:320). Fresh bone typically shows clean, smooth fractures at acute or obtuse angles to the bone surface and often has "spiral" fractures. Green-bone fractures can also have a flaked appearance, with lipping at the bone's cortical surface. Fractures on dried bone, on the other hand, have more of a stepped or ragged appearance and typically form at right angles to the bone surface. In general, humans fractured bone to obtain the nutrient-rich marrow.

Of the 11,158 bones in the sample, 1,332 (11.9%) showed classic signs of green-bone fracturing (Table 17). Eliminating fish, naiad (freshwater mussel), and other mollusk remains from the sample raises the proportion to 14.1 percent. Many of the other bone fragments, especially those of mammals, were probably fractured while fresh, but the fracture patterns could not be confirmed because they were obscured by weathering. Overall, green-bone fracturing seems common and widespread at the site, except for the Late Archaic area, where most of the bones were too small and weathered to show fracture patterns. Most of the confirmed green-bone fractures were on long-bone fragments of medium to large-sized mammals, and most of those fragments probably came from deer, although their identification cannot be confirmed. Most of the identified moose remains also displayed green-bone fracturing, especially several tibia fragments. This emphasis on fractured long bones suggests marrow extraction and possible bone-grease production. In general, information on this subject is lacking from northern Minnesota as well as much of the Midwest. It is thought to be a fall to winter activity, possibly associated with increased deer harvest rates during the fall (Baker 2001).

Cut Marks

Bones exhibiting cut marks were rare at Midway. Even including the identified Phase II materials, only 20 elements had cut marks. Of those, four were specimens with historic knife or saw marks (two moose elements, one pig phalanx, and one piece of unidentified mammal bone), and all were from disturbed contexts sampled during the Phase II excavations. Only 16 pieces (13 mammal, two bird, and one turtle) had cut marks caused by stone tools. Of the mammal bones, two were deer (a naviculo-cuboid and a distal metapodial), one was moose (a first phalanx), one was an artiodactyla (a metapodial), one was a muskrat, and eight were unidentified. Except for the muskrat, all of the cut marks were on the extremities of large ungulates and might be associated with deboning the animal at the kill site (see earlier discussion). Both of the bird pieces with cut marks were small, unidentified fragments. The turtle element was a small carapace fragment with cut marks on the interior at one of the vertebral attachments, perhaps resulting from converting the carapace into a bowl or some similar artifact. Overall, the number of cut marks was too small to provide reliable information on butchering practices.

Gnawing and Ingestion

A total of 178 bones showed signs of rodent gnawing, 118 had carnivore puncturing or pitting, and 7 had gnawing of an indeterminate type. Gnawing was almost exclusively seen on mammal and bird remains, which is not surprising, since gnawing tends to completely destroy bone from the other classes, especially fish.

Only 34 specimens showed clear indications of ingestion, and they included mammal, fish, and bird bone. More of the bone fragments might have been ingested, with the evidence obscured by weathering (see below). Ingested bone is recognized by erosion resulting in smoothing and rounded shallow pitting on compact bone surfaces (Klippel et al. 1987:158-159). The smoothed cortical bone surfaces often exhibit a distinct polish or sheen and the thin surfaces covering trabecular (spongy) bone are nearly completely eroded.

Both carnivore gnawing and bone ingestion are characteristic of carnivore scavenging (Binford

1981). Domestic dogs were probably responsible for most of the carnivore gnawing and ingestion seen at the site. The gnawing is primarily on the ends of long bones, typically the first portions destroyed by dogs and similar carnivores. No differential distribution of gnawed or ingested bone was noted at the site, except that in the Archaic area, the bones were in too poor of a condition to identify these forms of modification.

Weathering

Many of the Midway specimens show considerable surface wear and, in some cases, polish. Although the cause is difficult to determine, exposure on a beach/shoreline setting seems likely. Many landmarks and surface features are worn or polished as though they had been subjected to water action. It would have been difficult for the specimens to acquire these characteristics if they had remained in situ from the time they were first deposited. Most of the bone fragments in the assemblage are also much smaller than would typically be expected, perhaps another reflection of exposure to the turbulence of a beach environment. Unfortunately, the literature offers little information on these taphonomic processes.

Distribution Patterns

The faunal data were sorted in numerous ways to try to find patterning in the vertical or horizontal distributions of different species, different elements, or cultural modifications. In terms of vertical stratigraphy, no significant patterning was observed other than changes in the number of bones per level. Usually about three or four adjacent levels contained more bone than the others in the same unit, but interpreting these concentrations as possible occupation zones would require comparison to the distributions of ceramics and other artifacts.

In terms of horizontal patterning, two important differences were observed. The first was the small size of the fragments and much higher proportion of calcined bone in Area F, as discussed earlier in the section on burned bone. These Area F remains might represent earlier deposits.

The second difference was observed in Units 42, 43, 44, and 45, all of which were in Area A, on the western portion of the isthmus. These four units were the closest to the river channel and had a higher density of faunal remains than any other proveniences. Together, they contained 6,884 pieces of bone, or 30 percent of the entire Phase III assemblage. These units were also different from the others in terms of their fish remains. To examine this difference, several fish species were grouped together by family or genus, and the numbers of identified specimens (NISP) were compared to those from the other units at the site. Ideally, this comparison would have used MNI rather than NISP, but the sample sizes were too small.

Using NISP, these four units had a higher percentage of suckers (Catostomidae) and bullheads (*Ictalurus* sp.) than the site as a whole (Table 18). In fact, 63 percent of all of the bullhead bones and 42.3 percent of all of the sucker bones from the entire site came from these four units. Walleye (*Stizostedion vitreum*) were still the most abundant remains in these four units but ranked very close to the bullheads. In addition, the percent of pike (*Esox* sp.) remains is smaller, while that of the yellow perch (*Perca* flavescens) remains is about the same. These four units are closest to the river and might represent a different activity area or perhaps a different seasonal or cultural occupation. From the large number of bullheads, this portion of the site might represent a more summer-focused activity area or occupation. Comparison with the other cultural materials might help to clarify the differences.

Discussion and Conclusions

The Midway site produced a large and diverse faunal assemblage. Given the general scarcity of analyzed faunal material from northern Minnesota, the remains from this site are particularly significant. Unfortunately, the lack of a conclusive analysis of the Midway cultural material makes the assemblage rather difficult to interpret and place into a regional perspective. As mentioned above, Phase II excavations at the site produced evidence of Late Archaic, Brainerd, Laurel, St. Croix, Blackduck, Sandy Lake, and Oneota-like components (Kluth and Kluth 2000). Preliminary analysis of the diagnostic lithics and ceramics from the Phase III mitigation supports this initial observation and indicates that the Brainerd, Blackduck, and Sandy Lake peoples were the primary occupants of the site (LLHSP 2002). The additional recovery of a Hi-Lo projectile point from Area F pushes the site's initial occupation back to Late Paleoindian/Early Archaic times (LLHSP 2002:38). As such, we see that the site has been occupied for nearly 10,000 years, although the greatest density of occupation appears to have occurred during the Woodland Tradition.

With little to no data available for correlating the faunal remains to a particular cultural component, we must consider these remains as a composite assemblage. It is important to note that in doing so, we may be masking a great deal of variability in seasonal occupations and resource exploitation at the site. Therefore, the following discussion will reflect a generalized analysis for the site as a whole. Further study of the cultural remains will undoubtedly help to refine these interpretations.

Subsistence & Seasonality

Based upon rough estimates of useable meat weight, it can be postulated that large mammals (moose, white-tailed deer, elk, black bear, and caribou) provided most of the animal protein in the local diet prior to the arrival of Europeans (see Table 19). Moose might have been taken along lake margins or in shallow-water marshes during the warm season, or at nearby refuges in the closed coniferous forest during the winter. For deer, tooth eruption evidence (Table 5) indicates harvest in the fall to early winter; this is the mating period, during which they are less cautious and therefore more vulnerable.

As noted above, an examination of the skeletal-part frequencies of deer and moose indicates a disproportionate number of limb extremities. This is probably the result of the deboning of the animal at the kill locality to aid in transportation of the meat and hide back to the site. Ethnographic accounts demonstrate that native peoples frequently subdivide kills for ease of transport (Binford 1978:47-59). In this instance, the low utility extremities were likely left attached to the hide, while the heavier elements were stripped of their meat and left behind. This differential transport of ungulate skeletal elements has been reported from numerous sites elsewhere in the upper Midwest (Theler 2000:127) and is closely mirrored by the skeletal part representations at Midway.

The exploitation of large mammals was heavily supplemented by a wide range of medium to small mammals that were likely obtained from a variety of environments. Based upon MNI and NISP, we see that the beaver and muskrat are the second most abundant mammals at the site. Both of these animals live exclusively in aquatic habitats and would have likely been available in the immediate vicinity of the site. Historic documents (Pike 1966 appendix I:54,56; Schoolcraft 1966:223-224, 244-245) and other northern Minnesota archaeological sites (Lukens 1963, 1973; Whelan 1990; Morey et al. 1996) attest their importance in the prehistoric diet. The presence of the river otter and raccoon at Midway also indicate the exploitation of lacustrine and riverine zones. Other mammals from the site are found in a variety of habitats. The snowshoe hare, porcupine, and pine marten are commonly found in coniferous forests, while the badger was likely taken from a more open environment. Although a majority of the canid material was not identifiable to the species level, most of it likely comes from domestic dogs that would have been maintained and utilized by the Midway inhabitants.

The fish remains from Midway are dominated by pike and walleye, both of which are easily harvested during spring spawning. Other species in the assemblage, including the suckers and yellow perch, also might have been taken during spawning. Based on their sizes, the Midway specimens were primarily mature fish. The temperatures at which spawning occurs suggest a several-week period of fish harvest, beginning with northern pike at ice-out in March and continuing with walleye, suckers, and perhaps perch into May. Schoolcraft reported that when their winter store of wild rice was exhausted, the Ojibwe lived on fish (1966:229). Given the relatively poor bone preservation at the Midway site it is quite possible that the actual dietary contribution of fish may be extremely underestimated.

The relatively small sample of preserved fish remains makes it difficult to quantitatively evaluate how they may have been procured. At the nearby Horseshoe Bay Site, on Leech Lake in Cass County, significant amounts of fish bones and scales have been recovered from historic fur trade components (Shane 1996). These assemblages, like Midway, are dominated by large walleye and pike remains. Estimates of total lengths, through regression analysis, indicates that the Horseshoe Bay walleyes and pikes where generally of a consistent size and probably harvested through gill-netting during the spawn (Shane 1996:14-16). Significant historic, ethnographic, and archaeological data have documented the use of this technique throughout the Great Lakes area and demonstrate its role in the inland shore fishery (Cleland 1982). Although this technique may have been employed by the prehistoric occupants at Midway, other harvest methods, particularly spearing during the spawn, could have also been utilized. In addition to fish, another probable spring resource was turtles, especially snapping turtles, which could have been harvested while they were laying their eggs.

Birds seem to have been an important dietary supplement. All of the Midway birds, except for the ruffed grouse, migrate north for the summer and were probably taken between March and November. These migratory species are strongly associated with lake and riverside environments and were probably available very near the site. Ruffed grouse, the only non-aquatic species represented, prefers a landscape with greater cover but also could have been taken nearby.

Besides animal resources, certain plant species also probably played an important role in the ancient diet. The position of the Midway site in the Headwater Lakes region places it in the heart of wild rice country. A study of five ceramic rim sherds from the Midway site produced evidence of wild rice (*Zizania palustris*) phytoliths on four of the sherds (Thompson 2000). Analysis of macrobotanical remains from the Phase III excavations has also produced remains of wild rice, along with chenopods (*Chenopodium* spp.), amaranth (*Amaranthus retroflexus*), and smartweeds (*Polygonum* spp.), which may have served as food sources (Valppu 2002).

Environmental Setting

A further discussion of the composition of Midway's large mammal assemblage provides some interesting insights about the site's environmental setting. There has been much discussion about the significance of the prairie-forest border ecotone in shaping the diets and cultural manifestations of the prehistoric occupants of Minnesota (Hickerson 1970; Shay 1978; Spector and Johnson 1985; Anfinson and Wright 1990; cf. Michlovic 1980). This ecotone generally runs from the northwest to the southeast through the center of the state, and represents a physiographic transition from the prairies and grasslands of the south and west to the forests of the north and east. It should be noted that the ecotone is far from static and varies greatly in both geographic width and vegetational composition. Furthermore, the extent and position of the ecotone have experienced substantial temporal changes, commensurate with climate-induced succession of floral and faunal communities (Anfinson and Wright 1990:216-218).

Before extirpation at the hands of European hunters, bison were common in the prairies of southwest Minnesota (Faunmap 1994:461; Hazard 1982:168-169, Map 76). Archaeological sites demonstrate that bison were a significant economic resource in southern Minnesota, northern Iowa, and the eastern Dakotas (Lukens 1963; Shay 1978, 1985). The bison also appears to have flourished in the grasslands and deciduous edge habitats of the prairie-forest ecotone. Mather (2002:19-20) briefly reviews several sites from Minnesota's prairie-forest border where bison are present and in several cases quite abundant. In the Mille Lacs area bison were also found in limited numbers (Whelan 1990).

Early Holocene bison species (*Bison occidentalis*) ranged to the east of Beltrami County during warm, dry climatic phases (Shay 1971), but during later Holocene times, the coniferous and deciduous vegetational communities that dominated the region would not have favored *Bison bison*. Interestingly, bison remains have been recovered from Woodland contexts at the McKinstry Mound in Koochiching County and the Pike Bay Mound in St. Louis County (Lukens 1973), as well as the White Oak Mounds in Itasca County (Lukens 1963). It should be noted, however, that in all of these instances bison make up a very limited portion of the faunal assemblage and, given their possible mortuary association, it is difficult to ascertain their position in the local economy. No bison remains were identified from the Midway site. Although the absence of bison could be attributed to cultural or seasonal factors, it is most likely due to the lack of appropriate habitat within the vicinity of the site.

Another prairie-plains species missing from the Midway assemblage is the pronghorn antelope (*Antilocarpra americana*). This species is found in the short-grass steppe of the western Great Plains, with western Minnesota at the extreme eastern margin of its potential historic range. Pronghorn has been reported occasionally in the tall-grass prairies of southwestern Minnesota, where they are presumed to have wandered from the west (Hazard 1982:167, Map 75). The coniferous and deciduous forest setting of the Midway site would place it just east of the pronghorn's potential range. Pronghorn elements have not been recorded at archaeological sites in Minnesota, but this species is documented from a late prehistoric context in northwestern Iowa (Faunmap 1994:457, 645; Tiffany et al.1988:238-239).

The lack of pronghorn and, more importantly, bison remains, demonstrates that the Midway site is situated beyond the grasslands and open deciduous forests of the prairie-forest ecotone. Most maps of Minnesota's pre-European/early historic floral communities show that the area near Midway was comprised of a coniferous or coniferous-hardwood forest (Wendt and Coffin 1988; Borchert and Yaeger 1969; Kuchler 1964). Pollen sequences from extensive investigations of varved lake sediments at Elk Lake (40 km to the west of the Midway site in Clearwater County), indicate that by the end of the Altithermal, mixed deciduous and coniferous forests had begun to replace the oak savanna habitat (Whitlock et al. 1993). Following the onset of cooler climatic conditions, white pine (*Pinus strobus*) appeared in the pollen record at 2700 BP and came to dominate the forests by 2000 BP.

Although most evidence indicates that the Midway site is beyond the large expanses of prairie/savanna habitat, additional evaluation of its mammal assemblage shows that the area was part of the ecotonal environment representing a shift from more open deciduous habitats to the coniferous-hardwood forests of the north. Prior to A.D. 1860, white-tailed deer were uncommon to rare in most of northern Minnesota and Wisconsin (De Vos 1964:Fig. 7, 220-221; Swanson et al. 1945:15; Schorger 1953:197-199, 233, 241). According to one estimate, in the year 1800 there were no deer in northern Minnesota, including what is now Beltrami County (De Vos 1964:Fig. 7:220). After the Euro-American logging boom of the mid-nineteenth century, deer populations increased dramatically, commensurate with the development of successional stages of deciduous edge habitats (Swanson et al. 1945:26; Schorger 1953:197, 212; Swift 1946:18-23).

The region's deep winter snow cover would have placed white-tailed deer at a distinct disadvantage. In the Beltrami County area, annual snowfall from 1899 to 1938 (post Neo-Boreal era) was 100 cm (USDA 1941:727). Deer movements are sharply limited when snow is more than 50 cm deep or crusted with ice (Hazard 1982:163). At such times, deer are forced into small "yards" with some available forage (Schorger 1953:209-211). This vulnerability in deep snow virtually insured a low deer population density, perhaps with cyclical variation corresponding to climate and vegetation changes.

White-tailed deer are the normal and tolerant host of the nematode parasite *Parelaphostrangylus tenuis* (Karns 1967:299). This parasite is widespread in high-density deer populations and readily infects moose when large numbers of deer spread northward as a result of favorable habitat changes associated with logging, climatic conditions, or predator reduction. In moose, *P. tenuis* causes a fatal neurological disorder. The spread of this parasite accompanying northern shifts in deer range has led to a sharp decline in the numbers of moose along the southern fringe of moose habitat. To maintain a viable moose population, deer density should be 12 or fewer per square mile (Karns 1967:302).

The southern margins of the native range for moose include northwest to south-central Minnesota (Hazard 1982:163, Fig. 73). Moose prefer a boreal forest habitat with abundant deciduous browse and often take cover in closed coniferous or deciduous woodlands during winter (Hazard 1982:163). Prior to the twentieth century, the ranges of white-tailed deer and moose showed little overlap (Karns 1967:299). The moose's large body and long legs allowed it to move through snow up to 100 cm deep (Hazard 1982:163). In good habitat, moose density was probably about 1 to 1.5 animals per square mile (Karns 1967:299; Peek et al. 1976:19). Early European travelers into the Mississippi Headwaters region reported that moose was a principal food item from Leech Lake north in the Headwaters region (Pike 1966:62; Schoolcraft 1966:223-224, 244-252).

The region to the north of Bemidji was in coniferous forest, one of the poorest habitats for deer in the early Euro-American contact era. The few analyzed faunal assemblages from northern Minnesota support this assertion. At the Knutson Dam site, in southeast Beltrami County, deer comprise only 7.3 percent (NISP) of the mammal assemblage (Hohman-Caine and Goltz 1998). Low numbers of deer are also observed at the McKinstry Mounds (0.6 percent of NISP) and Smith Mounds (7.0 percent of NISP) in Koochiching County (Lukens 1973; see also Morey et al. 1996). Conversely, McKinstry Mounds and Knutson Dam both have abundant moose remains, comprising 25 percent and 67 percent of the respective mammal assemblages.

At Midway, however, deer make up 56 percent of the mammal remains (those identified to at least the genus level) while moose, although still present, comprise only 4 percent of the mammal NISP. Given the proportion of deer in the Midway assemblage, it seems unlikely that the area surrounding the site would have been strictly comprised of a coniferous-hardwood forest, as some sources seem to indicate. The quantity of deer, along with the presence of other mammals, such as elk, Plains pocket gopher, and badger implies that there was an abundance of deciduous edge habitat. At the same time, the occurrence of moose, caribou, snowshoe hare, porcupine, and pine marten indicate that there were substantial stands of coniferous-hardwood forest.

The Bemidji area, with its lakes, marshes, and deciduous forest margin located at the southern margin of Beltrami County (see Borchert and Yaeger 1969), may have furnished an optimal ecotonal niche to be exploited by prehistoric peoples. Although this region lies beyond what has been traditionally defined as the prairie-forest border, it is clear that the ecotonal nature of its environment may have provided a rich resource base for Woodland cultural manifestations. Further analysis of the cultural remains from Midway along with comparison to other Headwater Lakes sites will hopefully elaborate upon the interaction of this environment to its prehistoric occupants.

Conclusion

In sum, the overall subsistence patterns represented in the site are fall-winter deer harvest, use of moose (probably along with wild rice) during the winter, and spring harvest of riparian animals, spawning fish, and turtles. In terms of patterning within the assemblage, the bone fragments from Area F are compatible with the Phase II interpretations of this area as representing an earlier occupation, and the Area A units closest to the river are noticeably different from the other units in terms of both abundance of faunal remains and proportions of fish types. Comparisons of these findings with patterning in ceramics, other diagnostic artifacts, or other lines of evidence could provide additional information on activity areas or changes in subsistence activities through time.

Acknowledgments. As it is with any large faunal analysis, this project would not have been possible without the help many individuals. First and foremost, thanks go to Dr. Kathrine Stevenson and Elizabeth Schultz. Kathy created the database, assisted with some of the identifications, and helped in preparation of the report. Elizabeth was responsible for labeling the remains, completing all the database entry and paperwork, and conducting background research on the regional environment and species distributions. Dr. Constance Arzigian (MVAC) oversaw the administrative aspects of the faunal analysis. Dr. Paul Parmalee of the McClung Museum, University of Tennessee, identified some of the bird species, and Dr. Holmes Semken, Jr. of the Department of Geology, University of Iowa, identified certain small mammals. Dr. Terrance Martin and the Illinois State Museum furnished several comparative fish specimens, and the Leech Lake Band of Ojibwe and LLHSP provided several fresh fish specimens for creating comparative specimens. William Yourd of the Chippewa National Forest provided a copy of Knutson Dam site report. David Mather provided valuable comments and information on Minnesota zooarchaeology. David and Rose Kluth, as well as the LLHSP, provided the opportunity to work on this project and supplied much support throughout its course.

Editors' Note. As our readers are aware, proper taxonomic names at the genus-species level are conventionally set in italic typeface: *Marmota monax*. In this paper, such names sometimes occur in section headers that are also set in italic typeface: *Snapping Turtle (Chelydra serpentina)*. In these cases the editors chose to follow a typographic convention that reverses the italicization. What would normally be plain typeface is italicized, and what would normally be italicized is set as plain typeface: *Snapping Turtle (*Chelydra serpentina*)*. The authors of this paper have correctly pointed out that this is a problematic solution. The editors therefore wish to acknowledge responsibility for this stylistic choice and emphasize that the authors' original manuscript followed the convention of italicizing all genus-species names.

Table 1. Identified Mammal Remains from the Midway Site (21BL37)

Taxon	Common Name	Good Context NISP	Good Context MNI	Fill/Disturbed NISP	Fill/Disturbed MNI	Total Live Weight (kg)	Total Useable Meat (kg)
*Sorex cinereus	Masked shrew	1	1	-	-	+	+
Leporidae	Hare & rabbit family	3	-	-	-	-	-
Lepus americanus	Snowshoe hare	1	1	-	-	1.6	.8
cf. Lepus americanus	Snowshoe hare ?	1	-	-	-	-	-
Tamias striatus	Eastern chipmunk	6	1	1	-	+	+
cf. Tamias striatus	Eastern chipmunk ?	1	-	-	-	-	-
Marmota monax	Woodchuck	1	1	-	-	4.6	2.3
Sciuridae	Squirrel family	2	-	-	-	-	-
Geomys bursarius	Plains pocket gopher	24	4	-	-	+	+
Geomys cf. G. bursarius	Plains pocket gopher ?	7	-	-	-	-	-
Castor canadensis	Beaver	98	4	3	-	88.0	44.0
cf. Castor canadensis	Beaver ?	9	-	-	-	-	-
Peromyscus sp.	Mouse	2	1	-	-	+	+
cf. Peromyscus sp.	Mouse ?	3	-	-	-	-	-
*Clethrionomys gapperi	Southern red-backed vole	2	1	-	-	+	+
*Microtus pennslyvanicus	Meadow vole	1	1	-	-	+	+
Microtus sp.	Meadow vole/Prairie vole	2	-	-	-	-	-
Ondatra zibethicus	Muskrat	57	5	2	-	6.0	3.0
cf. Ondatra zibethicus	Muskrat ?	6	-	-	-	-	-
Erethizon dorsatum	Porcupine	2	1	-	-	6.8	3.4
Rodentia	Rodent order	7	-	-	-	-	-
Canis lupus	Wolf	2	1	-	-	31.8	15.9
Canis cf. C. lupus	Wolf ?	1	-	-	-	-	-
Canis sp.	Dog/coyote	16	3	-	-	18.0	9.0
cf. Canis sp.	Dog/coyote?	2	-	-	-	-	-
Vulpes vulpes	Red fox	1	1	-	-	5.0	2.5
Ursus americanus	Black bear	9	2	1	-	312.0	156.0
cf. Ursus americanus	Black bear ?	-	-	1	-	-	-
Procyon lotor	Raccoon	1	1	-	-	9.0	4.5
Martes americana	Pine marten	-	-	1	1	1.2	.6
cf. Mustela vison	Mink ?	1	1	-	-	1.0	.5
Taxidea taxus	Badger	1	1	-	-	9.0	4.5
Mephitis mephitis	Striped skunk	1	1	-	-	3.2	1.6
Lutra canadensis	River otter	3	1	-	-	9.0	4.5
Felis cattus (D)	Domestic cat	2	1	-	-	+	+
Sus scrofa (D)	Domestic pig	1	1	1	-	+	+
Cervus canadensis	American elk	3	1	1	-	320.0	160.0
cf. Cervus canadensis	American elk ?	2	-	-	-	-	-
Odocoileus sp.	Deer	354	6	11	-	456.0	228.0
cf. Odocoileus sp.	Deer ?	38	-	4	-	-	-
Alces alces	Moose	23	2	2	-	818.2	409.1
cf. Alces alces	Moose ?	6	-	1	-	-	-
Rangifer tarandus	Caribou	1	1	-	-	91.0	45.5
Cervidae	Cervid family	1	-	-	-	-	-
Artiodactyla	Even-toed ungulates	91	-	1	-	-	-
	Subtotal	796	42	30	3	2191.4	1095.7
	Unid. mammal > ¼ inch	7722	-	321	-	-	-
	TOTAL	8518	42	351	3	2191.4	1095.7

cf. = compares favorably/probable identification
D = domestic animal associated with European settlement
* = specimens identified by Holmes A. Semken, Jr.
+ = species not considered a dietary item

Table 2. Deer (Odocoileus sp.) Remains, by Element, from the Midway Site (21BL37)

ELEMENT	R*	L	A/U	ELEMENT	R	L	A/U
SKULL				TIBIA			
occipital condyle	1	-	-	proximal	1	-	-
auditory meatus	2	1	-	distal	4	2	-
frontal	1	1	-	METATARSAL			
maxilla	1	-	1	proximal	5	1	-
mandibular condyle	1	2	-	distal	-	2	-
horizontal ramus	-	5	-	shaft	1	3	4
coronoid process	1	-	-	CALCANEUM			
gonial angle	1	-	-	complete	-	1	-
isolated mandibular teeth	21	15	9	anterior	-	2	-
isolated maxillary teeth	26	16	2	posterior	2	1	-
AXIS VERTEBRA	-	-	1	ASTRAGALUS			
SCAPULA	-	2	-	complete	3	4	-
HUMERUS				proximal	1	-	-
shaft	1	-	-	distal	-	1	-
distal	-	1	-	NAVICULO-CUBOID			
ULNA				complete	-	1	-
proximal	2	1	-	lateral	-	1	-
RADIUS				medial	2	1	-
proximal	3	3	-	anterior	3	-	-
distal	-	2	-	1st TARSAL	-	1	-
RADIAL CARPAL	2	-	-	FUSED 2nd/3rd TARSAL	3	5	-
ULNAR CARPAL	1	-	-	4th TARSAL	1	-	-
INTERMEDIATE CARPAL	2	2	-	LATERAL MALLEOLUS	4	1	-
FUSED 2nd/3rd CARPAL	1	-	-	METAPODIAL			
4th CARPAL	3	1	-	distal	-	1	20
ACCESSORY CARPAL	-	1	-	RESIDUAL METAPODIALS			
METACARPAL				& PHALANGES	-	-	18
proximal	2	1	-	SESAMOIDS	-	-	21
shaft	-	-	1	1st PHALANX			
INNOMINATE				complete	-	-	1
ilium	2	-	-	proximal	-	-	14
pubis	-	2	-	distal	-	-	12
ischium	1	1	-	misc. fragments	-	-	11
ischium/ilium	-	1	-	2nd PHALANX			
FEMUR				proximal	-	-	21
proximal	-	-	1	distal	-	-	12
distal	1	-	-	misc. fragments	-	-	3
shaft	-	2	-	3rd PHALANX			
PATELLA	2	1	-	complete	-	-	5
				proximal	-	-	1
				misc. fragments	-	-	1

*R = right   L = left   A/U = axial/unsided

Table 3. Element Distribution of Limb Extremities and Cranial/Dentition Fragments of Deer (Odocoileus sp.) from the Midway Site (21BL37)

Limb Extremities		**NISP**
Carpals		13
Tarsals		15
Metacarpals		4
Metatarsals		16
Calcaneus		6
Astragalus		9
Naviculo-cuboid		8
Dew claw complex		18
Metapodials		21
Phalanges		81
Sesamoids		21
Distal tibia		2
Distal ulna, radius		2
	Total	220 -- of 354 identified deer remains
		= 62 % of deer remains
Cranial & Dentition		**NISP**
Mandibular fragments & teeth		55
Maxillary fragments & teeth		46
Other cranial fragments		6
	Total	107 -- of 354 identified deer remains
		= 30 % of deer remains
Limb Extremities		62 %
Cranial & Dentition		30 %
	Total	92 %

Table 4. Deer (Odocoileus sp.) Dentition from the Midway Site (21BL37)

Mandibular Dentition	R*	L	U
Isolated Teeth			
i1	-	1	-
i2	-	1	-
i3	1	-	-
i2 or i3	1	1	-
i3 or canine	1	-	-
dp4	1	1	-
p2	1	1	-
p3	5	3	-
p4	3	-	-
m1 or m2	2	5	-
m3	5	-	-
molars – position?	1	2	-
premolars – position?	-	-	9
Mandibular Rami			
ramus w/ p2, p3	-	1	-
ramus w/ p2, p3, p4	-	1	-
ramus w/ p4, m1	-	1	-
ramus w/ m1, m2	-	1	-
Maxillary Dentition			
Isolated Teeth			
dP2	1	-	-
dP3 or dP4	1	-	-
dP4	1	-	-
P2	4	1	-
P3	4	1	-
P3 or P4	1	2	-
P4	-	1	-
M1 or M2	4	5	-
M3	3	-	-
molars – position ?	4	5	1
premolars – position ?	2	2	1
Maxilla w/ Teeth			
maxilla w/ dP2, dP3, dP4, M1	1	-	-
maxilla w/ M1, M2	-	-	1
maxilla w/ M2, M3	1	-	-

*R = right   L = left   U = unsided

Table 5. Ages and Seasonal Dates Obtained from Deer (Odocoileus sp.) Remains from Various Proveniences at the Midway Site (21BL37)

Age	Season	Tooth	Side
5-6 mos.	Oct-Nov	Upper P3	R
5-6 mos.	Oct-Nov	Lower p3	L
6-7 mos.	Nov-Dec	Lower p4	R
6-7 mos.	Nov-Dec	Maxilla w/ dP2, dP3, dP4, M1	R
1.5 yrs.	Oct-Dec	Lower dp4	R
1.5 yrs.	Oct-Dec	Lower dp4	L
1.5 yrs	Oct-Dec	Upper dP4	R
1.5 yrs.	Oct-Dec	Lower p2	R
1.5 yrs.	Oct-Dec	Upper P4	R
1.5-2.5 yrs.		Upper P3	L
2-2.5 yrs.		Lower p2	R
2-2.5 yrs.		Lower p3	R
2-2.5 yrs.		Lower p3	R
2.5 yrs.		Mandible w/ p4 & m1	L
2-3 yrs.		Lower m3	R
3.5-4.5 yrs.		Mandible w/ p2 & p3	L
3+ yrs.		Lower p3	R
4-5 yrs.		Mandible w/ p2, p3, & p4	L
4+ yrs.		Lower p3	L
4+ yrs.		Indet. upper molar	R
4.5+ yrs.		Upper M2 or M3	R
5+ yrs		Indet. upper molar	Indet.
5+ yrs.		Lower p4	R
5+ yrs.		Indet. upper molar	L
7+ yrs.		Upper M1 or M2	R
7+ yrs.		Upper M1 or M2	L
7-8+ yrs.		Lower m1 or m2	L
Estimate not available	Late summer to early winter	Male deer frontal with attached fully grown antler	L

Table 6. Probable Deer (cf. Odocoileus sp.) Remains from the Midway Site (21BL37)

ELEMENT	R*	L	U
CRANIAL			
maxillary molar/premolar	-	1	-
mandibular condyle	-	1	-
mandibular premolar	-	-	1
incisor	1	-	-
molar/premolar fragments	-	-	18
HUMERUS			
proximal	1	-	-
FUSED 2nd/3rd CARPAL	1	-	-
INNOMINATE			
pubis	-	1	-
METATARSAL			
proximal	-	2	-
METAPODIAL			
distal	-	-	4
posterior	-	-	1
CUBOID			
medial	-	1	-
1st PHALANX			
misc. fragments	-	-	3
2nd PHALANX			
misc. fragments	-	-	1
3rd PHALANX			
misc. fragments	-	-	1

*R = right   L = left   U = unsided

Table 7. Moose (Alces alces) Remains, by Element, From the Midway Site (21BL37)

ELEMENT	R*	L	A/U
MOLAR			
upper M3	1	-	-
HUMERUS			
^distal	1	-	-
TIBIA			
distal	-	2	-
posterior	1	-	-
METATARSAL			
proximal	2	1	-
distal	-	-	1
CALCANEUS			
posterior	-	1	-
ASTRAGALUS			
complete	-	1	-
RESIDUAL DEW CLAW			
PHALANX	-	-	1
SESAMOIDS	-	-	4
1st PHALANX			
complete	-	-	1
distal	-	-	2
lateral	-	-	2
2nd PHALANX			
complete	-	-	1
^distal	-	-	1
3rd PHALANX			
complete	-	-	1
proximal	-	-	1

*R = right   L = left   A/U = axial/unsided
^ = elements from redeposited A horizon or other disturbed contexts

Table 8. Probable Moose (cf. Alces alces) Remains, by Element, from the Midway Site (21BL37)

ELEMENT	R*	L	A/U
ULNA			
proximal	-	1	-
FEMUR			
distal (lateral condyle)	-	1	-
TIBIA			
shaft	2	-	-
METATARSAL			
shaft	-	-	1
RESIDUAL DEW CLAW			
PHALANX	-	-	1
1st PHALANX			
^distal	-	-	1

*R = right   L = left   A/U = axial/unsided
^ = elements from redeposited A horizon or other disturbed contexts

Table 9. Elk (Cervus canadensis) Remains, by Element, from the Midway Site (21BL37)

ELEMENT	R*	L	A/U
SESAMOID	-	-	1
RESIDUAL DEW CLAW			
2nd PHALANX	-	-	1
^1st PHALANX	-	-	1
3rd PHALANX	-	-	1
Probable (cf.) Identifications			
TIBIA			
distal	1	-	-
2nd PHALANX			
distal	-	-	1

*R = right   L = left   A/U = axial/unsided
^ = elements from redeposited A horizon or other disturbed contexts

Table 10. Black Bear (Ursus americanus) Remains, by Element, from the Midway Site (21BL37)

ELEMENT	R*	L	A/U
CRANIAL			
maxilla (no dentition)	-	1	-
upper canine	1	1	-
upper I3	-	1	-
^occipital condyle		1	-
2nd METATARSAL			
proximal	1	-	-
3rd METATARSAL			
proximal	-	1	-
4th METATARSAL			
proximal	1	-	-
METAPODiAL			
distal	1	-	-
ASTRAGALUS	1	-	-
Probable (cf.) Identifications			
CRANIAL			
^canine fragment	-	-	1

*R = right   L = left   A/U = axial/unsided
^ = elements from redeposited A horizon or other disturbed contexts

Table 11. Dog/Coyote/Wolf (Canis sp.) Remains, by Element, from the Midway Site (21BL37)

ELEMENT	R*	L	A/U
MAXILLARY DENTITION			
upper I3	2	-	-
upper P2 or P3	-	1	-
MANDIBULAR DENTITION			
ramus w/ p2, p3, p4, & m2	-	1	-
ramus w/ sockets for c, p2, p3, p4, & m1	1	-	-
ramus w/ no dentition	1	-	-
lower i3	1	-	-
lower canine	-	1	-
lower p3	1	-	-
lower p3 or p4	1	-	-
lower p4	2	-	-
indet. premolar	-	-	1
ATLAS VERTEBRA			
left ½	-	-	1
FEMUR			
distal	-	1	-
METAPODIAL			
distal	-	-	1
Probable (cf.) Identifications			
ATLAS VERTEBRA			
anterior fragment	1	1	-

*R = right   L = left   A/U = axial/unsided

Table 12. Beaver (Castor canadensis) Remains, by Element, from the Midway Site (21BL37)

ELEMENT	R*	L	A/U	ELEMENT	R	L	A/U
SKULL				ULNA			
maxilla (no dentition)	1	-	-	complete	1	-	-
upper dentition (isolated)				proximal	-	2	
P4	1	-	-	shaft	-	2	-
M1 or M2	3	1	-	RADIUS			
molar – position?	1	5	-	proximal	1	-	-
incisor fragments	1	1	-	METACARPAL			
lower dentition (isolated)				complete	1	-	-
p4	1	1	-	INNOMINATE			
m2	1	-	-	ilium	-	1	-
m3	2	-	-	ischium	1	-	-
m1 or m2	-	1	-	FEMUR			
molar or premolar	-	4	-	distal	1	-	-
incisor fragments	3	4	-	shaft	1	1	-
mandibles w/ dentition				TIBIA			
w/ m1, m2, m3	-	1	-	distal	1	-	-
w/ p4, m1, m2, m3	-	1	-	shaft	-	1	-
fragments w/ p4, m1 or m2, m2 or m3	1	-	-	FIBULA			
				distal	-	1	-
molar or premolar	-	-	6	METATARSAL			
incisor fragments	-	-	18	proximal	1	-	-
ATLAS VERTEBRA	-	-	1	4th METATARSAL			
SCAPULA				distal	-	1	-
distal	1	1	-	CALCANEUS			
posterior	-	1	-	complete	1	-	-
HUMERUS				ASTRAGALUS			
proximal	1	1	-	complete	1	1	-
distal	-	1	-	1st PHALANX	-	-	5
complete	2	-	-	2nd PHALANX	-	-	2
				3rd PHALANX	-	-	3
				METAPODIAL			
				distal		1	-
							1

*R = right   L = left   A/U = axial/unsided

Table 13. Muskrat (Ondatra zibethicus) Remains, by Element, from the Midway Site (21BL37)

ELEMENT	R*	L	U/A
CRANIAL			
maxilla fragments	2	2	-
mandible fragments	6	5	-
upper teeth	1	1	-
lower teeth	3	-	1
incisor fragments	6	-	-
AXIS VERTEBRA	-	-	1
SCAPULA			
proximal	1	-	-
distal	1	-	-
HUMERUS			
proximal	2	-	-
distal	-	2	-
ULNA			
proximal	-	3	-
distal	1	-	-
INNOMINATE			
illium	-	1	-
COCCYXGEAL VERTEBRA	-	-	3
FEMUR			
proximal	3	-	-
distal	-	1	-
TIBIA			
shaft	1	2	-
distal	-	1	-
CALCANEUS	2	1	-
ASTRAGALUS	1	2	-
3rd PHALANX	-	-	1

*R = right   L = left   U/A = unsided

Table 14. Plains Pocket Gopher (Geomys bursarius) Remains, by Element, from the Midway Site (21BL37)

ELEMENT	R*	L	U/A
CRANIAL			
premaxilla	-	-	1
maxilla	-	-	1
incisor (isolated)	1	1	-
mandible	3	4	-
SCAPULA			
complete	1	1	-
HUMERUS			
complete	1	2	-
ULNA			
complete	1	1	-
RADIUS			
complete	1	-	-
FEMUR			
complete	1	-	-
INNOMINATE			
complete	1	2	-
SACRUM	-	-	1

*R = right   L = left   U/A = unsided

Table 15. Identified Bird Remains and their Estimated Weights, from the Midway Site (21BL37)

Taxon	Common Name	NISP	MNI	Total est. live weight (kg)	Total est. useable meat (kg)
*Gavia immer	Common loon	2	1	[a]4.1	2.9
*Phalacrocorax auritus	Double-crested cormorant	4	3	[b]5.1	3.5
*Ardea herodias	Great blue heron	3	1	[b]2.4	1.7
Anatidae	Ducks	29	3	-	-
cf. Anatidae	Ducks ?	2	-	-	-
Anas sp.	Dabbling ducks	2	-	-	-
Anas sp. (crecca/discors)	Green-winged teal/Blue-winged teal	1	1	[c].4	.3
Anas sp. (platyrhynchos/rupripes)	Mallard/Black duck	1	1	[c]1.2	.8
Anas cf. A. strepa	Gadwall ?	1	1	[c].9	.6
Aythya sp.	Diving ducks	2	-	-	-
*Haliaeetus leucocephalus	Bald eagle	3	1	+	+
*Haliaeetus cf. H. leucocephalus	Bald eagle ?	2	-	+	+
*cf. Eagle (Haliaeetus leucocephalus/Aquila chrysaetos)	Bald eagle/Golden eagle ?	1	-	+	+
cf. Bonasa umbellus	Ruffed grouse	1	1	[d].6	.4
Gallus gallus (D)	Domestic chicken	2	1	+	+
	Subtotal	56	14	14.7	10.2
	Unidentified bird	202	-	-	-
	TOTALS	258	14	14.7	10.2

* = specimens identified by Paul W. Parmalee
cf. = compares favorably/probable identification
D = domestic animal associated with European settlement
+ = not considered to be a dietary item
-- Individual live weights from: [a] McIntyre (1988) and Sibley (2000), [b] Sibley (2000), [c] Bellrose (1976), and [d] Johnsgard (1975)

Table 16. Identified Fish Remains and their Estimated Live Weights from the Midway Site (21BL37)

Taxon	Common Name	NISP	MNI	Total est. live weight (kg)	Range of est. live weights (kg)
Esox sp.	Northern pike/muskie	74	15	32.6	.05 to 6.0
cf. *Esox* sp.	Northern pike/muskie ?	3	-	-	-
Catostomus commersoni	White sucker	2	1	1.0	-
cf. *Catostomus commersoni*	White sucker ?	2	1	1.2	-
Moxostoma sp.	Redhorse suckers	6	2	5.3	2.3 to 3.0
Catostomidae	Sucker family	16	-	-	-
Ictalurus sp.	Bullhead group	43	-	-	-
Ictalurus melas	Black bullhead	4	3	1.0	.3 to .4
Ictalurus nebulosus	Brown bullhead	7	4	1.6	.3 to .5
cf. *Ambloplites rupestris*	Rock bass ?	1	1	.5	-
Lepomis gibbosus	Pumpkinseed	1	1	.4	-
Micropterus cf. *M. dolomieui*	Smallmouth bass ?	1	1	.1	-
Perca flavescens	Yellow perch	20	4	1.6	.1 to .5
cf. *Perca flavescens*	Yellow perch ?	7	-	-	-
Stizostedion vitreum	Walleye	118	14	21.0	.7 to 4.5
cf. *Stizostedion vitreum*	Walleye ?	13	-	-	-
	Subtotal	**318**	**47**	**66.3 kg**	
	Unid. Fish > ¼ inch	1444			
	TOTAL	**1762**	**47**	**66.3 kg**	

cf. = compares favorably/probable identification

Table 17. Bone Attributes for the Site Total and for the "Archaic" Units (33-41) of the Midway Site (21BL37)

Prov.	NISP >¼"	Scorched NISP	%	Burned NISP	%	Calcined NISP	%	GBF NISP	%	Rodent Gnaw NISP	%	Carniv. Gnaw NISP	%
*SiteTotal	11,158	36	.3	642	5.6	693	6.2	1332	11.9	178	1.2	118	1.1
Units													
33	3	0	0	0	0	2	66.6	0	0	0	0	0	0
34	2	0	0	0	0	0	0	0	0	0	0	0	0
35	1	0	0	0	0	1	100.0	0	0	0	0	0	0
36	16	0	0	0	0	14	87.5	1	6.3	0	0	0	0
37	7	0	0	0	0	7	100.0	0	0	0	0	0	0
38	16	0	0	1	6.3	13	81.3	0	0	0	0	0	0
39	3	0	0	0	0	1	33.3	0	0	0	0	0	0
40	4	0	0	0	0	1	25.0	0	0	0	0	0	0
41	4	0	0	0	0	3	75.0	0	0	0	0	0	0
Total of Units 33-41	**56**	**0**	**0**	**1**	**6.3**	**42**	**75.0**	**1**	**6.3**	**0**	**0**	**0**	**0**

* The site total includes only the Phase III material greater than 1/4 inch.

Table 18. Fish Remains for Total Site Compared to Those from Units 42, 43, 44, and 45 of the Midway Site (21BL37)

	Site Total NISP	%	Units 42-45 NISP	%	Units 42-45 as % of the Site Total
Pikes (*Esox* sp.)	77	24.2	20	18.0	26.0
Suckers (Catostomidae)	26	8.2	11	10.0	42.3
Bullheads (*Ictalurus* sp.)	54	17.0	34	31.0	63.0
Perch (*Perca flavescens*)	27	8.5	10	9.0	37.0
Walleye (*Stizostedion vitreum*)	131	41.2	36	32.0	27.5
Other species	3	.9	0	0	0
Total	**318**	**100.0**	**111**	**100.0**	

Table 19. Totals by Class for Remains from Good Contexts at the Midway Site (21BL37)

Class	NISP	# of Taxa	Est. MNI	Est. Useable Meat (kg)
Mammals	8515	27	45	1095.1
Birds	246	10	13	10.2
Reptiles	535	2	3	11.8
Amphibians	36	1	2	-
Fishes	1732	9	33	33.2
Mollusks	26	2	3	-
Vertebrate Class Unknown (< ¼ inch)	11,780	-	-	-
Historic Domestic Species	5	3	3	-
TOTAL	**22,875**	**54**	**102**	**1150.3**

References Cited

Anfinson, Scott F. and H.E. Wright, Jr.
  1990 Climatic Change and Culture in Prehistoric Minnesota. In *The Woodland Tradition in the Western Great Lakes: Papers Presented to Elden Johnson*, ed. by Guy E. Gibbon, pp. 213-232. Publications in Anthropology 4. University of Minnesota, Minneapolis.

Baker, Jonathan D.
  2001 Bone Grease Processing at the Krause Site (47 Lc 41). Paper presented at the Midwest Archaeological Conference, La Crosse, Wisconsin, October 10-14.

Banfield, A.W.F.
  1974 *The Mammals of Canada*. University of Toronto Press, Toronto.

Becker, George C.
  1983 *The Fishes of Wisconsin*. University of Wisconsin Press, Madison.

Bellrose, Frank C.
  1976 *Ducks, Geese and Swans of North America*. Stackpole, Harrisburg, Pennsylvania.

Binford, Lewis R.
  1978 *Nunamiut Ethnoarchaeology*. Academic Press, New York.
  1981 *Bones: Ancient Men and Modern Myths*. Academic Press, New York.

Blue, Kathleen
  2000 Osteological Analysis of the Human Skeletal Remains from the Gull Lake Dam Site (21CA37) Cass County, Minnesota. Paper presented at the Joint Midwest Archaeological/ Plains Anthropological Conference, St. Paul, Minnesota, November 9-12.

Borchert, John R. and Donald P. Yaeger
  1969 *Atlas of Minnesota Resources and Settlement*. Minnesota State Planning Agency, St. Paul.

Clarke, Arthur H.
  1981 *The Freshwater Molluscs of Canada*. National Museum of Natural Sciences, National Museums of Canada, Ottawa.

Cleland, Charles E.
  1982 The Inland Shore Fishery of the Northern Great Lakes: Its Development and Importance in Prehistory. *American Antiquity* 47:761-784.

De Vos, Antoon
  1964 Range Changes of Mammals in the Great Lakes Region. *American Midland Naturalist* 71(1):211-231. Faunmap Working Group (co-directors and principal authors, Russell W. Graham and Ernest L. Lundelius Jr.; compilers, Mary Ann Graham, Ralph F. Stearley and Erich K. Schroeder)
  1994 *Faunmap: A Data Base Documenting Late Quaternary Distributions of Mammal Species in the United States*. Scientific Papers 25(1, 2). Illinois State Museum, Springfield.

Green, Janet C. and Robert B. Janssen
  1975 *Minnesota Birds: Where, When, and How Many*. University of Minnesota Press, Minneapolis.

Grim, Leland H. and Larry W. Kallemeyn
  1995 *Reproduction and Distribution of Bald Eagles in Voyageurs National Park, Minnesota, 1973–1993*. Biological Science Report 1. U.S. Department of the Interior, Washington, D.C.

Hall, E. Raymond and Keith R. Kelson
  1959 *The Mammals of North America, Volume 2*. Ronald Press, New York.

Hannes, Sheri M.
  1994 The Faunal Analysis of the Horseshoe Bay Site: A Subsistence Study of a Nineteenth-Century Fur Trading Post. Unpublished Master's thesis, Department of Anthropology, University of Iowa, Iowa City.

Hargrave, Lyndon L.
  1972 *Comparative Osteology of the Chicken and American Grouse*. Prescott College Studies in Biology 1. Prescott College Press, Prescott, Arizona.

Hatch, Jay T. and Konrad Schmidt
  2004 Fishes of Minnesota: Distribution in 8 Major Drainage Basins. Available at http://www.gen. umn.edu/research/fish/fishes/distribution_table. html.

Hazard, Evan B.
  1982 *The Mammals of Minnesota*. University of Minnesota Press, Minneapolis.

Hickerson, Harold
  1970 *The Chippewa and Their Neighbors: A Study in Ethnohistory*. Holt, Rinehart, and Winston, New York.

Hohman-Caine, Christy A. and Grant E. Goltz
  1998 *Final Report: Knutson Dam Site, 21-BL-4 (FS #09-03-02-069), and Knutson Dam Blufftop Site (FS #09-03-02-575)*. Copy on

file at Chippewa National Forest, Cass Lake, Minnesota.

Jackson, H.T. Hartley
1961 *Mammals of Wisconsin.* University of Wisconsin Press, Madison.

Johnsgard, Paul A.
1975 *North American Game Birds of Upland and Shoreline.* University of Nebraska Press, Lincoln.

Karns, Patrick D.
1967 *Pneumostrongylus tenuis* in Deer in Minnesota and Implications for Moose. *Journal of Wildlife Management* 31(2):299-303.

Kaufman, Kenn
1996 *Lives of North American Birds.* Houghton Mifflin, New York.

Klippel, Walter E., Lynn M. Snyder and Paul W. Parmalee
1987 Taphonomy and Archaeologically Recovered Mammal Bone from Southeast Missouri. *Journal of Ethnobiology* 7(2):155-169.

Kluth, Rose A. and David W. Kluth
2000 *Phase II Archaeological & Geomorphological Evaluation of Site 21-BL-37 and Phase I Archaeological & Geomorphological Assessment of the TH 197 Bridge Abutments & Portions of Area E, (S.P. 0416-19) in the City of Bemidji, Beltrami County, Minnesota.* Leech Lake Heritage Sites Program. Copy on file, LLHSP, Cass Lake, Minnesota.

Kuchler, A.W.
1964 *Potential Natural Vegetation of the Conterminous United States.* Special Publication Number 36. American Geographical Society, New York.

Leech Lake Heritage Sites Program
2002 *Phase III Data Recovery of Site 21BL37, The Midway Site, Beltrami County, Minnesota.* Report submitted to the Minnesota Department of Transportation. Copy on file, LLHSP, Cass Lake, Minnesota.

Lukens, Paul W. Jr.
1963 *Some Ethnozoological Implications of Mammalian Faunas from Minnesota Archaeological Sites.* Ph.D. dissertation, Department of Anthropology, University of Minnesota, Minneapolis.
1973 The Vertebrate Fauna from the Pike Bay Mound, Smith Mound 4, and McKinstry Mound 1. In *The Laurel Culture of Minnesota,* by James B. Stoltman, pp. 37-45. Minnesota Historical Society, St. Paul.

Lyman, R. Lee
1994 *Vertebrate Taphonomy.* Cambridge University Press, Cambridge.

Mather, David
1998 Faunal Analysis. In *A Spring Piscary in the Headwaters Region: The Third River Bridge Site, 12-IC-46 (CNF #09-03-01-109),* by C.A. Hohman-Caine and G.E. Goltz, pp. 20-34. Hamline University, St. Paul.
2002 Zooarchaeology of the Lake Lida Site (21OT109), Otter Tail County, Minnesota. *The Minnesota Archaeologist* 61:9-21.

McIntyre, Judith W.
1988 *The Common Loon: Spirit of Northern Lakes.* University of Minnesota Press, Minneapolis.

Michlovic, Michael G.
1980 Ecotonal Settlement and Subsistence in the Northern Midwest. *Midcontinental Journal of Archaeology* 5(2):151-168.

Morey, Darcy F., Carl R. Falk and Holmes A. Semken Jr.
1996 Vertebrate Remains from the McKinstry Site. In *The McKinstry Site (21 KC 2): Final Report of Phase III Investigations for Mn/DOT S.P. 3604-44, Replacement of Bridge 5178 over the Little Fork River, Koochiching County, Minnesota,* by M.M. Thomas and D. Mather, pp. 15.1-15.56. Loucks Project Report No. 93512, Loucks & Associates, Maple Grove, Minnesota.

Oldfield, Barney and John J. Moriarty
1994 *Amphibians & Reptiles Native to Minnesota.* University of Minnesota Press, Minneapolis.

Peek, James M., David L. Urick and Richard J. Mockie
1976 *Moose Habitat Selection and Relationships to Forest Management in Northern Minnesota.* Wildlife Monographs 48. Wildlife Society, Washington, D.C.

Pike, Zebulon M.
1966 An Account of Expeditions to the Sources of the Mississippi, and Through the Western Parts of the Arkansaw, Kaws, La Platte, and Pierre Jaun, Rivers. Readex Microprint Corporation. [Originally published 1810]

Schoolcraft, Henry R.
1966 *Narrative Journal of Travels from Detroit Northeast Through the Great Chain of American Lakes to the Sources of the Mississippi in the Year 1820.* March of America Facsimile Series 66. University Microfilms, Ann Arbor, Michigan. [Originally published 1821]

Schorger, A.W.
1953 The White-tailed Deer in Early Wisconsin. *Transactions of the Wisconsin Academy of Sciences, Arts, and Letters* 42:1-10.

Shane, Orrin C. III
1996 *Identification and Analysis of Fish Remains from the Horseshoe Bay Site: North and South Buildings.* Unpublished Manuscript. Copy on file at Archaeology Department, Minnesota Historical Society.

Shay, C. Thomas
1971 *The Itasca Bison Kill Site: An Ecological Analysis.* Minnesota Historical Society, St. Paul.
1978 Late Prehistoric Bison and Deer Use in the Eastern Prairie Forest Border. Memoir 14, Bison Procurement and Utilization: A Symposium. *Plains Anthropologist* 23(82, part 2):194-212.
1985 Late Prehistoric Selection of Wild Ungulates in the Prairie-Forest Transition. In *Archaeology, Ecology, and Ethnohistory of the Prairie-Forest Border Zone in Minnesota and Manitoba*, ed. by Janet Spector and Elden Johnson, pp. 31-65. Reprints in Anthropology, Volume 31. J&L Reprint Company, Lincoln, Nebraska.

Sibley, David A.
2000 *National Audubon Society: The Sibley Guide to Birds.* Chanticleer Press, New York.

Spector, Janet and Elden Johnson (editors)
1985 *Archaeology, Ecology, and Ethnohistory of the Prairie-Forest Border Zone in Minnesota and Manitoba.* Reprints in Anthropology, Volume 31. J&L Reprint Company, Lincoln, Nebraska.

Stevenson, Katherine P., Edward Swanson and Jonathan D. Baker
n.d. MS Access Database for the Analysis of Archaeological Faunal Remains. Unpublished report. Copy on file, Mississippi Valley Archaeology Center, University of Wisconsin–La Crosse, La Crosse.

Stoltman, James B.
1973 *The Laurel Culture in Minnesota.* Minnesota Historical Society, St. Paul.

Surber, T.
1932 *The Mammals of Minnesota.* Minnesota Department of Conservation, St. Paul.

Swanson, Gustav A., Thaddeus Surber and Thomas S. Roberts
1945 *The Mammals of Minnesota.* Technical Bulletin No. 2. Minnesota Department of Conservation, St. Paul.

Swift, Ernest
1946 *A History of Wisconsin Deer.* Publication 323. Wisconsin Conservation Department, Madison.

Synder, Lynn M.
1991 Barking Mutton: Ethnohistoric, Ethnographic, Archaeological, and Nutritional Evidence Pertaining to the Dog as a Native American Food Resource on the Plains. In *Beamers, Bobwhites, and Blue-Points: Tributes to the Career of Paul W. Parmalee*, ed. by James. R. Purdue, Walter. E. Klippel, and Bonnie W. Styles, pp. 359-378. Scientific Papers 23. Illinois State Museum, Springfield.

Theler, James L.
1987 *Woodland Tradition Economic Strategies: Animal Resource Utilization in Southwestern Wisconsin and Northeastern Iowa.* Report 17. Office of the State Archaeologist, University of Iowa, Iowa City.
2000 Animal Remains from Native American Archaeological Sites in Western Wisconsin. *Transactions of the Wisconsin Academy of Sciences, Arts, and Letters* 88:121-142.

Theler, James L. and Jonathan D. Baker
2002 Chapter 11: Animal Remains from the Midway Site (21-BL-37), Beltrami County, Minnesota. In *Phase III Data Recovery of Site 21BL37, The Midway Site, Beltrami County, Minnesota*, complied by Leech Lake Heritage Sites Program, pp. 62-103. Report submitted to the Minnesota Department of Transportation. Copy on file, LLHSP, Cass Lake, Minnesota.

Thomas, Jack W. and Dale Toweill
1982 *Elk of North America: Ecology and Management.* Stackpole, Harrisburg, Pennsylvania.

Thompson, Robert G.
2000 Chapter 8: Phytolith Analysis. In *Phase II*

Archaeological & Geomorphological Evaluation of Site 21-BL-37 and Phase I Archaeological & Geomorphological Assessment of the TH 197 Bridge Abutments &Portions of Area E, (S.P. 0416-19) in the City of Bemidji, Beltrami County, Minnesota, ed. by Rose A. Kluth and David W. Kluth, pp. 169-201. Leech Lake Heritage Sites Program. Copy on file, LLHSP, Cass Lake, Minnesota.

Tiffany, J.A., S.J. Schermer, J.L. Theler, D.W. Owsley, D.C. Anderson, E.A. Bettis III and D.M. Thompson

1988 The Hanging Valley Site (13HR28): A Stratified Woodland Burial Locale in Western Iowa. *Plains Anthropologist* 33(120):219-259.

Turgeon, Donna D., J.F. Quinn Jr., A.E. Bogan, E.V. Coan, F.G. Hochberg, W.G. Lyons, P.M. Mikkelsen, R.J. Neves, C.F.E. Roper, G. Rosenberg, B. Roth, A. Scheltema, F.G. Thompson, M. Vecchione and J.D. Williams

1998 *Common and Scientific Names of Aquatic Invertebrates from the United States and Canada: Mollusks,* 2nd edition. Special Publication 26. American Fisheries Society, Bethesda, Maryland.

United States Department of Agriculture [USDA]

1941 *Climate and Man.* Yearbook of Agriculture, U. S. Department of Agriculture, Government Printing Office, Washington.

Valppu, Seppo H.

2002 Chapter 12: Archaeobotanical Analysis. In *Phase III Data Recovery of Site 21BL37, The Midway Site, Beltrami County, Minnesota,* complied by Leech Lake Heritage Sites Program, pp. 104-116. Report submitted to the Minnesota Department of Transportation. Copy on file, LLHSP, Cass Lake, Minnesota.

Wendt, Keith M. and Barbara A. Coffin

1988 *Natural Vegetation of Minnesota: At the Time of the Public Land Survey 1847-1907.* Biological Report No. 1. Natural Heritage Program, Minnesota Department of Natural Resources, St. Paul.

White, Theodore E.

1953 A Method of Calculating the Dietary Percentage of Various Food Animals Utilized by Aboriginal Peoples. *American Antiquity* 18:396-398.

Whitlock, Cathy, Patrick J. Bartlein and William A. Watts

1993 Vegetation History of Elk Lake. In *Elk Lake, Minnesota: Evidence for Rapid Climate Change in the North-Central United States,* ed. by J. Platt Bradbury and Walter E. Dean, pp. 251-274. Special Paper 276. Geological Society of America, Boulder, Colorado.

Whelan, Mary K.

1990 Late Woodland Subsistence Systems and Settlement Size in the Mille Lacs Area. In *The Woodland Tradition in the Western Great Lakes: Papers Presented to Elden Johnson,* ed. by Guy E. Gibbon, pp. 55-75. Publications in Anthropology 4. University of Minnesota, Minneapolis.

The 1860-1873 Mound Surveys made by Alfred J. Hill in Minnesota, Wisconsin, and South Dakota

Fred A. Finney, Ph.D., RPA
fafinney@aol.com
Upper Midwest Archaeology, PO Box 106, St. Joseph, IL 61873

Alfred J. Hill (1833-1895) is best known for sponsoring the late nineteenth century Northwestern Archaeological Survey (NAS) in the Upper Mississippi River valley. For this endeavor, and the related winter surveys in the mid-south and southeast called the Southern Archaeological Survey, Hill hired archaeologist Theodore H. Lewis to conduct the fieldwork. Prior to meeting Lewis in 1880, Hill had made a limited number of his own mound surveys in Minnesota, Wisconsin, and South Dakota (then Dakota Territory). Documentation exists for 15 sites that Hill personally investigated between 1860 and 1873. It has been assumed that Lewis revisited these sites and that Winchell's Aborigines of Minnesota *published the survey results. However, an inspection of Hill's surveys in the NAS paperwork revealed that this was not always the case. The last survey in 1873 included a brief note that summarized the prospects and problems of survey, and anticipated the subsequent NAS. Hill's personal efforts to conduct archaeological surveys comprised a significant precursor to the NAS. These efforts are described in this paper.*

Introduction

Present-day knowledge of mounds and mound groups in Minnesota began with a remarkable privately-funded effort called the Northwestern Archaeological Survey (NAS). The survey was conducted in the Upper Mississippi River valley during the last two decades of the nineteenth century. It was sponsored by Alfred J. Hill (1833-1895) of St. Paul, Minnesota, who hired Theodore H. Lewis (1856-1930) to make the actual field site surveys (Dobbs 1991; Finney 2000, 2001, 2004, 2005a, 2005b; Lewis 1898). It was based on a written proposal by Hill (n.d.a). Although the NAS mound survey effort featured just one field archaeologist, it succeeded in recording, in a series of 41 field notebooks, over 17,000 mounds and earthworks from over 2,000 sites between 1880 and 1895. (In contrast Lewis [1898] used a figure of 12,000 mounds in his brief NAS summary. Later writers repeated this figure until Dobbs [1991] revised it.) This total includes approximately 1,000 earthworks. The field notes for this massive survey are held at the Minnesota Historical Society (MHS).

The NAS began as a mound survey in the Upper Mississippi River valley that after a few years expanded its scope to much of the Midwest. Minnesota (n=7791) and Wisconsin (n=4090) accounted for more than two-thirds (ca. 70 percent) of this mound total. By mound count, Iowa (n=771), South Dakota (n=671), Illinois (n=593), and North Dakota (n=567) also represent substantial survey efforts. Only sporadic work was done south of northeast Iowa and northern Illinois (Lewis 1898). The NAS notebooks contain sparse notes from Kansas, Nebraska, Missouri, Indiana, Ohio, and Michigan sites. These figures are based on the comprehensive NAS site finder aid (Dobbs 1991). (The Illinois mound count includes many examples not attributed to a specific state [Dobbs 1991].) Only the Minnesota surveys have been published in full (Winchell 1911). Hill and Lewis also collaborated on surveys made during the winter in the mid-south and southeast, an endeavor named the Southern Archaeological Survey (Finney 2004). Their efforts remain the largest privately funded archaeological project undertaken in this country (Dobbs 1991; Finney 2001).

Prior to meeting Lewis in 1880, Hill made his own mound surveys at 15 sites between 1860 and 1873. This unpublished and poorly known effort can be found buried in the NAS records at the Minnesota Historical Society (MHS). Hill's field surveys comprise a significant precursor to the NAS as he determined the need for a field archaeologist, field survey methods, and the size and scope of the project (Hill n.d.a).

Alfred James Hill

Born at St John's Wood, London, England, in 1833, Hill was educated as a civil engineer (Fig. 1). He immigrated to Red Wing, Minnesota in 1854, and purchased 40 acres in the NW 1/4, NW 1/4, Section 1, T111N, R16W, Goodhue County from the federal government (Certificate No. 2462 issued by the Red Wing land office). Hill moved on to St. Paul in 1856, where he worked as draftsman for a railroad land office. Thereafter Hill resided in St. Paul, except for his Civil War military service. He enlisted August 14, 1862, in Company E of the 6th Minnesota Volunteer Infantry. This regiment was raised to serve in the south but stayed in the state when the Dakota Conflict started in the Minnesota River Valley. Later Hill was detached from his regiment and sent to Washington, D.C. for service with the Office of Topographic Engineers. He returned as the clerk of Company E in July 1864 when the regiment traveled to Arkansas and Louisiana (Hill 1899). By investing in St. Paul real estate during the initial beginnings of the city when land was inexpensive, he accumulated the personal wealth that funded the NAS (Anonymous 1895).

During the 1860s Hill became concerned about the ongoing destruction of mounds and other sites as the result of expanding urban development of the Twin Cities. In 1860 he initially wrote to the MHS about mounds. By 1862 he was a member of the MHS and its Committee on Archaeology (MHS n.d.). After the MHS disbanded this committee in 1873, Hill retained a fascination with mounds. He decided to continue recording basic site data such as the diameter, height, and arrangement of the mounds at a site. The NAS was based on Hill's (n.d.a) written research proposal, which clearly stated the project goals, initially restricted to the state of Minnesota. To complete these goals Hill hired Lewis, a land surveyor with prior archaeological experience, as the field archaeologist. Over the 1880 to 1895 duration of the NAS, this association produced remarkable results. The unexpected 1895 death of Hill ended the NAS (Anonymous 1895, 1905; Dobbs 1991; Finney 2000; Keyes 1928, 1930, 1977; Winchell 1911).

Methods

The primary sources used for reconstructing Hill's mound surveys are housed at the MHS. They include the Alfred J. Hill papers (Hill n.d.b), Hill's correspondence as secretary of the MHS Archaeological Committee (Hill n.d.c), his mound records in the NAS records (Hill n.d.c), the Hill Geographic Notebooks (Hill n.d.b), his one published article on mounds (Hill 1894), and other resources that largely duplicated the information found in the above sources.

MHS Committee on Archaeology

Winchell (1911:vi) presented the best available summary for this committee, which existed between 1862 and 1873. Other notable participants were Col. D.A. Robertson, Dr. Charles DeMontreville, Dr. R.O. Sweeney, Edward D. Neill, William H. Kelley, and William Wallace. None of the committee members could devote fulltime efforts to its objectives. The committee had a brief period of fieldwork at St. Paul's Indian Mounds Park in 1862 before the Civil War drained away manpower and state resources for the MHS. After the war, the committee's activity peaked in 1867 with a burst of fieldwork around Lake Minnetonka. Scattered fieldwork then took place in the Twin Cities region until 1873.

Nearly all of Hill's archaeological investigations occurred as a member of the MHS committee. He quickly became the committee secretary and eventually the chairman. As secretary his major duty consisted of handling the committee's correspondence. The available records indicate that Hill carried out an extensive correspondence with numerous informants. The committee devised a printed flyer or circular in 1867 asking for archaeological site information (reproduced by Arzigian and Stevenson 2003:10). Such a postal inquiry method for surveys was common practice before the instigation of institution-based archaeological research programs. In particular the circulars were sent to surveyors working for the U.S. government and for railroads. Hill mailed the circulars and copied the written responses received into two notebooks that became the first two volumes of his mound records. The responses typically divulged mound and mound group

Figure 1. Alfred J. Hill (Winchell 1911:viii).

locations. Some data was received about habitation sites.

The secretary's correspondence, or more properly copies of the responses to the circular, comprise the bulk of the first two notebooks in the Mound Records preserved in the NAS paperwork. These two notebooks also contain a few of the Hill surveys. Of particular interest to this paper are the seven mound groups surveyed by Hill that are copied into in the fourth Mound Records notebook. In summary, Hill's most significant contribution to the MHS committee was the preservation of its records.

Other Sources

The Alfred J. Hill Papers include his Geographic Notebooks that are numbered 1 to 37. Notebook No. 37 contains a copy of his 1860 letter describing three mound groups east of Sioux Falls in Dakota Territory (Hill n.d.b). Other than this entry, Hill's personal papers proved to be the least useful source since they contain only scattered archaeological information. The letters in his personal papers were scanned for mentions of mounds. The slight archaeological or ethnological data noticed, but not relevant to this paper, included the 1860s and 1870s correspondence with the missionary Stephen R. Riggs and a young Thomas S. Roberts (later director of the Museum of Natural History at the University of Minnesota.). Finally, it was discovered that the MHS committee correspondence is duplicated in the Alfred J. Hill Record Books with the Minnesota Academy of Science records held in the MHS Archives.

Hill's Fieldwork

Except for the 1860 report, Hill's mound surveys were done as part of the work accomplished by the MHS Committee on Archaeology. Hill (1860) wrote a letter to the MHS dated August 20, 1860, reporting three mound groups that he had recently observed near Sioux Falls, Dakota Territory. Copies of this letter exist in the Hill Geographic Notebooks Vol. 37 in the Alfred J. Hill papers (Hill n.d.b) and on legal-sized paper among the miscellaneous materials in the NAS records. However, this survey information was not included by Hill with the data in the next source.

The microfilmed NAS records contain Hill's four notebooks of his Mound Records (Hill n.d.c). Winchell (1911) cited these notebooks as the "Hill records." Much of Hill's first two notebooks represent hand copied letters written in reply to his MHS committee postal inquiries for archaeological information. Entry 1 in Mound Record No. 1 is a copy of his 1860 letter about three mound groups in South Dakota. There are a total of 106 entries in Mound Records No. 1. By the end of this notebook, Hill is abstracting archaeological site information from the published reports of explorers (e.g., Long, Schoolcraft, Nicollet, Featherstonehaugh) and geologists. The 64 entries in Mound Records No. 2 include five Hill surveys:

- Suburban Hills Mound Group (Entry 107),
- Dayton's Bluff Mound Group (Entry 108),
- Lake Minnetonka Mounds (Entry 109),
- Lake Calhoun Mounds (Entry 110), and
- Mound one mile north of Red Rock (Entry 111).

Mound Records 3 and 4 are largely site information gathered after 1873 and used for planning fieldwork on the NAS surveys. However, near the end of the fourth notebook Hill copied his own field notes for some of the surveys he personally made between 1862 and 1873 as Entries 279 to 285. (The repeated sites from the entries in Mound Record No. 2 were presented in a clearer manner in Mound Records No. 4.) Each was labeled as "Delayed Record" to indicate the time gap between the fieldwork and their presence in the fourth notebook of the mound records. The majority of these sites are in Hennepin and Ramsey counties, although Anoka County and Pierce County, Wisconsin are also represented. The mound surveys made by Hill (n.d.c) as reported in Mound Records No. 4 include the following sites:

- Suburban Hills Mound Group (Entry 279),
- Dayton's Bluff Mound Group (Entry 280),
- Harrington Mound near Wayzata (Entry 281),
- Centerville Mound Group (Entry 282),
- Phelps Island Mound Group at Lake Minnetonka (Entry 283),
- Cook's Bay Mound Group at Lake Minnetonka (Entry 284), and
- Prescott Mound Group (Entry 285).

The entries in Mound Records Nos. 1, 2, and 4 represent the extent of fieldwork claimed by Hill. In particular the 1873 entry for Prescott, Wisconsin ends with a note stating that Hill would not personally make mound surveys again. However, one additional survey appears in his 1894 article (Hill 1894).

The following presentation of the Hill mound surveys is organized by date of the investigation or documentation. The site descriptions are brief in length since nearly all of this information has been superseded by subsequent surveys. In addition some of the Minnesota site names have been changed since Hill's surveys took place. For this reason the site numbers have been included with the descriptions.

Mounds near Sioux Falls, South Dakota

As a result of a trip to Sioux Falls, Dakota Territory in 1860, Hill made brief notes on three mound groups in the vicinity. They were

- a mound group (n=6) in T101N, R49W, Sections 19 and 30,
- the Eminiga Mound Group (n=26) in T101N, R48W, and

- another mound group located to the north-northwest of the Eminiga Mound Group.

In a letter to the Secretary of the MHS dated August 31, 1860, Hill wrote:

> With a view to increasing the collection of facts concerning the aboriginal tribes of the north-west, or their supposed predecessors the "Mound Builders," I here send you a description of certain artificial earthworks – two groups of circular tumuli – in the valley of the Big Sioux River, which I saw and examined a week or two ago whilst on a flying visit to Dakota Territory.
>
> Being unprovided with instruments, with the exception of a small pocket compass the case of which was warped so that the degrees of the circle by no means corresponded with each other, the results of my examination are merely approximate, but they will serve to definitely describe these works, which has not yet been done, so far as I am aware.
>
> The first group is situated in the bend which gives the river its name, which now has returned to its natural solitude. Here is built the extensive group of mounds referred to, partly on the townsite the north line of which passes through the largest one (No. 17).
>
> The main group extends for about a quarter of a mile north and south and consists of twenty six mounds varying in height from two to twelve feet. To the north at some distance are two isolated ones, of but little height. To the N.N.W., about a furlong off, commences a series of smaller mounds, overlooking the Sioux River, which I was unable to examine and ascertain the number of, by reason of the approach of sunset, having to return to the [Sioux] Falls before dark. Map No. 3 shows the relative position of the mounds of this group according to the best examination my time and means would allow.
>
> There are no trees growing either on or near these mounds except in the river bottoms. Map No. 1 herewith gives the general position of the two groups; possibly there are others on the river bluffs between these, which would be a very desirable thing to ascertain by some future examination of the country. [Hill 1860:1-2]

Hill included sketch maps of the first two mound groups but apparently did not visit, or at least did not count and map, mounds in the third site (Hill 1894, n.d.a: Geographic Notebooks Vol. 37, n.d.c: Mound Records 1, Entry 1). These sites were later visited by Lewis who made maps for the NAS (per a handwritten note later added by A.J.Hill to the Mound Records.).

Suburban Hills Mound Group (21RA10)

Before the Civil War halted work, the MHS Committee began work on the mounds that occurred on Dayton's Bluff overlooking the Mississippi River Valley in the city of St. Paul in Ramsey County. This work followed 1850s investigations made by Edward Neill and others. The mounds from the lower and upper ends of the bluff were considered two distinct sites. Today the extant mounds on Dayton's Bluff are in Indian Mounds Park and are designated as sites 21RA5 and 21RA10. The following description is directed only at noting the fieldwork that Hill accomplished in Indian Mounds Park. Lewis (1896a, 1896b) reported the excavations made by Hill and associates. A complete history of the archaeological investigations made at these sites is available elsewhere (Anfinson 1982; Arzigian and Stevenson 2003).

The MHS committee initially worked at the Suburban Hills Mound Group. Today this site is called the Lower Dayton's Bluff Mound Group or Indian Mounds Park (21RA10). This investigation was headed by William Wallace and Alfred Hill on May 7, 1862. Members of the committee returned in June 1866 for excavations in Mounds 7, 8, and 9. The committee report was signed by William H. Kelley. Lewis prepared a report on these excavations (Anfinson 1982; Arzigian and Stevenson 2003; Hill 1894:313, n.d.c: Mound Records No. 4, Entry 279; Lewis 1896a:207, 1896b:314; Winchell 1911:261-263).

Dayton's Bluff Mound Group (21RA5)

The MHS committee initially worked the Dayton's Bluff Mound Group on May 8, 1862, with Wallace and Hill. Today this site is known as the Upper Dayton's Bluff Mound Group (21RA5). A note in the

Mound Records indicates that this mound survey was never finished at that time.

> It was the intention of Mr. Wallace and myself to complete the survey of this group of earthworks (and of the one previously described) by the making of very careful measurements for the outline and height of each mound, but other things took precedence and we enlisted in the Union army three months later. The work thus remained incomplete till Mr. Lewis finished it in 1881. [Hill n.d.c: Mound Records No. 4, Entry 280; a handwritten note later added by Hill stated that Wallace died in the spring of 1883.]

As noted, the 21RA5 survey was completed by Lewis in 1881 (Anfinson 1982; Arzigian and Stevenson 2003; Hill 1894:313, n.d.c: Mound Records No. 4, Entry 280; Lewis 1896a, 1896b; Winchell 1911:264-266).

Harrington Mound near Wayzata (21HE29)

This site is one of several isolated mounds reported from the north side of Lake Minnetonka in Hennepin County. It was a round mound. The Harrington Mound was examined September 18, 1867, by Dr. DeMontreville of the MHS Archaeological Committee (Winchell 1911:229). In *Aborigines of Minnesota*, Winchell used the DeMontreville site description. According to the Mound Records (No. 4, Entry 281), Hill visited the Harrington Mound on June 22, 1869: "Having a few leisure hours at Wayzata I visited this mound with a view to measuring it" (Hill 1894, n.d.c: Mound Records No. 4, Entry 281). Winchell did not mention Hill with regard to the Harrington Mound.

Lake Calhoun Mounds (21HE-z)

The Lake Calhoun Mounds (21HE-z) in Hennepin County represent three round mounds recorded September 30, 1867. At that time this lake was five miles from Minneapolis. Hill was following an anonymous report of mounds at this location published in the *Pioneer Press* (Hill n.d.c: Mound Records No. 2, Entry 110). This site was never formally entered in the Minnesota site file. Winchell (1911:223) indicated that it was surveyed by Hill (1894). The site location is believed to be inside the limits of Lakewood Cemetery. There is no evidence that the Lake Calhoun Mounds were ever examined by Lewis and presumably they had been destroyed by the time of the NAS surveys.

Halpin Mound Group at Starvation Point (21HE3)

The Halpin Mound Group (21HE3) was found at Starvation Point on Lake Minnetonka in Hennepin County (Hill 1894). Site 21HE3 consisted of 20 mounds. They were 13 circular and 7 elongated mounds. Hill did not include this site in his list of surveys. However, it was attributed to Hill by Winchell (1911:229). Apparently the investigation consisted of a major excavation effort in Mounds 2, 5, and 7 by the MHS committee on September 30, 1867. Winchell (1911:232) illustrated human skeletal material from the dig. The published site description in *Aborigines of Minnesota* is the 1868 description made by Dr. R.O. Sweeney for the MHS Archaeological Committee (Winchell 1911:229-233). The Halpin Mound Group was surveyed in 1883 by Lewis. In fact Winchell (1911:230) used the Lewis map and mound numbering system in his book.

Wayzata Mound Group (21HE28)

The Wayzata Mound Group (21HE28) is another Hennepin County mound group not included in the Hill list of surveys. It consisted of two round and one elongated mounds. One of the round mounds was situated in the public square. This mound was reported to have yielded human bones. The September 30, 1867 site examination was by Hill for the MHS Archaeological Committee. Two of the mounds were excavated by Dr. DeMontreville (Hill 1894, n.d.c: Mound Records No. 2, Entry 109; Winchell 1911:233). Site 21HE28 was surveyed by Lewis in 1883, but this fact is not noted in *Aborigines of Minnesota* (Winchell 1911:233).

Mound One Mile North of Red Rock (21RA3)

Surprisingly this Ramsey County mound is only covered in Mound Records No. 2 despite its appearance in his one published article on mounds (Hill 1894). This isolated mound was positioned one mile north of Red Rock on the east side of the Mississippi River. Wallace assisted by determining the elevation of the 21RA3 mound in relation to the known datum on the nearby railroad line. It was surveyed April 30, 1868, by Hill and on April 16, 1887, by Lewis (Hill 1894:315, n.d.c: Mound Records No. 2, Entry 111; Winchell 1911:267).

Centerville Mound Group (21AN2)

The Centerville Mound Group in Anoka County consisted of seven conical mounds. As listed in the Mound Records (No. 4, Entry 282) the largest mound was 13 feet tall. Hill made his site survey on July 5, 1869.

> Having an hour or two to spare at this place, I devoted the time to making such rough survey as a pocket compass and tape line enabled me to make, of some mounds that had been described to me as situated near the lake there. [Hill n.d.c: Mound Records No. 4, Entry 282]

This mound group was resurveyed by Lewis, who reported more mounds and a height of 12 feet for the largest one. Winchell referred to this site as the Centerville Lake Mounds (Hill 1894:318; Winchell 1911:280).

Phelps Island Mound Group at Lake Minnetonka (21HE36)

This Hennepin County mound group was surveyed by Hill on October 6, 1872. Site 21HE36 had 10 conical mounds and another two mounds positioned a quarter of a mile to the west. All of the mounds were positioned adjacent to the lake shore. This landform was called Nobles Island when Hill made his survey (Hill n.d.c: Mound Records No. 4, Entry 283). When Lewis surveyed the site in 1883 he found 11 mounds in the main group (Hill 1894:316; Winchell 1911:241-242).

Cook's Bay Mound Group at Lake Minnetonka (21HE65)

Hill mapped 13 conical mounds at this site on October 7, 1872 (Mound Records No. 4, Entry 284). The tallest mound was five feet. This site name and number of mounds is not approximated by any mound groups in Winchell's (1911) section of the Hennepin County discussion "Mounds of Lake Minnetonka." He did report a "Cook's Group" consisting of four circular mounds, according to Lewis' May 12, 1883 investigation (Winchell 1911:224). The Cook's Bay Mound Group of Hill is reported by Winchell as the "First Bartlett Group." It had 18 mounds when mapped by Lewis on May 5, 1883. They were 15 circular, 2 elongated, and 1 elongated irregular mounds. Lewis found the additional mounds in the area Hill (1894) delineated as "dense and tangled thickets" at the west end of the site. Hill's survey at this site was not mentioned in *Aborigines of Minnesota* (Winchell 1911:224).

Prescott Mound Group

Hill's next survey was his only foray into Wisconsin. At Prescott in Pierce County, he mapped a total of 29 conical mounds that were strung out along the bluff edge at the confluence of the St. Croix and Mississippi rivers. The tallest was Mound 14 at 5 feet high (Hill 1894). The mounds began on the north side of the intersection of Elm and Kinnikinnic streets and extended past Sycamore Street to the south into the unplatted countryside south of Prescott. The number of mounds and length of the site caused Hill to deviate from his typical tape-and-compass method of mapping.

> I accordingly commenced with tape line and pocket compass but soon found that time would not allow of that method of examination, so I went along the bluffs to the end of the series, and merely paced distance and estimated dimensions in the majority of cases. [Hill n.d.c: Mound Records No. 4, Entry 285]

There was a gap in the Prescott Mound Group between South and Sycamore Streets. Presumably mounds had once existed on this block at the bluff edge. Hill noted the presence of, but did not precisely survey, a series of low and irregular mounds and embankments paralleling the bluff line south of Sycamore Street. These embankments resembled elongated or linear mounds and were placed ca. 150 feet east of the conical mounds at the bluff edge. Hill mapped several "rifle pits" at the south end of the site overlooking the Mississippi River. This survey took place on May 13, 1873 and included an abrupt comment at the end of the site description (Mound Records No. 4, Entry 285). The note made by Hill after the Prescott survey stated:

Special Remark

This was the last attempt I made to survey or personally note any mounds. The job was too large for much impression to be made by getting only a group at long intervals, as the leisure of an employee only could permit. After this, I told my friends that I was only keeping the place warm till a real archaeologist should turn up.

Alfred J. Hill [Hill n.d.c: Mound Records No. 4, Entry 285]

Pine City (21PN-q)

Despite having made the above statement, Hill made one more survey. In August 1873 he discovered that a large mound was being destroyed by grading at Pine City in Pine County. From the remaining portion, Hill estimated the mound dimensions to have originally been 8 feet high and 70 feet in diameter. He received reports that it had contained human bones. The mound location was south of Third Avenue between Ninth and Tenth Streets, and Hill noted that more mounds existed in Pine City but were never formally surveyed. This represents another case where Hill was the only observer to record a mound group.

Summary and Conclusions

The mound surveys made by Hill have two particularly significant aspects. First, the site descriptions and maps include one or two sites in the Twin Cities region that were never seen by Lewis during the subsequent NAS investigations. Their absence marks the advance of development in the 10 to 15 years since Hill conducted fieldwork. Another site was renamed by Winchell when published in *Aborigines of Minnesota*. Winchell further missed Hill's involvement with this site. He did not miss the entries containing Hill's surveys in Mound Records Nos. 2 and 4 for the Minnesota sites. Each page of the Minnesota surveys has a pencil line drawn through it from the upper right to the lower left. This is the method that Winchell used to mark NAS materials included in *Aborigines of Minnesota*. However, in a few cases he must not have carefully compared the Hill surveys to the later ones.

Second, the 1873 survey at Pine City marked the end of Hill's active participation in fieldwork. After determining he no longer wished to personally survey mounds, Hill turned his attention to historical research, ethnohistory, and planning an archaeological survey of Minnesota that eventually expanded into the NAS and the SAS. Thus Hill's mound surveys, while scant in number, functioned as a critical prelude to the NAS. With the MHS Committee on Archaeology, Hill established procedures for gathering archaeological site information using a postal inquiry method. He continued similar procedures during the NAS by using this information to devise a plan of campaign for survey locations for each field season in advance of the actual investigations (see the entries in Mound Records Nos. 3 and 4.). As a result of his personal surveys and work with the MHS committee, Hill (n.d.a) knew what he wanted to accomplish with the NAS and how to go about achieving those objectives. The only exception is the absence of a publication covering the entire survey. Lewis' numerous published articles formed a beginning toward that goal, which was prevented by the unexpected death of Hill in 1895.

Acknowledgments. I thank Kent Bakken for his interest in this topic. Part of the Lewis background information has previously appeared in *The Minnesota Archaeologist*, *The Wisconsin Archeologist*, and *Illinois Archaeology*.

References Cited

Anfinson, Scott F.
  1982 *1981 Annual Report: Minnesota Municipal and County Highway Archaeological Reconnaissance Study*. Archaeology Department, Minnesota Historical Society. Copy on file, State Historic Preservation Office, Minnesota Historical Society, St. Paul.

Anonymous
  1895 Alfred J. Hill: Death of a Noted Archaeologist and Engineer [obituary]. *St. Paul Pioneer Press*. June 16, p. 7.

1905 Northwestern Archaeological Survey: State Historical Society will get Possession of the Result of the Work of Mr. Hill and Prof. Lewis. *St. Paul Pioneer Press.* August 6, Section 2, p.2.

Arzigian, Constance M. and Katherine P. Stevenson

2003 *Minnesota's Indian Mounds and Burial Sites: A Synthesis of Prehistoric and Early Historic Archaeological Data.* Publication No. 1. The Minnesota Office of the State Archaeologist, St. Paul.

Dobbs, Clark A.

1991 *The Northwestern Archaeological Survey: An Appreciation and Guide to the Field Notebooks.* Reports of Investigation No. 135. Institute for Minnesota Archaeology, Minneapolis.

Finney, Fred A.

2000 Theodore H. Lewis and the Northwestern Archaeological Survey's 1891 Fieldwork in the American Bottom. *Illinois Archaeology* 12(1-2):244-276.

2001 An Introduction to the Northwestern Archaeological Survey by Theodore H. Lewis. *The Minnesota Archaeologist* 60:13-29.

2004 Reconstructing the 1878-1895 "Southern Archaeological Survey" of Theodore H. Lewis. Paper presented at the joint Meeting of the Southeastern Archaeological Conference and the Midwest Archaeological Conference, St. Louis. Upper Midwest Archaeology, St. Joseph, Illinois.

2005a Theodore H. Lewis (1856-1930). *The Minnesota Archaeologist* 64.

2005b Introduction. *Mounds, Humbugs, and De Soto: The Archaeological Legacy of Theodore H. Lewis from North Dakota to Florida.* Upper Midwest Archaeology, St. Joseph, Illinois.

Hill, Alfred J.

1860 Letter dated August 31, 1860, to the Secretary of the Minnesota Historical Society. Unpublished manuscript in the Mound Records, Northwestern Archaeological Survey, Pre-1880, 1880-1895, Archives, Minnesota Historical Society, St. Paul.

1894 Indian Mounds in Dakota, Minnesota and Wisconsin. *Minnesota Historical Society Collections* 6:311-319.

1899 *History of Company E, of the Sixth Minnesota Regiment of Volunteer Infantry.* Published by T.H. Lewis. Pioneer Press, St. Paul.

n.d.a Proposal for a Survey of the Ancient Earthworks of Minnesota. Unpublished manuscript in the Mound Records, Northwestern Archaeological Survey, Pre-1880, 1880-1895, Archives, Minnesota Historical Society, St. Paul.

n.d.b Alfred James Hill Papers (7 boxes). Manuscript on file, Minnesota Historical Society, St. Paul.

n.d.c Northwestern Archaeological Survey. Related Volumes, pre-1880, 1880-1895. Mound Records Nos. 1-4. Archives, Minnesota Historical Society, St. Paul.

Keyes, Charles R.

1928 The Hill-Lewis Archaeological Survey. *Minnesota History* 9:96-108.

1930 A Unique Survey. *The Palimpsest* 11(5):214-226.

1977 The Hill-Lewis Archaeological Survey. *The Minnesota Archaeologist* 36(4):146-155. Reprinted. Originally published 1928 in *Minnesota History*.

Lewis, Theodore H.

1896a Pre-Historic Remains at St. Paul, Minnesota. *The American Antiquarian* 18(4):207-210.

1896b Mounds and Stone Cists at St. Paul, Minnesota. *The American Antiquarian* 18(6):314-320.

1898 *The Northwestern Archaeological Survey.* Pioneer Press, St. Paul.

n.d. Unpublished Field Notes Notebook Numbers 1-41. Manuscript on file, Minnesota Historical Society, St. Paul.

MHS (Minnesota Historical Society)

n.d. Membership Records before 1900. Archives, Minnesota Historical Society, St. Paul.

Winchell, Newton H.

1911 *The Aborigines of Minnesota: A Report Based on the Collections of Jacob V. Brower, and on the Field Surveys and Notes of Alfred J. Hill and Theodore H. Lewis.* Minnesota Historical Society, St. Paul.

Zooarchaeology of the Third River Bridge Site (21IC46), a Late Woodland Fishing Camp in Itasca County, Minnesota

David Mather
Mather Heritage Group, LLC
45881 US Highway 169, Onamia, MN 56359

Chippewa National Forest archaeologists conducted excavations at the Third River Bridge site in 1983, recovering a rich assemblage of fish and other animal bone. Suckers of the genus Catostomus *are the dominant fish represented. It appears that most are the white sucker,* Catostomus commersoni. *Pits and other features containing massive quantities of fish bone suggest that sucker spawning runs were the reason for repeated Late Woodland occupations here, spanning more than 800 years. The suckers and other spring-spawning fish are clear seasonal indicators. The composition and distribution of faunal materials within the site features are discussed, as are methodological issues for dealing with large quantities of fish bone. In this case, the ceratohyal bone was the basis for determination of the* Catostomus *MNI.*

Introduction

Minnesota's lakes and rivers are well known for their abundance of fish, but this resource is often overlooked in the archaeological record. Fish bones are fragile, so they are often not preserved or recovered. When they are found, they are often not analyzed in detail. Such is not the case at the Third River Bridge site (21IC46), however. It is clear from the site's structure, artifacts and location that this is a place that's all about fish. More specifically, it is all about suckers.

The archaeology of the Third River Bridge site includes multiple Woodland-tradition components represented by Blackduck and Sandy Lake ceramics, ranging from approximately 600 to 1400 A.D. (Hohman-Caine and Goltz 1998). The site is located on both banks of the Third River, a short distance north of Lake Winnibigoshish (Fig. 1). This setting is clearly advantageous for harvest of water resources. Moreover, the faunal assemblage demonstrates the site's use, at least in part, as a fish processing area (Table 1). The predominant fish taxon represented, *Catostomus* sp. (probably the white sucker, *Catostomus commersoni*), is proposed as a seasonal indicator due to its dramatic spawning migrations in the early spring (e.g., Eddy and Underhill 1974; Becker 1983; Middlemis 1984; Phillips, Schmid and Underhill 1982).

The Late Woodland date of the site suggests the existence of climatic conditions generally similar to

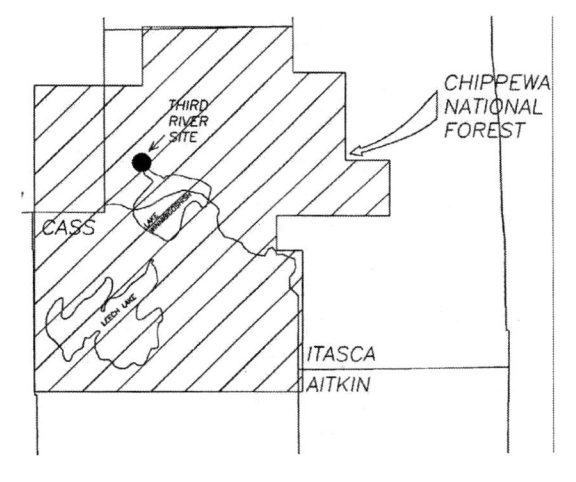

Figure 1. Location of the Third River Bridge site (21IC46) within Chippewa National Forest (from Hohman-Caine and Goltz 1998).

the present day. The site is located in the northern coniferous forest, where it is expected that white-tailed deer, moose, bear, wolves, elk and other large terrestrial mammals would be significant faunal resources. The site is also within the former range of caribou in Minnesota (Tester 1995; Hazard 1982). Notable changes to the local environment since Euroamerican settlement include lumbering and establishment of the reservoir level of Lake Winnibigoshish.

This article is adapted from a zooarchaeological report (Mather 1998) prepared as part of the Third River Bridge site analysis. The reader is referred to

Hohman-Caine and Goltz (1998) for discussion of the site as a whole.

Methods

The Third River Bridge site faunal assemblage was sorted by taxonomic class, and then to family, genus and species through use of the author's osteological comparative collection and that of the Archaeology Department of the Minnesota Historical Society. Standard osteological texts were also utilized (Gilbert 1993; Gilbert, Martin and Savage 1996; Olsen 1968; Brown and Gustafson 1979; Rojo 1991). References particularly useful in identification of the sucker remains include Eastman (1977), Gregory (1933), Harrington (1955), Manzano and Dickinson (1991), Nelson (1948, 1949) and Weisel (1960). The taxonomic nomenclature used here follows Hazard (1982) for the mammals and Eddy and Underhill (1974) for the fishes.

The faunal data was recorded as lot numbers specific to particular identifications within each provenience. These were numbered sequentially starting with the suffix "00." For example, the first identification within provenience 11-3 is identified by number 11-300, the second by 11-301, the third by 11-302, etc. The quantity of bone fragments within each lot number is variable. A lot number may designate a single identified element, or thousands of unidentified fish bone fragments. This recording system was selected to facilitate future study of the Third River faunal assemblage, as additional lot numbers can be added for each provenience where the present analysis leaves off. Faunal data recorded for each lot number include Quantity, Feature, Class, Identification, Element, Side, Representation and Taphonomy. The full faunal catalog is curated with the collection at the Chippewa National Forest headquarters in Cass Lake.

Research Context

As a faunal assemblage dominated by fish and within a secure cultural context, the Third River Bridge site is a welcome addition to the regional zooarchaeological inventory. Comprehensive faunal studies in Minnesota are relatively rare, in some cases due to poor bone preservation in acidic soils. Perhaps equal blame falls to regional archaeologists, who have either focused on large-mammal remains or left faunal assemblages unanalyzed in favor of other artifact classes. Fish and other faunal remains can be well preserved in Minnesota archaeological sites, and several relevant studies are summarized here to provide some context for the present analysis.

Morey, Falk and Semken's (1996) study of the McKinstry site (21KC2) Phase III faunal assemblage is among the premier zooarchaeological analyses conducted to date in Minnesota. The McKinstry assemblage is dominated by fish when quantified by NISP, and mammals when quantified by weight. Sturgeon are the prevalent fish taxon, followed by suckers, northern pike/muskellunge, walleye/sauger, and mooneye/goldeye. Beaver is the prevalent mammalian species, followed by moose and other cervids. Other mammals, turtles and birds are present in small amounts. Comparison of these taxa between Initial Woodland (Laurel) and Terminal Woodland (primarily Blackduck) components demonstrates a shift from intensive sturgeon fishing to a greater proportional diversity of resources, notably beaver and sucker. The suckers from the McKinstry assemblage are mainly of the genus *Moxostoma*, with specific identifications of silver, shorthead and greater redhorse suckers. Quillback (*Carpiodes cyprinus*) and *Catostomus* sp. (white/longnose sucker) are present in trace amounts (Morey, Falk and Semken 1996).

Also in the Rainy River region, large numbers of fish remains in Blackduck contexts are reported at the Hannaford site (21KC25) by Rapp et al. (1995). Fish account for 92.9 percent of the Phase III assemblage. Mammal remains, including moose, elk, bear, beaver and numerous small mammals comprise only 6.6 percent of the assemblage. Reptiles and birds are present in trace amounts (less than 1% combined). Suckers and sturgeon are the dominant fish remains in the assemblage, although northern pike/muskellunge, walleye, perch, bullhead, channel catfish, rock bass and large/smallmouth bass are also present. The suckers are primarily of the genus *Moxostoma* (redhorse suckers), with specific identifications of northern redhorse, golden redhorse, greater redhorse, and silver redhorse. "Common sucker," a name suggesting the white sucker but identified only to the genus *Catostomus*, is present in trace amounts. Various subareas of the Hannaford site are identified as fish harvesting and potentially processing areas. However, this conclusion is based on intrasite lithic distributions rather than zooarchaeological evidence. None of the faunal remains are identified by element in the report or appendices, making independent assessment of body part representation per species impossible.

In the Mille Lacs area, Whelan (1990) has analyzed the Late Woodland faunal assemblages from the Vineland Bay (21ML7), Cooper (21ML9) and Wilford (21ML12) sites, and compared the results with the Historic Dakota village at Little Rapids (21SC27). Deer are the primary upland animal resource at the three Mille Lacs sites, with elk and bison also important. Beaver and muskrat are prevalent with other small mammals also present. A diverse fish assemblage is dominated by bullheads and walleye/sauger. In combination, the identified taxa suggest year-round occupation of the Mille Lacs sites, apparently facilitated by surplus stores of wild rice. A shift to a seasonal occupation (summer) is seen at Little Rapids. Deer and elk are still the dominant species, but muskrat has the greatest NISP count of the assemblage. The diverse fish assemblage is led by the freshwater drum (Whelan 1990, 1987).

The Horseshoe Bay site (21CA201) on Leech Lake provides a valuable Historic era comparison for the Third River Bridge assemblage. Fish remains from late Fur Trade building features include large quantities of walleye/sauger, pike/muskellunge and multiple species of suckers, including buffalo fish, redhorse, quillback and white suckers. Shane (1996) discusses the Horseshoe Bay faunal assemblage relative to the environmental impacts of the late nineteenth and early twentieth centuries, and local extirpation of the redhorse sucker species (genus *Moxostoma*).

The investigations cited above are the most comprehensive extant faunal studies incorporating fish remains. Fish remains at other sites have been studied with varied degrees of success, particularly in the prairie-forest ecotone, where the importance of seasonal fishing has been recognized but not quantified. Michlovic (1979), for example, notes the primary focus of the Dead River site (21OT51) as a fishing camp, but the fish remains themselves have not been studied. Thus, while relatively few studies provide context for the present effort, the Third River Bridge site can be seen to contribute to a growing body of regional data.

Table 1. Percentage of Total Faunal Assemblage by Class, 21IC46

Class	Count	Percentage
Fish	73,986	95.86%
Mammal	246	0.31%
Bird	28	0.04%
Reptile	19	0.02%
Other	11	0.01%
Unidentified	2,916	3.70%

The Third River Bridge Faunal Assemblage

The Third River Bridge site faunal assemblage is clearly dominated by fish, and the most prevalent are suckers (Tables 1-2). Of secondary importance are walleye/sauger, followed by trace amounts of northern pike/muskellunge and bullheads. Other identified taxa include beaver, muskrat, porcupine, deer, elk, turtles and marsh ducks. The suckers may be interpreted as the focus of resource procurement at this site. The other fish species are viewed as opportunistic catches during exploitation of the sucker spawning runs by Late Woodland peoples spanning the use of Blackduck and Sandy Lake ceramics. The faunal assemblage is discussed first in its entirety, inclusive of species present and taxonomic abundance, followed by presentation of faunal data from identified cultural features.

Species Present and Taxonomic Abundance

Table 2 presents the Number of Identified Specimens (NISP) and Minimum Number of Individuals (MNI) for each taxon. NISP and MNI determinations are standard features of osteological investigations despite continuing general debate regarding their individual utility. The NISP can overemphasize the representation of certain animals by not taking taphonomic concerns of differential fragmentation into account. Calculations of MNI tend to result in underestimation of abundance due in part to differential preservation between faunal classes and skeletal elements. When used in tandem, however, these figures do provide a range of potential abun-

Table 2. Total Site Assemblage, NISP and MNI by Taxon, 21IC46

TAXON	NISP	MNI
Unidentified:	2,916	--
Mollusca and Gastropoda:		
shell fragments, unidentified	6	--
Class Osteichthyes (total=73,986):		
fish, undifferentiated	72,490	--
Family Catostomidae:		
sucker, undifferentiated	777	--
Catostomus sp. (white/longnose sucker)	488	208
Catostomus cf. *commersoni* (white sucker?)	15	4
Family Percidae:		
Stizostedion sp. (walleye/sauger)	176	22
cf. *Stizostedion* sp. (walleye/sauger?)	16	--
Perca flavescens (yellow perch)	1	1
Family Esocidae:		
Esox sp. (northern pike/muskellunge)	16	3
Family Ictaluridae:		
Ictalurus cf. *melas* (black bullhead?)	3	2
Ictalurus sp. (bullhead/catfish)	3	--
cf. *Ictalurus* sp. (bullhead/catfish?)	1	--
Class Amphibia (total=5):		
amphibian, undifferentiated	5	--
Class Reptilia (total=19):		
Order Testudinia:		
turtle, undifferentiated	19	--
Class Aves (total=28):		
bird, undifferentiated	22	--
Family Anatinae:		
marsh ducks, undifferentiated	6	--

TAXON	NISP	MNI
Class Mammalia (total=246):		
mammal, undifferentiated	169	--
small mammal	4	--
medium mammal	2	--
large mammal	1	--
Order Lagomorpha:		
cf. *Sylvilagus floridanus* (eastern cottontail?)	1	1
Order Rodentia:		
rodent, undifferentiated	7	--
Castor canadensis (beaver)	19	1
cf. *Castor canadensis* (beaver?)	11	--
Castor/Erethizon (beaver or porcupine)	7	--
Erethizon dorsatum (porcupine)	1	1
Ondatra zibethicus (muskrat)	10	1
Order Carnivora:		
Canis sp.	1	1
Order Artiodactyla:		
artiodactyl, undifferentiated	3	--
Odocoileus sp. (deer)	8	1
cf. *Odocoileus* sp. (deer?)	1	--
Cervus elaphas (elk)	1	1
Total Fauna	*77,206*	*247*

dance for each taxon, with MNI the minimum and NISP the maximum (Lyman 1994; Hesse and Wapnish 1985; Davis 1987).

Combined numbers of identified fragments and entire bones are the basis for the NISP figures presented here, as opposed to the number of individual skeletal elements (cf. Lyman 1994:38). The MNI figures presented here are fairly crude, being simply the minimum number of animals necessary to account for the identified remains by taxon based on skeletal structure. Differences in size and age (e.g., unfused epiphyses) were incorporated when apparent, but were generally not an issue in an assemblage dominated by fish.

MNI calculations were generally only made for taxa that could be identified to the species level. A notable exception is the white/longnose sucker category (*Catostomus* sp.). As is described in greater detail below, the spawning migrations of suckers appear to be the primary reason for occupation of the Third River Bridge site. Simple establishment of the minimum number of fish (i.e. suckers) represented in the assemblage is therefore a matter of archaeological importance, whether or not the fish in question are of one or two closely related species. For similar reasons, MNI calculations were also made for the categories of *Stizostedion* sp. (walleye/sauger) and *Esox* sp. (northern pike/muskellunge).

Fishes

The Third River Bridge site faunal assemblage is dominated by fish, primarily suckers, followed by walleye/sauger and trace amounts of northern pike/muskellunge, bullhead/catfish and other fish. The analytical challenges presented by the massive quantities of sucker remains in particular require further discussion of taxonomic identification and methodological issues.

White Sucker (and Sucker Family): The suckers (Family Catostomidae) are widespread in North America, ranging from the arctic to Mexico, and the longnose sucker (*Catostomus catostomus*) is also known in Siberia, "but nowhere are there so many large suckers, of so many different genera and species, and in such abundance as in the waters of the Mississippi River system, the great breeding center of this common herd of the native American fish population" (Rostlund 1952:31). Suckers are distinguished by their "thick, fleshy lips" (Banister 1995:100) and pharyngeal bone with its single line of teeth (e.g., Eastman 1977). This latter feature is shared with the minnow family (Family Cyprinidae). These families together comprise the Order Cypriniformes.

Sixteen species of sucker have been documented as native to the Minnesota fauna, and it should be noted that comparative osteological specimens were not available for all the possible species. Available specimens covered five of the seven extant sucker genera. The two missing genera are each represented by only one species in the state. The historical distribution of the northern hog sucker (*Hypentelium nigricans*) includes the St. Croix River, the Minnesota River and its tributaries, and the Mississippi River below Hastings (Eddy and Underhill 1974:284-285). The spotted sucker (*Minytrema melanops*) is found in the St. Croix and lower Mississippi River (Phillips, Schmid and Underhill 1982:157-158). Based on their historical distributions, these species are not likely candidates for the Third River Bridge site.

Sucker genera for which comparative specimens were available include *Catostomus* (white and longnose suckers), *Ictiobus* (bigmouth and smallmouth buffalo fish), *Carpiodes* (river and highfin carpsuckers, and quillback), and *Moxostoma* (shorthead, silver, river, golden, greater, and black redhorse). A specimen of the blue sucker (*Cycleptus elongatus*) was also available. On the basis of modern species distributions, the most likely genera in the Third River Bridge site area are *Catostomus* and *Moxostoma*, as the other native genera (*Hypentelium, Minytrema, Ictiobes, Carpiodes*, and *Cycleptus*) are most prevalent in the southern part of the state (Phillips and Underhill 1971; Eddy and Underhill 1974; Phillips, Schmid and Underhil 1982).

While the full range of comparative specimens would have been welcome during the analysis, all identified Catostomidae remains compared favorably with the genus *Catostomus*. The more pressing issue in species identification therefore became differentiation between the white sucker, *Catostomus commersoni*, and the longnose sucker, *Catostomus catostomus*. Two white sucker specimens were available in the Minnesota Historical Society collections, and one longnose sucker specimen was available through loan from the Canadian Museum of Nature. While the skeletal features of these animals appeared very similar, differentiation of the species appeared feasible for the dentary, maxilla, hyomandibular, and to a lesser degree, the opercle. (For all of the fish taxa, including the Catostomidae, secure identifications to element are primarily from cranial bones. Tentative identifications of vertebrae have been made in some cases, but the vast majority were left at the class level of Osteichthyes.) Unfortunately, the most prevalent sucker bone in the Third River Bridge assemblage, the ceratohyal, appeared essentially identical. The ceratohyal was therefore identified only to the genus level, and the MNI count of 208 suckers could be from a combination of white and longnose suckers. The more diagnostic elements were identified as white sucker, but the species designation was left as tentative because only one longnose sucker specimen was available.

It should be noted that the NISP counts of Catostomidae, *Catostomus* sp. and *Catostomus* cf. *commersoni* are under-represented in this analysis. Due to the sheer volume of the fish bone, identifications of all bones of sucker proceeded until the ceratohyal was observed to be the most prevalent element (see Fig. 2). After that point, the fish bone was sorted to separate only the *Catostomus* ceratohyals to obtain the MNI count, and all material from other genera and/or species.

The white sucker has a broad geographical range, and is more tolerant of a variety of environmental conditions than many suckers. The longnose sucker is relatively rare in Minnesota, being found mainly in the northeastern border country. The potential presence of longnose suckers at the Third River Bridge site is therefore a matter of zoological and paleoecological importance, but is probably peripheral to the archaeological analysis. Obviously, the people harvesting the spring spawning runs

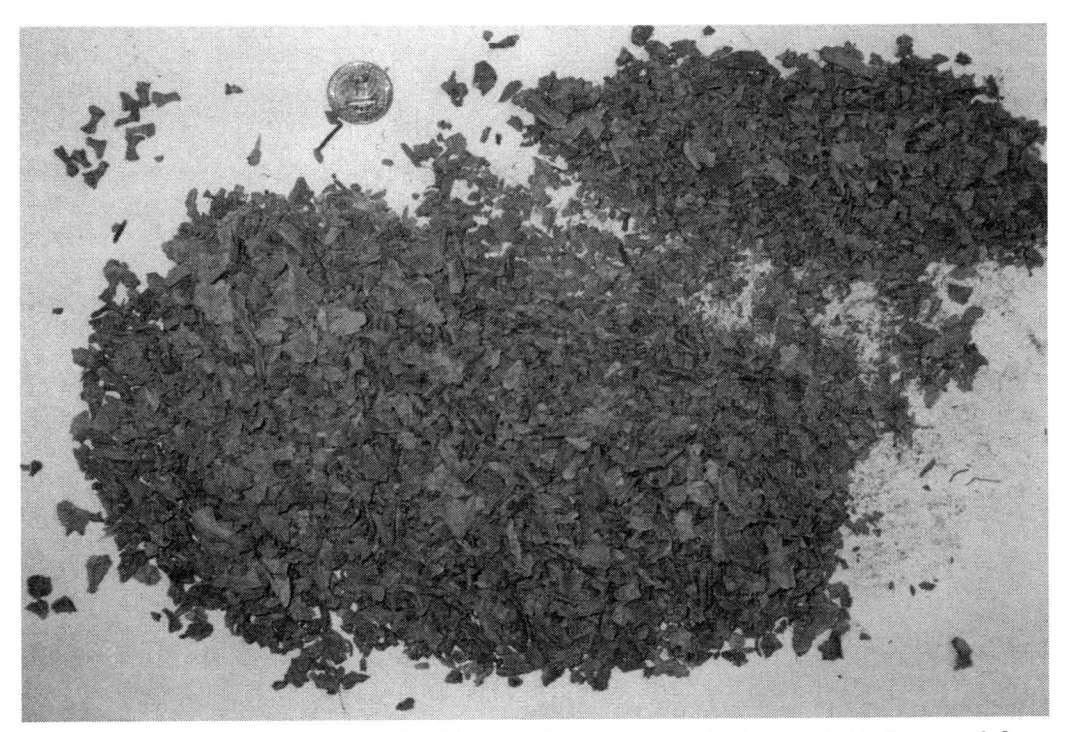

Figure 2. Fish bone (Feature F, 21IC46), with some *Catostomus* ceratohyals separated to the upper left.

at Third River Bridge were there to gather all the fish they could, regardless of taxonomy. White and longnose suckers have been documented within the same spawning runs in places where their distributions overlap (Middlemis 1984; Eddy and Underhill 1974). This issue is discussed at greater length below.

Walleye/Sauger: Walleye (*Stizostedion vitreum*) and sauger (*S. canadense*) are predatory fishes common to large lakes and rivers of north-central North America. They are the largest members of the Percidae (Perch Family). Walleye typically range in weight from 2 to 8 pounds, but can reach 15 pounds. Sauger can reach 3 pounds. On this basis, it is suggested that most of the Third River Bridge *Stizostedion* are walleyes, but the two species are virtually impossible to distinguish osteologically. Both species make mass spawning migrations in the spring up rivers and smaller tributaries. They are highly prized sportfish, because of their fine taste and fighting qualities (Eddy and Underhill 1974). Their frequent appearance on Minnesota archaeological sites suggests that they were similarly valued in prehistory. A minimum number within the Third River Bridge faunal assemblage is 22, based on equal counts of *Stizostedion* left dentary and angular fragments. The NISP count is 176 and 16 tentative identifications.

Northern Pike/Muskellunge: Northern pike (*Esox lucius*) and muskellunge (*E. masquinongy*) are both large, predatory fish, sometimes reaching weights of 50 pounds or more. They are nearly impossible to distinguish osteologically, possibly due in part to the occasional hybridization of the species. Northern pike are typically more widespread and abundant than the muskellunge, but historically both have been found throughout the state. Northerns and muskies spawn in the spring immediately after the ice melts, at the edges of lakes or after ascending small streams (Eddy and Underhill 1974). A total of 16 *Esox* specimens (NISP) were identified in the Third River Bridge assemblage. An MNI count of 3 is based on right dentary fragments.

Bullhead and Other Fishes: It is considered likely that all of the *Ictalurus* remains are of the various species of bullhead, rather than catfish. Three tentative identifications of black bullhead (*Ictalurus melas*) suggest a MNI of 2, based on two fragments of the left pectoral spine. Three other *Ictalurus* specimens could not be identified beyond the generic level. Bullheads spawn in the spring, making a nest in shallow water on a sand or mud bottom. They otherwise are known to travel in large schools, sometimes containing all three bullhead species. Black bullheads are the smallest of the genus, reaching a maximum length of 15 inches (Eddy and Underhill 1974). It is possible that the elements identified as *Ictalurus* sp. could be from an immature channel catfish (*Ictalurus punctatus*), or any of the three bullhead species.

The only other fish species in the Third River Bridge assemblage is one specimen of the yellow perch (*Perca flavenscens*). This element accounts for a NISP and MNI count of 1. Perch can reach 15 inches in length and just over a pound in weight. They are predatory fish and can overwhelm a lake in numbers. Perch spawn in the spring, in shallow, open water (Eddy and Underhill 1974).

Mammals

Mammals account for less than one percent of the site assemblage by count, but several species of clear economic importance are present. Beaver are most prevalent, followed by muskrat, deer, elk and porcupine. Small rodents are present in small amounts. Isolated identifications were made of cottontail rabbit and *Canis* sp. (dog/wolf/coyote).

Beaver, Muskrat and Other Rodents: Small rodent remains are present in the Third River assemblage (n=7) but all appear to be of recent origin, and were not analyzed in greater detail. Larger rodents of probable economic importance include beaver (*Castor canadensis*) and muskrat (*Ondatra zibethicus*). The presence of these animals is not unexpected in Lake Winnibigoshish and the Third River, where they would have been readily accessible to the site inhabitants. The faunal remains of beaver and muskrat account for one animal of each (MNI). Beaver are represented by loose teeth, mandible, scapula, femur and metacarpal/metatarsal fragments. The NISP count for beaver is 19. Muskrats are represented by 10 elements (NISP). One scapula fragment was identified as porcupine (*Erethizon dorsatum*), for a MNI of one. Finally, seven rodent incisor fragments are classified as *Castor/Erethizon*, because of the similarity of the incisor in these animals. Beaver and muskrat are aquatic animals, while the porcupine is largely arboreal (Hazard 1982). All three species are valued for their fur or quills, and for food.

Deer and Elk: Because of their size, deer and elk are animals of major economic importance, but in this assemblage they are still peripheral to fish. Deer are represented by eight elements and one tentative identification, for minimum number of one animal. The Third River Bridge deer could be either white-tailed deer (*Odocoileus virginianus*) or mule deer (*O. hemonius*). These species are generally associated with the forest or prairie, respectively, but both were once common along the ecotone (Hazard 1982). They are generally not distinguishable osteologically.

The elk (*Cervus elaphas*) is osteologically similar to the bison (cf. Brown and Gustafson 1979), but in truth is a closer relative to deer. Elk were once common in Minnesota on the prairie and along the prairie-forest border, but have been absent except as managed herds since the early twentieth century (Hazard 1982). Elk are represented in the Third River Bridge assemblage by one second-phalanx fragment, for a NISP and MNI count of one.

Three bone fragments were not identified beyond the Artiodactyl category. Other artiodactyls that might be expected include moose, caribou, bison and, to a lesser extent, pronghorn (Shay 1985; Hazard 1982). These were not otherwise identified in the assemblage, however. It should be noted that comparative specimens of caribou and pronghorn were not available to the current investigation, but all Artiodactyl remains identifiable to element were consistent with the more expected taxa.

Birds and Reptiles

Birds and reptiles are minor components of the faunal assemblage, at less than one tenth of one percent each. The identified birds are all marsh, or dabbling, ducks (Family Anatinae), represented by six elements. This family includes mallards, teals, pintails, gadwalls and wood ducks, among others, many of which are common in the site area (e.g., Janssen 1987).

Reptiles are represented solely by 19 turtle carapace or plastron fragments. None were sufficiently intact to allow identification to genus or species, and were left at the Order level, Testudines. It is likely, however, that the softshell and snapping turtles can be ruled out on the basis of their distinctive carapace and plastron morphologies. The majority of

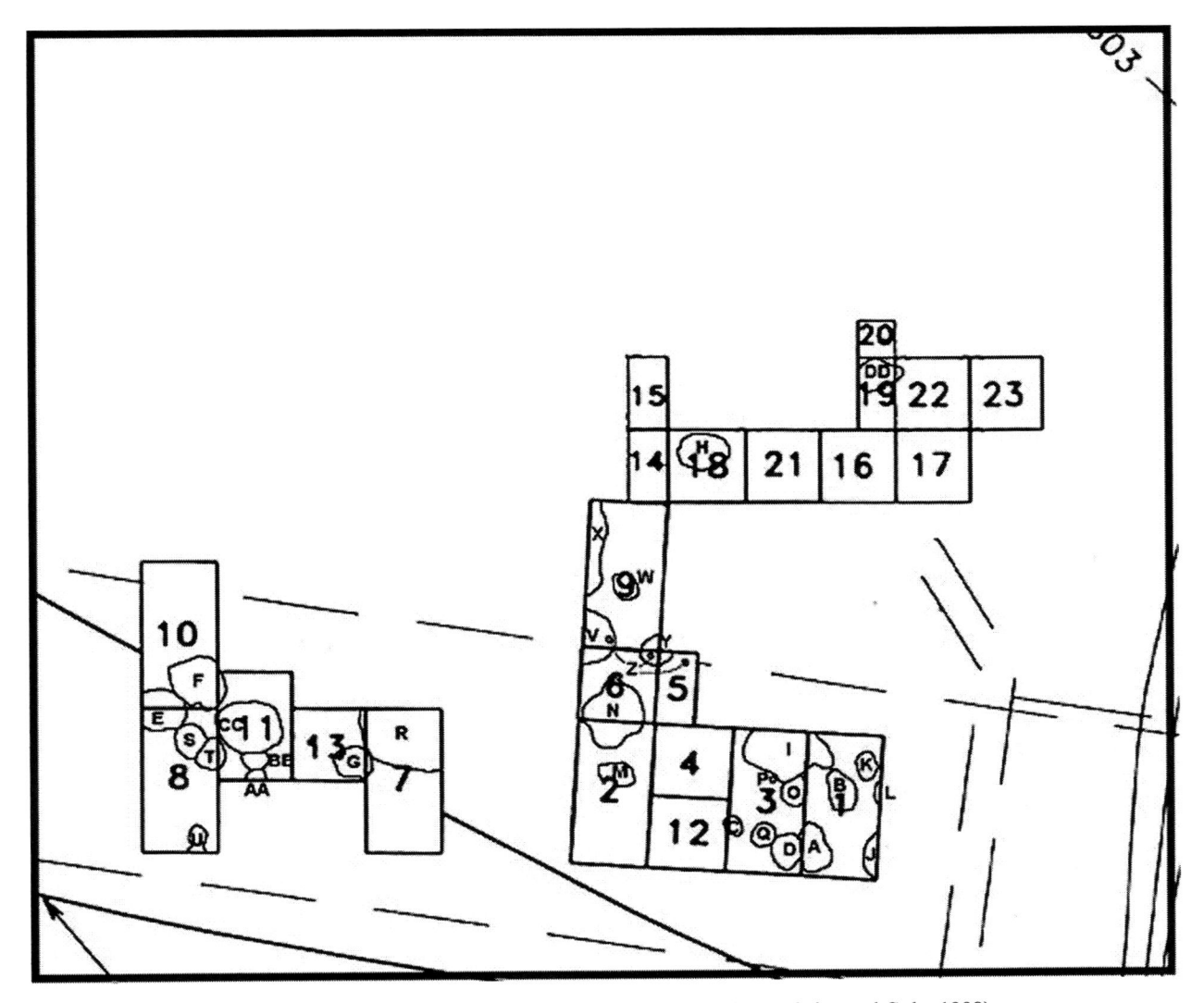

Figure 3. Excavation units and features, 21IC46 (from Hohman-Caine and Goltz 1998).

the Third River Bridge turtles are probably painted, map or Blanding's turtles, all of which could be expected in the vicinity of the site area (Oldfield and Moriarty 1994).

Intrasite Distribution of Faunal Remains

Excavation of the Third River Bridge site documented past disturbance to the upper levels of the site, but recovered distinct cultural features that could be clearly linked to varied Late Woodland cultural components. Eight of these features contained significant amounts of animal bone. These faunal remains are discussed here in the context of the individual features, and for the remainder of the site assemblage. The features have been assigned alphabetic designations (Features A through H). The location of these features within the Third River Bridge excavations is shown in Figure 3. Figures 4 and 5 illustrate the distribution of animal bone within the site. This clearly shows the provenience of the majority of the faunal assemblage as Feature F, the "fish pit" in Test Units 10 and 11. The faunal content is each feature is now described.

Feature A

Feature A is a pit feature in Unit 1. It is associated with Sandy Lake ceramics and dates to ca. A.D. 1420. (The reader is referred to the site report [Hohman-Caine and Goltz 1998] for full discussion of radiocarbon dates, features and related data.) The feature

Table 3. Feature A Faunal Identifications, 21IC46

Class	Identification	Element	Side	Quantity
bird	Anatinae	coracoid	left	1
bird	Anatinae	humerus	right	1
fish				3,508
fish		basioccipital	n/a	2
fish		scale		43
fish		vertebra		311
fish		vertebra	n/a	32
fish	Catostomidae			109
fish	Catostomidae	pharyngeal arch		39
fish	Catostomidae	pharyngeal arch	indet	4
fish	Catostomidae	weberian apparatus	n/a	11
fish	*Catostomus* sp.	ceratohyal	left	21
fish	*Catostomus* sp.	ceratohyal	right	23
fish	cf. *Stizostedion* sp.	opercle	right	2
fish	*Esox* sp.	dentary	left	1
fish	*Stizostedion* sp.	angular	left	3
fish	*Stizostedion* sp.	angular	right	2
fish	*Stizostedion* sp.	ceratohyal	indet	2
fish	*Stizostedion* sp.	dentary	left	6
fish	*Stizostedion* sp.	dentary	right	3
fish	*Stizostedion* sp.	premaxilla	left	4
fish	*Stizostedion* sp.	premaxilla	right	1
fish	*Stizostedion* sp.	preopercle	left	4
fish	*Stizostedion* sp.	preopercle	right	1
fish	*Stizostedion* sp.	quadrate	left	5
fish	*Stizostedion* sp.	quadrate	right	5
mammal				6

Table 4. Feature A Assemblage, NISP and MNI by Taxon, 21IC46

TAXON	NISP	MNI
Fish:	3,896	--
Catostomidae (Sucker Family)	163	--
Catostomus sp. (white/longnose sucker)	44	23
Stizostedion sp. (walleye/sauger)	36	6
cf. *Stizostedion* sp. (walleye/sauger?)	2	--
Esox sp. (northern pike/muskellunge)	1	1
Mammal:	6	--
Bird:		
Anatinae (Marsh Duck Family)	2	--
Total Fauna	**4,150**	**30**

Table 5. Feature B Faunal Identifications, 21IC46

Class	Identification	Element	Side	Quantity
bird	Anatinae	humerus	left	1
fish				1,632
fish		scale		28
fish		vertebra	n/a	217
fish	Catostomidae	pharyngeal arch	indet	20
fish	*Catostomus* sp.	ceratohyal	left	9
fish	*Catostomus* sp.	ceratohyal	right	6
fish	*Esox* sp.	palatine	indet	2
fish	*Stizostedion* sp.	angular	left	1
fish	*Stizostedion* sp.	angular	right	1
fish	*Stizostedion* sp.	dentary	left	6
fish	*Stizostedion* sp.	dentary	right	1
mammal				7
mammal	*Castor canadensis*	scapula	right	1

Table 6. Feature B Assemblage, NISP and MNI by Taxon, 21IC46

TAXON	NISP	MNI
Fish:	1,877	--
Catostomidae (Sucker Family)	20	--
Catostomus sp. (white/longnose sucker)	15	9
Stizostedion sp. (walleye/sauger)	9	6
Esox sp. (northern pike/muskellunge)	2	1
Mammal:	7	--
Castor canadensis (beaver)	1	1
Bird:		
Anatinae (Marsh Duck Family)	1	--
Reptile:		
Testudines (turtle)	2	--
Total Fauna	**1,934**	**17**

Table 7. Feature C Faunal Identifications, 21IC46

Class	Identification	Element	Side	Quantity
fish				263
fish		vertebra	n/a	158
fish	Catostomidae	epihyal		1
fish	Catostomidae	pharyngeal arch	indet	2
fish	Catostomidae	weberian apparatus		n/a 1
fish	*Catostomus* sp.	ceratohyal	left	1
fish	*Ictalurus* cf. *melas*	angular	right	1
fish	*Ictalurus* cf. *melas*	pectoral spine	left	2
fish	*Ictalurus* sp.	dentary	right	1
fish	*Perca flavescens*	dentary	left	1
fish	*Stizostedion* sp.	dentary	left	1
mammal				1
mammal	artiodactyl	tooth	indet	1
mammal	*Castor canadensis*	P1	left	1
unidentified				92

Table 8. Feature C Assemblage, NISP and MNI by Taxon, 21IC46

TAXON	NISP	MNI
Fish:	421	--
Catostomidae (Sucker Family)	4	--
Catostomus sp. (white/longnose sucker)	1	1
Ictalurus cf. *melas* (black bullhead)	3	2
Ictalurus sp. (bullhead/catfish)	1	--
Stizostedion sp. (walleye/sauger)	1	1
Perca flavescens (yellow perch)	1	1
Mammal:	1	--
Castor canadensis (beaver)	1	1
Artiodactyl	1	--
Unidentified:	92	
Total Fauna	**527**	**18**

Table 9. Feature D Faunal Identifications, 21IC46

Class	Identification	Element	Side	Quantity
fish				4,952
fish		vertebra	n/a	564
fish	Catostomidae			37
fish	Catostomidae	epihyal	indet	3
fish	Catostomidae	pharyngeal arch	indet	26
fish	*Catostomus* sp.	ceratohyal	left	12
fish	*Catostomus* sp.	ceratohyal	right	16
fish	cf. *Stizostedion* sp.	basioccipital	n/a	3
fish	cf. *Stizostedion* sp.	epihyal	indet	7
fish	cf. *Stizostedion* sp.	frontal	indet	4
fish	*Stizostedion* sp.	angular	left	17
fish	*Stizostedion* sp.	angular	right	7
fish	*Stizostedion* sp.	ceratohyal	indet	16
fish	*Stizostedion* sp.	cleithrum	left	1
fish	*Stizostedion* sp.	dentary	left	5
fish	*Stizostedion* sp.	dentary	right	9
fish	*Stizostedion* sp.	hyomandibular	left	3
fish	*Stizostedion* sp.	hyomandibular	right	5
fish	*Stizostedion* sp.	maxilla	left	8
fish	*Stizostedion* sp.	maxilla	right	9
fish	*Stizostedion* sp.	preopercle	left	1
fish	*Stizostedion* sp.	quadrate	left	8
fish	*Stizostedion* sp.	quadrate	right	10
mammal				3
unidentified				30

Table 10. Feature D Assemblage, NISP and MNI by Taxon, 21IC46

TAXON	NISP	MNI
Fish:	5,516	--
Catostomidae (Sucker Family)	66	--
Catostomus sp. (white/longnose sucker)	28	16
Stizostedion sp. (walleye/sauger)	99	17
cf. *Stizostedion* sp. (walleye/sauger?)	11	--
Mammal:	3	--
Unidentified:	30	--
Total Fauna	**5,756**	**33**

Table 11. Feature E Faunal Identifications, 21IC46

Class	Identification	Element	Side	Quantity
fish				312
fish		basioccipital	n/a	1
fish		ceratohyal		1
fish		scales		4
fish		vertebra	n/a	139
fish	Catostomidae			1
fish	Catostomidae	autopalatine		1
fish	Catostomidae	dentary		1
fish	Catostomidae	maxillary		1
fish	Catostomidae	opercle		1
fish	Catostomidae	pharyngeal arch		4
fish	Catostomidae	quadrate		1
fish	Catostomidae	supracleithrum		1
fish	Catostomidae	weberian apparatus	n/a	2
fish	Catostomidae	weberian process		2
fish	*Catostomus* sp.	ceratohyal	right	1
fish	*Esox* sp.	prevomer	n/a	1
mammal				1
mammal	*Castor/Erethizon*	incisor	indet	1
unidentified				23

Table 12. Feature E Assemblage, NISP and MNI by Taxon, 21IC46

TAXON	NISP	MNI
Fish:	457	--
Catostomidae (Sucker Family)	15	--
Catostomus sp. (white/longnose sucker)	1	1
Esox sp. (northern pike/muskellunge)	1	1
Mammal:	1	--
Castor/Erethizon (beaver/porcupine)	1	--
Artiodactyl	1	--
Unidentified:	23	--
Total Fauna	**499**	**2**

Table 13. Feature F Faunal Identifications, 21IC46

Class	Identification	Element	Side	Quantity
fish				52,360
fish		vertebra	n/a	415
fish	*C.* cf. *commersoni*	dentary	left	4
fish	*C.* cf. *commersoni*	dentary	right	2
fish	*C.* cf. *commersoni*	hyomandibular	left	1
fish	*C.* cf. *commersoni*	maxilla	left	1
fish	Catostomidae			360
fish	Catostomidae	parasphenoid	n/a	28
fish	Catostomidae	pharyngeal arch	indet	8
fish	Catostomidae	pharyngeal arch	left	1
fish	Catostomidae	pharyngeal arch	indet	6
fish	Catostomidae	supracleithrum	indet	20
fish	Catostomidae	supraethmoid	n/a	2
fish	Catostomidae	weberian apparatus		2
fish	Catostomidae	weberian apparatus	n/a	1
fish	*Catostomus* sp.	angular	left	1
fish	*Catostomus* sp.	angular	right	1
fish	*Catostomus* sp.	basioccipital	n/a	13
fish	*Catostomus* sp.	ceratohyal	left	157
fish	*Catostomus* sp.	ceratohyal	right	138
fish	*Catostomus* sp.	epihyal	left	1
fish	*Catostomus* sp.	frontal	right	1
fish	*Catostomus* sp.	hyomandibular	left	3
fish	*Catostomus* sp.	hyomandibular	right	2
fish	*Catostomus* sp.	maxilla	left	2
fish	*Catostomus* sp.	opercle	left	19
fish	*Catostomus* sp.	opercle	right	15
fish	*Catostomus* sp.	pharyngeal arch	left	1
fish	*Catostomus* sp.	quadrate	left	1
fish	*Catostomus* sp.	supraethmoid	n/a	1
fish	cf. *Ictalurus* sp.	pectoral spine	indet	1
fish	*Esox* sp.	cleithrum	left	1
fish	*Esox* sp.	dentary	left	1
fish	*Esox* sp.	dentary	right	1
fish	*Ictalurus* sp.	pectoral spine	indet	1
fish	*Stizostedion* sp.	angular	right	1
fish	*Stizostedion* sp.	dentary	right	1
mammal				3
mammal		caudal vertebra	n/a	1
mammal	*Castor canadensis*	metacarpal/tarsal	undifferentiated	1
mammal	*Castor canadensis*	P2	right	1
mammal	*Erethizon dorsatum*	scapula	left	1
mammal	*Odocoileus* sp.	3rd phalanx	right	1
mammal	*Ondatra zibethicus*	calcaneus	left	1
reptile	Testudines			1
unidentified				15

Table 14. Feature F Assemblage, NISP and MNI by Taxon, 21IC46

TAXON	NISP	MNI
Fish:	52,775	--
Catostomidae (Sucker Family)	428	--
Catostomus sp. (white/longnose sucker)	356	157
Catostomus cf. *commersoni* (white sucker)	8	4
Stizostedion sp. (walleye/sauger)	2	1
Esox sp. (northern pike/muskellunge)	3	1
Ictalurus sp. (bullhead/catfish)	1	--
cf. *Ictalurus* sp. (bullhead/catfish?)	1	--
Mammal:	4	--
Castor canadensis (beaver)	2	1
Erethizon dorsatum (porcupine)	1	1
Ondatra zibethicus (muskrat)	1	1
Odocoileus sp. (deer)	1	1
Reptile:		
Testudines (turtle)	1	--
Unidentified:	15	--
Total Fauna	**53,599**	**167**

Table 15. Feature G Faunal Identifications, 21IC46

Class	Identification	Element	Side	Quantity
fish				7
fish		vertebra	n/a	12
fish	*Catostomus* sp.	ceratohyal	right	1

Table 16. Feature G Assemblage, NISP and MNI by Taxon, 21IC46

TAXON	NISP	MNI
Fish:	19	--
Catostomus sp. (white/longnose sucker)	1	1
Total Fauna	**20**	**1**

Table 17. Feature H Faunal Identifications, 21IC46

Class	Identification	Element	Side	Quantity
bird				2
fish				17
fish		dentary	left	1
fish		vertebra	n/a	126
fish	C. cf. *commersoni*	opercle	left	1
fish	Catostomidae	angular	right	1
fish	Catostomidae	pharyngeal arch	indet	8
fish	Catostomidae	pharyngeal arch	right	1
fish	Catostomidae	supraethmoid	n/a	1
fish	*Esox* sp.	palatine	indet	2
fish	*Stizostedion* sp.	ceratohyal		1
mammal				4
mammal	*Castor/Erethizon*	incisor	indet	1
mammal	*Odocoileus* sp.	1st phalanx	indet	2
mammal	*Odocoileus* sp.	3rd phalanx	indet	1
reptile	Testudines	carapace/plastron		2
unidentified				122

Table 18. Feature H Assemblage, NISP and MNI by Taxon, 21IC46

TAXON	NISP	MNI
Fish:	144	--
Catostomidae (Sucker Family)	11	--
Catostomus cf. *commersoni* (white sucker)	1	1
Stizostedion sp. (walleye/sauger)	1	1
Esox sp. (northern pike/muskellunge)	2	1
Mammal:	4	--
Castor/Erethizon (beaver/porcupine)	1	--
Odocoileus sp. (deer)	3	1
Bird:	2	--
Reptile:		
Testudines (turtle)	1	--
Unidentified:	122	--
Total Fauna	**293**	**4**

Table 19. Non-Feature Faunal Identifications, 21IC46

Class	Identification	Element	Side	Quantity
amphibian				5
bird				19
bird		humerus	right	1
bird	Anatinae	coracoid	left	2
bird	Anatinae	ulna	left	1
fish				5,853
fish		epihyal		1
fish		quadrate	indet	1
fish		scale		5
fish		scale	n/a	1
fish		vertebra		147
fish		vertebra	n/a	1,377
fish	*C.* cf. *commersoni*	dentary	left	1
fish	*C.* cf. *commersoni*	dentary	right	1
fish	*C.* cf. *commersoni*	hyomandibular	left	1
fish	*C.* cf. *commersoni*	hyomandibular	right	1
fish	*C.* cf. *commersoni*	opercle	left	1
fish	*C.* cf. *commersoni*	opercle	right	1
fish	Catostomidae			19
fish	Catostomidae	angular		2
fish	Catostomidae	basioccipital	n/a	1
fish	Catostomidae	opercle		1
fish	Catostomidae	parasphenoid	n/a	6
fish	Catostomidae	pharyngeal arch		3
fish	Catostomidae	pharyngeal arch	indet	21
fish	Catostomidae	pharyngeal arch	n/a	4
fish	Catostomidae	prevomer	n/a	3
fish	Catostomidae	supracleithrum	indet	6
fish	Catostomidae	supraethmoid	n/a	1
fish	Catostomidae	weberian apparatus	n/a	1
fish	Catostomidae	weberian process	n/a	2
fish	*Catostomus* sp.	angular	left	6
fish	*Catostomus* sp.	angular	right	2
fish	*Catostomus* sp.	basioccipital	n/a	1
fish	*Catostomus* sp.	ceratohyal	left	8
fish	*Catostomus* sp.	ceratohyal	right	14
fish	*Catostomus* sp.	frontal	left	3
fish	*Catostomus* sp.	frontal	right	1
fish	*Catostomus* sp.	hyomandibular	left	1
fish	*Catostomus* sp.	hyomandibular	right	1
fish	*Catostomus* sp.	maxilla	left	1
fish	*Catostomus* sp.	maxilla	right	1
fish	*Catostomus* sp.	opercle	right	1
fish	*Catostomus* sp.	pharyngeal arch	left	1
fish	*Catostomus* sp.	supraethmoid	n/a	1
fish	*Esox* sp.	cleithrum	right	1
fish	*Esox* sp.	dentary	indet	1
fish	*Esox* sp.	dentary	right	2
fish	*Esox* sp.	palatine	n/a	1
fish	*Esox* sp.	tooth	indet	2
fish	*Ictalurus* sp.	pectoral spine	indet	1
fish	*Stizostedion* sp.	angular	left	6
fish	*Stizostedion* sp.	angular	right	3
fish	*Stizostedion* sp.	ceratohyal	indet	1
fish	*Stizostedion* sp.	cleithrum	right	1
fish	*Stizostedion* sp.	dentary	left	4
fish	*Stizostedion* sp.	dentary	right	5
fish	*Stizostedion* sp.	frontal	indet	1
fish	*Stizostedion* sp.	maxilla	right	1
fish	*Stizostedion* sp.	premaxilla	left	1
fish	*Stizostedion* sp.	quadrate	left	2
fish	*Stizostedion* sp.	quadrate	right	3

Class	Identification	Element	Side	Quantity
gastropoda		shell		1
mammal				130
mammal		tooth enamel		1
mammal		tooth enamel		7
mammal		tooth enamel	indet	4
mammal		vertebra, unfused	n/a	1
mammal	artiodactyl	phalanx	indet	1
mammal	artiodactyl	tooth	indet	1
mammal	*Castor canadensis*	1st phalanx	left	1
mammal	*Castor canadensis*	1st phalanx	right	1
mammal	*Castor canadensis*	femur	right	1
mammal	*Castor canadensis*	M1	left	1
mammal	*Castor canadensis*	m1	right	1
mammal	*Castor canadensis*	M2	left	2
mammal	*Castor canadensis*	M2	right	1
mammal	*Castor canadensis*	m3	right	1
mammal	*Castor canadensis*	mandible		1
mammal	*Castor canadensis*	molar		2
mammal	*Castor canadensis*	premolar/molar		1
mammal	*Castor canadensis*	premolar/molar	indet	2
mammal	*Castor/Erethizon*	2nd phalanx	undifferentiated	1
mammal	*Castor/Erethizon*	incisor		1
mammal	*Castor/Erethizon*	incisor	indet	1
mammal	*Castor/Erethizon*	incisor enamel	indet	1
mammal	*Castor/Erethizon*	phalanx	undifferentiated	1
mammal	*Cervus elaphas*	2nd phalanx	right	1
mammal	*Canis* sp.	astragulus	right	1
mammal	cf. *Castor canadensis*	incisor		1
mammal	cf. *Castor canadensis*	incisor	indet	2
mammal	cf. *Castor canadensis*	molar	indet	3
mammal	cf. *Castor canadensis*	premolar/molar	indet	5
mammal	cf. *Odocoileus* sp.	tooth	indet	1
mammal	cf. *Sylvilagus floridanus*	maxilla	indet	1
mammal	large mammal	rib	indet	1
mammal	medium mammal	metacarpal/tarsal	indet	1
mammal	medium mammal	rib	indet	1
mammal	*Odocoileus* sp.	1st phalanx	left	1
mammal	*Odocoileus* sp.	1st phalanx	right	1
mammal	*Odocoileus* sp.	2nd phalanx	right	1
mammal	*Odocoileus* sp.	i2	left	1
mammal	*Ondatra zibethicus*	calcaneus	right	1
mammal	*Ondatra zibethicus*	caudal vert. epiphysis	n/a	2
mammal	*Ondatra zibethicus*	caudal vertebra	n/a	5
mammal	*Ondatra zibethicus*	mandible	right	1
mammal	rodentia	cranium		1
mammal	rodentia	incisor		1
mammal	rodentia	mandible	right	1
mammal	rodentia	phalanx		2
mammal	rodentia	rib		2
mammal	small mammal	metacarpal/tarsal	indet	1
mammal	small mammal	ulna	indet	1
mammal	small mammal	ulna	left	1
mammal	small mammal	vertebra	n/a	1
mollusk		shell		5
reptile	Testudines	carapace/plastron		14
unidentified				2,634

Table 20. Non-Feature Faunal Identifications, NISP and MNI by Taxon, 21IC46

TAXON	NISP	MNI
Fish:	7,385	--
Catostomidae (sucker family)	70	--
Catostomus sp. (white/longnose sucker)	42	14
Catostomus cf. *commersoni* (white sucker?)	6	1
Stizostedion sp. (walleye/sauger)	28	6
Esox sp. (northern pike/muskellunge)	7	2
Ictalurus sp. (bullhead/catfish)	1	--
Mammal:	145	--
small mammal	4	--
medium mammal	2	--
large mammal	1	--
Castor canadensis (beaver)	15	2
cf. *Castor canadensis* (beaver?)	11	--
Castor/Erethizon (beaver or porcupine)	5	--
Ondatra zibethicus (muskrat)	9	1
cf. *Sylvilagus floridanus* (eastern cottontail?)	1	1
rodent, undifferentiated	7	--
Canis sp. (dog/wolf/coyote)	1	1
Artiodactyl	2	--
Odocoileus sp. (deer)	4	1
cf. *Odocoileus* sp. (deer?)	1	--
Cervus elaphas (elk)	1	1
Bird:	20	--
Anatinae (marsh ducks)	3	--
Reptile:		
Testudines (turtle)	14	--
Amphibian:	5	--
Mollusk and Gastropod:	6	--
Unidentified	2,916	--
Total Fauna	**10,428**	**30**

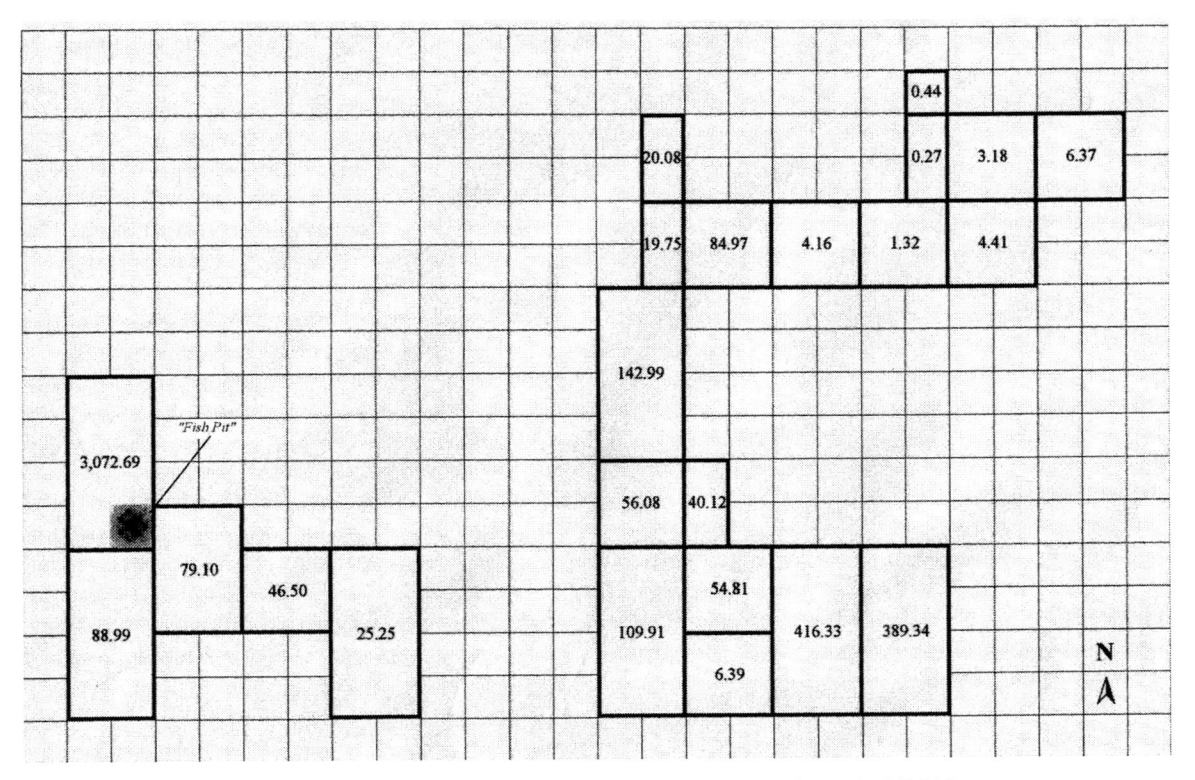

Figure 4. Weight of faunal material (in grams) per excavation unit, 21IC46.

includes proveniences 1-4, 1-5 and 1-6. A total of 4,150 bone fragments were recovered from Feature A, of which 99 percent are fish remains. The remaining 1 percent consists of 2 bird and 6 mammal bone fragments. Taxonomic identifications from Feature A are presented in Tables 3 and 4. It is important to note that the MNI counts by feature will total more than the MNI counts determined for the site assemblage as a whole, assuming that a single animal would not be represented in more than one feature. Suckers are the primary fish taxon, with a minimum of 23 individuals, followed by walleye/sauger, with a minimum of 6.

Feature B

Feature B is a separate feature in the center of Unit 1. It consists of provenience 1-11. It may relate to Feature A. Bone fragments from this feature total 1,934. Again, 99 percent are fish remains. The remaining 1 percent consists of 1 bird, 8 mammal and 2 turtle bone fragments. Taxonomic identifications from this feature are presented in Tables 5 and 6. There is less of a disparity here between suckers and walleye/sauger, with minimum numbers of 9 and 6, respectively. Also present are trace amounts of beaver, duck and turtle.

Feature C

Feature C dates to ca. A.D. 670. It is the "fish pot," an Early Blackduck ceramic vessel that had broken in place and contained a large amount of associated fish bone. It is therefore tempting to suggest that these remains represent a single meal. The assemblage was recovered from Unit 3. This feature includes proveniences 3-8, 3-9, 3-25 and 3-33. A total of 527 bone fragments were recovered from the pot, of which 82 percent (n=432) were fish remains. Unidentified fragments account for 17 percent (n=92), and the remaining 3 bone fragments are mammal. Taxonomic identifications from this feature are presented in Tables 7 and 8. A greater diversity of fish species is seen in this feature, with no individual taxon dominant. Bullheads are most prevalent with a minimum of 2 individuals. Suckers, walleye/sauger and perch are represented by a minimum of 1 individual each. One beaver and one fragment artiodactyl are also present.

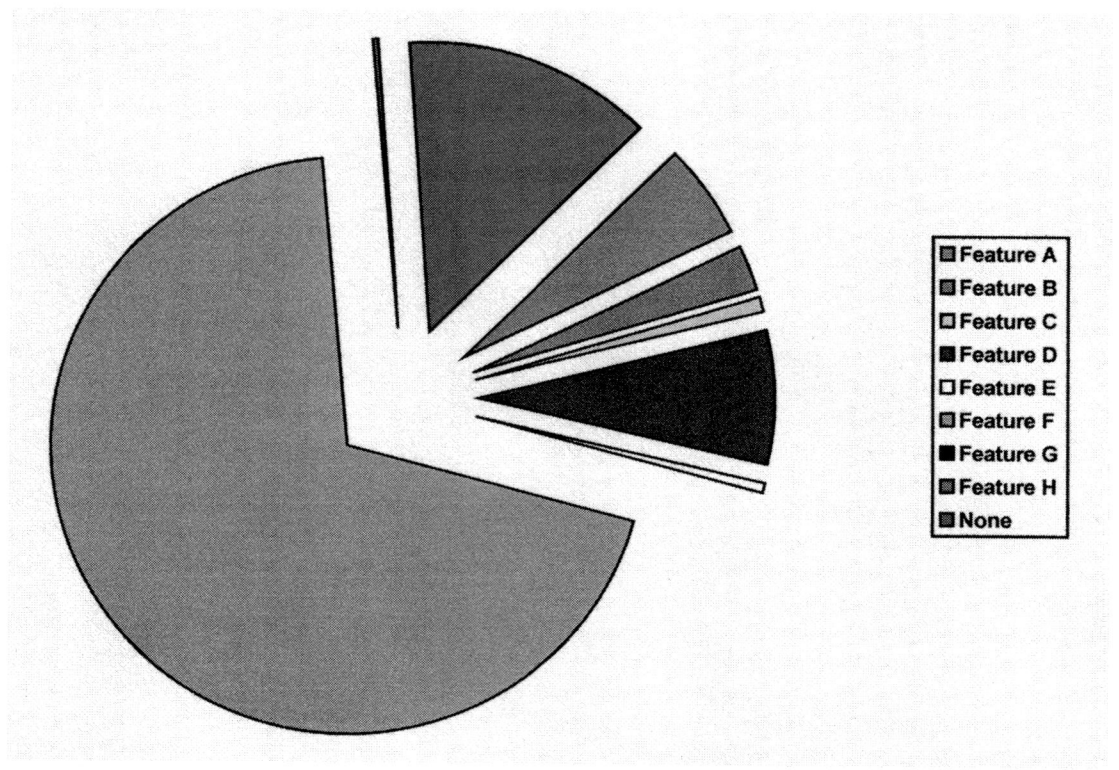

Figure 5. Intra-site distribution of faunal remains, features and non-feature material, by count, 21IC46.

Feature D

Feature D was also in Unit 3. It is a separate feature from Feature C, consisting of proveniences 3-26, 3-27, 3-28, 3-29, and 3-30. Feature D is associated with an early Sandy Lake component dating to ca. A.D. 1225. A total of 5,756 bone fragments were recovered from this feature, of which 99 percent are fish remains. The remaining 1 percent consists of 3 mammal and 30 unidentified bone fragments. Taxonomic identifications from this feature are presented in Tables 19 and 10. The fish in this feature are almost evenly divided between suckers and walleye/sauger, and a minimum of 16 and 17 individuals, respectively.

Directly relevant to Features C and D is the recovery of two antler tine projectile points (or harpoon heads) from Test Unit 3. These were unfortunately not in the clear context of either feature, but may offer a glimpse of the Late Woodland fishing technology utilized at the site.

Feature E

Feature E was discovered in Unit 8. It is associated with Blackduck ceramics but is not radiocarbon dated. It consists of proveniences 8-4, 8-5, 8-6, 8-7, 8-8 and 8-9. A total of 499 bone fragments were recovered from this feature, of which 95 percent are fish remains (n=474). Unidentified remains (n=23)

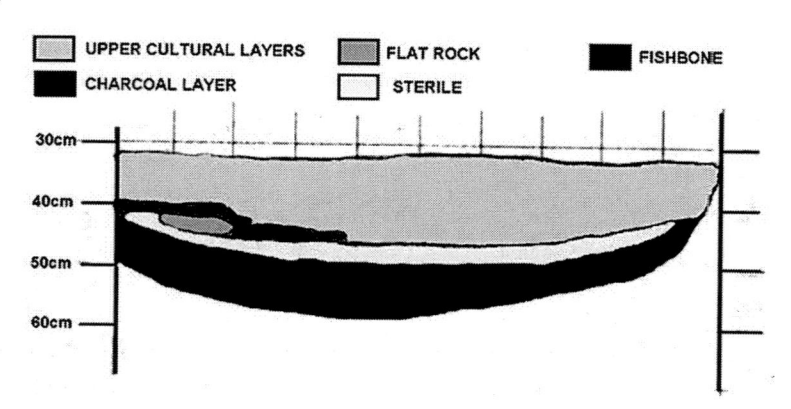

Figure 6. Feature F profile, 21IC46 (from Hohman-Caine and Goltz 1998).

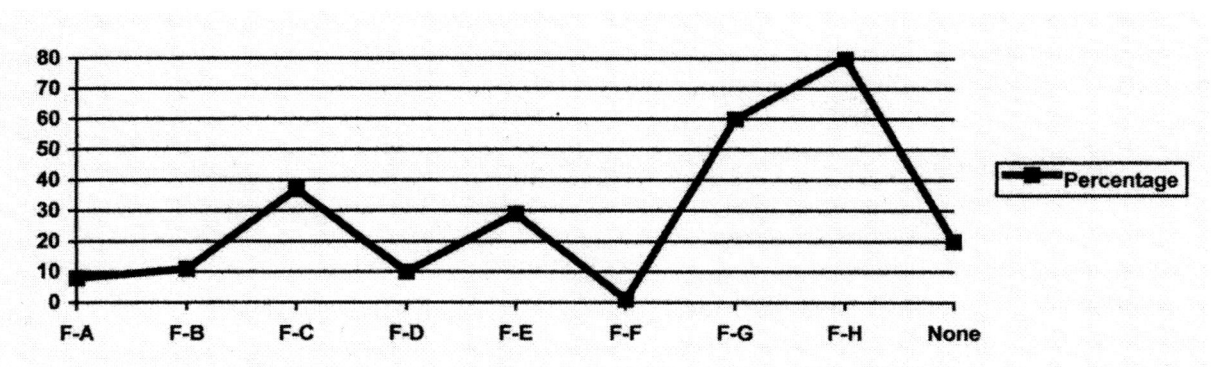

Figure 7. Percentage of vertebrae within total fish bone by provenience, 21IC46.

account for 4.6 percent, and 2 mammal bone fragments contribute the remaining less than 1 percent. Taxonomic identifications from this feature are presented in Tables 11 and 12. This feature contains sucker, pike/muskellunge and beaver at minimum numbers of one individual each. Suckers are most numerous by NISP count, however. One artiodactyl is also represented.

Feature F

Feature F is the "fishbone pit" from Units 10 and 11. It is a truly remarkable feature in terms of Minnesota zooarchaeology, as the faunal remains comprised a discrete stratigraphic level (Fig. 6). They were recovered without the necessity of screening, because virtually no sediment was included with the bone. As such, this feature offers a rare opportunity of complete recovery of faunal (primarily fish) remains. The research potential of this assemblage has only been touched upon in the present analysis, which focused on the issues of species composition and taxonomic abundance through MNI calculations. This is an ideal assemblage to investigate taphonomic topics such as differential body part preservation and representation (cf. Butler 1993, 1996; Butler and Chatters 1994; Lubinski 1996).

This is a Late Blackduck feature, dating to ca. A.D. 1005. It includes proveniences 10-8, 10-9, 10-16, 10-20, 10-21, 10-22, 10-24, 10-25, 10-26 and 11-32. An estimated total of 53,574 bone fragments were examined from this feature, of which 99 percent were fish. The remaining 1 percent consists of 15 unidentified, 9 mammal and 1 turtle bone fragments. Estimation of the total number of bone fragments was necessary, as the assemblage varied from virtually complete bone to tens of thousands of tiny fish bone fragments and finally to fish-bone dust.

Taxonomic identifications from this feature are presented in Tables 13 and 14. As previously mentioned, this feature contains the majority of the fish bone (and of the bone in general) from the site assemblage. Suckers, probably white suckers, are the predominant taxa. Minimum numbers of 157 suckers, and 4 probable white suckers are followed by trace amounts of pike/muskellunge and bullhead. Beaver, porcupine, muskrat, deer and turtle are also present.

It is important to note that provenience 10-26 was not available for study during the present analysis. The faunal material from this provenience was from the same fish bone dominated stratum as the remainder of the feature, however. If one assumes that the entire stratum is essentially homogenous in nature, rough estimation is possible of 2,588 additional fish bone fragments from the 10-26 fauna's known weight of 103.0 grams. By the same measure, this could add up to 4 additional suckers based on ceratohyal representation. These numbers have not been added to the site assemblage quantification in Table 2, however, pending examination of the actual 10-26 assemblage.

Feature G

Feature G was located in Unit 13. It consisted of a clay layer and an ashy layer, and includes proveniences 13-13 and 13-14. The feature has not been assigned to a cultural component. Taxonomic identifications from this feature are presented in Tables 15 and 16. Compared to the other contexts discussed here, this feature contains very little faunal material.

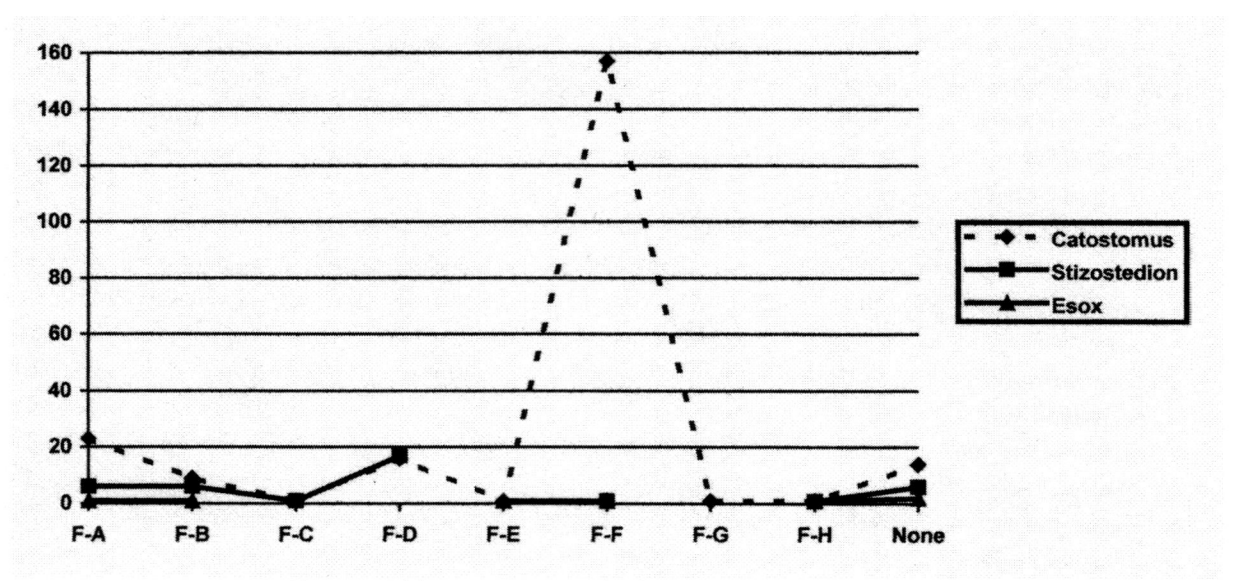

Figure 8. Fish genus representation by provenience (MNI), 21IC46.

Twenty fish bones are present, representing a minimum of one sucker.

Feature H

Feature H is a shallow pit feature with ash in Unit 18. It has not been assigned to a cultural component. Feature H includes proveniences 18-3, 18-4, 18-5, 18-6, 18-10 and 18-11. Taxonomic identifications from this feature are presented in Tables 17 and 18. The feature assemblage is dominated by fish remains, with identifications of sucker, pike/muskellunge and walleye/sauger at a minimum of one individual each. Deer bone and a beaver/porcupine incisor are also present, with trace amounts of bird and turtle bone.

Nonfeature Site Assemblage

The faunal assemblage recovered from outside identified features, or the nonfeature site assemblage, cannot be assigned to a particular cultural component. Like the feature assemblages, it is dominated by fish, including suckers, walleye/sauger, pike/muskellunge and bullhead in decreasing order of importance (Tables 19 and 20). Mammal, bird and turtle bone is better represented here than in any of the features. Mammalian species include beaver, muskrat, deer and elk. A single canid astragalus could be from domestic dog, wolf or coyote. Trace amounts of amphibian, mollusk and gastropod remains may be unrelated to the archaeological assemblage.

Despite the certainty that this subassemblage represents a mixture of the cultural components identified at the site, it is perhaps illustrative of a similarity in site function through the history of occupation. The taxonomic diversity of this subassemblage also shows the range of animal species gathered by the site inhabitants over time. It is proposed, however, that the feature contents, all clearly dominated by fish, represent the primary site activity. Thus, while the economic importance of mammals such as elk, deer and beaver cannot be denied, it is suggested that hunting of these and other animals was incidental to the recurring site occupations, which focused on fishing and fish processing.

Differential Element and Species Representation

The present analysis can only touch upon the topic of differential element representation within the fish assemblage, but some level of fish processing is clearly apparent. As mentioned previously, this study could not address the full range of Catostomidae remains, and instead focused on quantification of the total number of fish through isolation of the ceratohyal (the most frequently preserved catostomid bone). In this regard, the clearly archaeological context of the assemblage was a benefit. A well-preserved fish assemblage is often of doubtful provenience, necessitating detailed analysis of all ele-

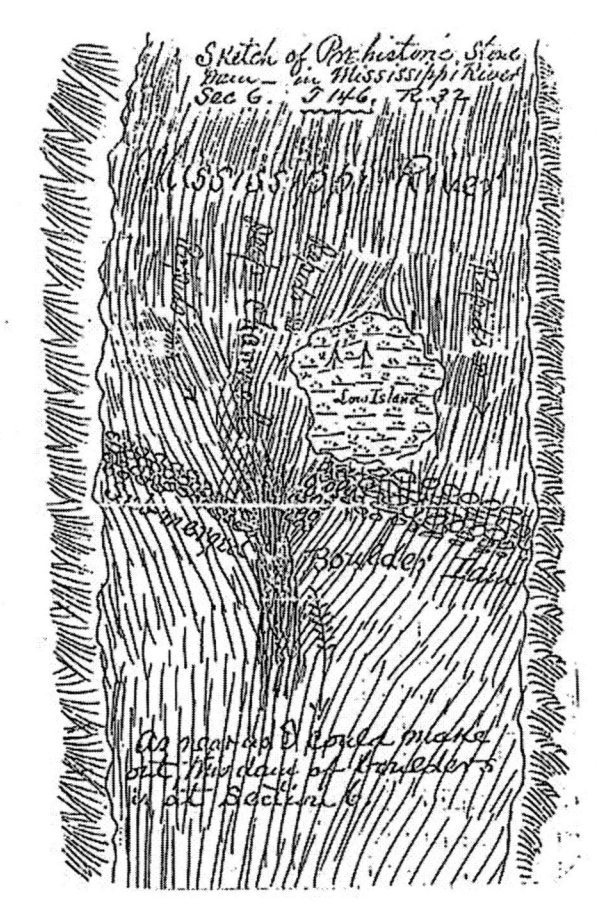

Figure 9. Jacob Brower's (1898) sketch of a stone formation (fish weir?) in the Mississippi River.

ments present to determine whether it is of cultural or natural occurrence (cf. Butler 1993, 1996). Such studies clearly demonstrate the benefit of further analysis of the Third River Bridge assemblage as well, particularly in regard to fish processing and assemblage taphonomy (Lubinski 1996; Butler and Chatters 1994).

Having not identified all possible fish bones, particularly among the Catostomidae, the best means to investigate fish processing is to compare the distribution of vertebrae, all of which were quantified, against all other fish bones (Fig. 7). The latter are assumed to mainly represent the cranial region of the skeleton. It should also be remembered that vertebrae are the most numerous and durable bone in the fish skeleton, so they should be expected to form the majority of a fish bone assemblage. These preliminary results are of interest in that features from the Sandy Lake component (Features A, D and possibly B) show values of only 11 percent vertebrae or lower. Blackduck Features C and E have slightly higher percentages, at 37 and 29 percent, respectively. Feature F, the "fish pit" from the Late Blackduck component, is particularly striking with a vertebra percentage of only one percent. The disproportionate presence of cranial bones in these features is believed to represent the processing or disposal of fish heads after removal of the body. This would be expected during drying or smoking fish meat for storage (e.g., Stewart 1977:135-138).

The non-meat portions of the fish may have been otherwise utilized prior to disposal, although the present analysis cannot provide verification. Kuhm (1928) describes the making and use of fish oil, although he unfortunately does not provide specific ethnographic examples or citations:

> The fish guts and heads that remained after the smoking process were boiled to obtain fish oil. When deer brains, used in the Indian process of softening buckskin, were scarce, fish oil was used as a substitute. Buckskin was prepared by placing the hides in hot water to remove the hair, which could then be scraped off. Then either deer brains or fish oil were rubbed over the hide to soften it. [Kuhm 1928:98]

The representation of different fish species is also of interest. Figure 8 presents minimum numbers (MNI) of suckers (*Catostomus* sp.), walleye/sauger (*Stizostedion* sp.) and northern pike/muskellunge (*Esox* sp.). While suckers dominate the assemblage throughout, the greatest species diversity is seen in the Sandy Lake component, Features A, D and possibly B. In Feature D in particular, suckers and walleye/sauger are present in roughly equal amounts. Blackduck Features C and E do not provide much basis for comparison, but Feature F shows a dramatic shift in favor of suckers.

Seasonal Indicators

Zooarchaeological studies can often suggest a season of site occupation based on the habits of identified animals, or on osteological criteria such as tooth wear or eruption sequences. In the case of the Third River Bridge assemblage, recurring spring occupations are strongly suggested by the clear predominance of spring spawning fish, including suckers, walleye/sauger, pike/muskellunge and bullheads (Eddy and Underhill 1974; Phillips, Schmid and Underhill 1982; Becker 1983). The spawning runs of suckers in particular are proposed as a likely reason for site occupation, as they are highly noticeable and memorable events. The dramatic behavior and coloration of the fish at these times has influenced their common names, particular in the case of the redhorse suckers (Eddy and Underhill 1974; Olson 1963).

The spawning behavior of white (and other) suckers is described in great detail by Becker (1983:683-684) and others (e.g., Middlemis 1984; Eddy and Underhill 1974; Phillips , Schmid and Underhill 1982; Olson 1963). Of perhaps greatest interest to the archaeology of the Third River Bridge site is the duration and timing of the spawning runs. Becker notes that male suckers are generally more numerous in the spawning areas, and arrive two to three days earlier than the females. The runs are believed to be precipitated by initiation of the spring melt, when the water temperature reaches approximately 45 degrees Fahrenheit. Kohl (1985:120) notes that among the Ojibwe of Lake Superior, February was called "the moon of the suckers, because those fish begin going up the rivers then." During the migration, more activity occurs at night, reaching its peak between 10:00 and 11:00 PM (Becker 1983). Olson (1963) states that the spawning run of white suckers often follows that of the walleyes, a matter that is also of direct relevance to the Third River Bridge site.

A second possibility must be mentioned in discussion of the Third River Bridge sucker assemblage. Eddy and Underhill (1974:294) describe "summerkills" of white suckers in Minnesota lakes. The cause of death has not been determined but mortality due to natural causes has been proposed, as the affected fishes are large and show no visible signs of trauma. These events take place in late summer in northern Minnesota (Eddy and Underhill 1974). Scavenging of dead fish is not considered a likely explanation for the Third River Bridge faunal assemblage, however, for several reasons. First, the site is located on the banks of the river, not along the lakeshore, which would be closer to "summerkilled" suckers. Perhaps more telling is the presence of other fish species in the site assemblage, including walleye/sauger, northern pike/muskellunge, bullheads and perch. Finally, the greatest potential for all of these species to be captured together would be during the spring spawning runs, particularly in the case of suckers and walleye/sauger, the dominant taxa of the assemblage.

The Late Woodland Fishery

When considering the Late Woodland fishery represented by the Third River Bridge site, one must abandon present notions of fishing as sport angling, and instead consider the hunter-gatherer's need for intensive resource procurement at the end of a long, cold winter. At such a time, the nutritional resource provided by sucker spawning runs could literally be a matter of life or death. Angling is but one of many fishing methods utilized by Indian and Euroamerican peoples, and is probably the least efficient (especially in pursuit of suckers). Harvesting of suckers during their spawning runs was fairly common into Historic times, with much of the meat salted for later use. This practice apparently led to the expression, "thirsty as a sucker in a salt bale" (Tomelleri and Eberle 1990:95).

By the Late Woodland period, harvesting of spring- and fall-spawning fish had achieved the status of both an art and a science, and made quite an impression on early European explorers (e.g., Cleland 1982). Alexander Henry provides one example from the Great Lakes:

> These rapids (of Sault de Sainte-Marie) are beset with rocks of the most dangerous description; and yet they are the scene of a fishery in which all their dangers are braved and mastered with singular expertness. They are full of whitefish, much larger and more excellent than those at Michilimakinac, and which are found here during the greater part of the season, weighing, in general, from six pounds to fifteen.
>
> The method of taking them is this: each canoe carries two men, one of whom steers with a paddle, and the other is provided with a pole, ten feet in length, and at the end of which is affixed a scoop-net. The steersman sets the canoe from the eddy of one rock to that of another; while the fisherman in the prow, who sees through the pellucid element the prey of which he is in pursuit, dips his net, and sometimes brings up, at every

succeeding dip, as many as it can contain. The fish are often crowded together in the water in great numbers; and a skillful fisherman, in autumn, will take five hundred in two hours.

This fishery is of great moment to the surrounding Indians, whom it supplies with a large proportion of their winter's provision; for, having taken the fish in the manner described, they cure them by drying in the smoke, and lay them up in large quantities. [Henry 1809, as quoted by Rau 1884:273-274]

The spawning runs of suckers and other fish at the Third River Bridge site could have been harvested by netting, spearing, clubbing, or even by hand. Ethnographic accounts suggest that spearing was a prominent method of taking fish. Lewis (1967:167) describes the Ojibwe spearing fish at night from shore and from boats, using bonfires or torches to attract the fish. Arrows attached to a line were also used. Clubbing is also an effective means of gathering fish in shallow waters. This method is reported to have been used at night by torchlight, and sometimes during the course of fish "drives" by organized parties. Kuhn (1928:30) quotes an anonymous source as saying, "Suckers came up this creek in former days from the river and these the natives captured by clubbing." The fish harvest itself often captured the notice of observers, rather than any one fishing method. Pond (1986:30) notes that "In the spring many fish were killed in the lakes and rivers, and in the small streams where they went in immense numbers to deposit their spawn. The suckers which they took at such times they preserved by drying them over fires."

Finally, it is tempting to consider that the Third River Bridge fish harvests might have been aided by a fish weir fashioned of stone or wood. Jacob Brower noted stone formations in the rivers of the Mississippi Headwaters region during his explorations in the late nineteenth century (Fig. 9). He described one such formation as

> extending from shore to shore... with an opening at the centre of the stream through which a deep swift channel passes. The stone boulders of the glacial drift have been gathered and systematically placed in the bed of the Mississippi so as to force the current of the river in low water to a central channel. [Brower, Field Book No. 6, 1898]

Brower considered the formations to be aids to navigation. It seems equally likely that they might have been fish weirs. Unfortunately, the Lake Winnibigoshish reservoir had been established prior to Brower's visit to the Third River so it is likely that such a stone formation, if present, would not have been noticeable.

Conclusion

The incredible fish bone assemblage of the Third River Bridge site offers a unique opportunity for continued zooarchaeological study. Much of the animal bone was recovered from well-documented cultural contexts, in association with diagnostic artifacts. The present analysis has only touched upon the research potential of this assemblage, which is well suited for further study of taphonomy and differential element preservation and representation, paleoecology, and regional Late Woodland fishing and resource management.

The present effort has documented the dominance of suckers (*Catostomus* sp.) within the site assemblage, and suggested a specific identification of *Catostomus commersoni*, the white sucker. Walleye or sauger (*Stizostedion* sp.) are the fish species of secondary importance, followed by small numbers of northern pike/muskellunge (*Esox* sp.), bullheads (*Ictalurus* sp.) and perch (*Perca flavescens*). The fish harvest appears to have been supplemented by hunting of beaver, muskrat, deer, elk, ducks and turtles, among other animals. The dramatic spring spawning runs of suckers in particular are believed to provide a strong indication of the period of site occupation. Comparison of intrasite species and element distribution has also suggested the site's continued focus as a fishing camp throughout the Late Woodland Blackduck and Sandy Lake occupations, and provided indications of on-site fish processing.

In the midst of the technical quantification necessary for a study such as this, it is often easy to forget the vivid images of the events represented here. The sights and sounds of the fish spawning runs coinciding with the melting snows, the pace of activity surrounding the fish harvest at the site, and the possible construction and maintenance of a fish weir are all components of this story. These events are more dramatic when considering that the best fish procurement may have occurred at night by torchlight, in the midst of the ongoing activities and attendant smells of cleaning, processing and preserving fish. Because of the sucker runs harvested here, the Third River Bridge site was probably also a place of relief and feasting following a hard winter. Along with the technical and economic research topics proposed above, these aspects of the site occupation clearly merit further consideration.

Acknowledgments. I am grateful to Christy Hohman-Caine and Grant Goltz for sharing their research on the Third River Bridge site, and creating an opportunity for me to contribute to the site analysis. Thanks also to Andrea LeVasseur, Bill Yourd and the staff of Chippewa National Forest for their continuing stewardship of heritage sites. Darcy Morey was a great help to the study with his advice concerning sucker anatomy. Darlene Balkwill and Robert Clouse facilitated the loan of a longnose sucker (*Catostomus catostomus*) specimen from the Canadian Museum of Nature for purposes of this analysis. Kent Skaar helped obtain a blue sucker (*Cycleptus elongatus*) after its untimely demise at Underwater Adventures in the Mall of America. Randy Peterson was of great assistance in quantifying the massive quantities of fish bone in Test Units 10 and 11 by weight and count. This analysis was conducted at Loucks Associates, and was made possible through a contract with Hamline University.

References Cited

Banister, K.E.
  1995 Carps and their Allies. In *Encyclopedia of Fishes*, edited by J.R. Paxton and W.N. Eschmeyer, pp. 96-100. Academic Press, San Diego.

Becker, G.C.
  1983 *Fishes of Wisconsin*. The University of Wisconsin Press, Madison.

Brower, J.V.
  1898 Field Book No. 6. Manuscript curated at the Minnesota Historical Society, St. Paul, MN.

Brown, C.L. and C.E. Gustafson
  1979 *A Key to Postcranial Skeletal Remains of Cattle/Bison, Elk, and Horse*. Washington State University, Laboratory of Anthropology, Reports of Investigations, No. 57, Pullman.

Butler, V.L.
  1993 Natural Versus Cultural Salmonid Remains: Origin of The Dalles Roadcut Bones, Columbia River, Oregon, U.S.A. *Journal of Archaeological Science*, 20:1-24.

  1996 Tui Chub Taphonomy and the Importance of Marsh Resources in the Western Great Basin of North America. *American Antiquity*, 61(4):699-717.

Butler, V.L. and J.C. Chatters
  1994 The Role of Bone Density in Structuring Prehistoric Salmon Bone Assemblages. *Journal of Archaeological Science*, 21:413-424.

Cleland, C.E.
  1982 The Inland Shore Fishery of the Northern Great Lakes: Its Development and Importance in Prehistory. *American Antiquity*, 47(4):761-784.

Davis, S.J.M
  1987 *The Archaeology of Animals*. Yale University Press, New Haven.

Eastman, J.T.
  1977 The Pharyngeal Bones and Teeth of Catostomid Fishes. *American Midland Naturalist*, 97:68-88.

Eddy, S. and J.C. Underhill
  1974 *Northern Fishes*, third edition. University of Minnesota Press, Minneapolis.

Gilbert, B.M.
  1993 *Mammalian Osteology*. Missouri Archaeological Society, Columbia.

Gilbert, B.M., L.D. Martin and H.G. Savage
  1996 *Avian Osteology*. Missouri Archaeological Society, Columbia.

Gregory, W.K.
  1933 Fish Skulls: A Study in the Evolution of Natural Mechanisms. *Transactions of the American Philosophical Society*, 23(2).

Harrington, R.W., Jr.
  1955 The Osteocranium of the American Cyprinid Fish, Notropis bifrenatus, with an Annotated Synonymy of Teleost Skull Bones. *Copeia* 4:267-290.

Hazard, E.B.
  1982 *The Mammals of Minnesota*. The University of Minnesota Press, Minneapolis.

Hesse, B. and P. Wapnish
  1985 *Animal Bone Archaeology*. Taraxacum, Washington D.C.

Hohman-Caine, C.A. and G.E. Goltz
  1998 *A Spring Piscary in the Headwaters Region: The Third River Bridge Site, 12-IC-46 (CNF #09-03-01-109)*. Hamline University, St. Paul. Report prepared for Chippewa National Forest.

Janssen, R.B.
1987 *Birds in Minnesota.* University of Minnesota Press, Minneapolis.

Kohl, J.G.
1985 *Kitchi-Gami: Life Among the Lake Superior Ojibway* [originally published in 1885]. Minnesota Historical Society Press, St. Paul.

Kuhm, H.W.
1928 Wisconsin Indian Fishing. *The Wisconsin Archaeologist*, 7(2):61-113.

Lewis, H.
1967 *The Valley of the Mississippi Illustrated*, translated by A.H. Poatgieter, edited by B.L. Heilbron [originally published ca. 1850]. Minnesota Historical Society, St. Paul.

Lubinski, P.M.
1996 Fish Heads, Fish Heads: An Experiment on Differential Bone Preservation in a Salmonid Fish. *Journal of Archaeological Science*, 23:175-181.

Lyman, R.L.
1994 Quantitative Units and Terminology in Zooarchaeology. *American Antiquity,* 59:36-71.

Manzano, B.L. and W.C. Dickinson
1991 Archaeological Occurrences of the Extinct Harelip Sucker, *Lagochila lacera* Jordan and Brayton (Pisces: Catostomidae). In *Beamers, Bobwhites, and Blue-Points: Tributes to the Career of Paul W. Parmalee*, edited by J.R. Purdue, W.E. Klippel and B.W. Styles, pp. 81-89. Illinois State Museum Scientific Papers, Volume 23, Springfield, and The University of Tennessee, Department of Anthropology Report of Investigations Number 52, Knoxville.

Mather, D.
1998 Faunal Analysis. In *A Spring Piscary in the Headwaters Region: The Third River Bridge Site, 12-IC-46 (CNF #09-03-01-109)*, by C.A. Hohman-Caine and G.E. Goltz, pp. 20-34. Hamline University, St. Paul.

Michlovic, M.G.
1979 *The Dead River Site (21 OT 51).* Occasional Publications in Minnesota Anthropology No. 6, Minnesota Archaeological Society, St. Paul.

Middlemis, S.A.
1984 *A Description of Catostomus catostomus and Catostomus commersoni Spawning Adults and Early Life History in Selected Minnesota Tributaries of Lake Superior.* M.S. Thesis, University of Minnesota, St. Paul.

Morey, D., C. Falk and H. Semken, Jr.
1996 Vertebrate Remains from the McKinstry Site. In *The McKinstry Site (12 KC 2): Final Report of Phase III Investigations for Mn/DOT S.P. 3604-44, Replacement of Bridge 5178 over the Little Fork River, Koochiching County, Minnesota,* by M.M. Thomas and D. Mather, pp. 15.1-15.56. Loucks Project Report 93512. Loucks & Associates, Inc., Maple Grove.

Nelson, E.M.
1948 The Comparative Morphology of the Weberian Apparatus of the Catostomidae and its Significance in Systematics. *Journal of Morphology*, 83:225-252.

1949 The Opercular Series of the Catostomidae. *Journal of Morphology*, 85:559-568.

Oldfield, B. and J.J. Moriarty
1994 *Amphibians & Reptiles Native to Minnesota.* University of Minnesota Press, Minneapolis.

Olsen, S.J.
1968 Fish, Amphibian and Reptile Remains from Archaeological Sites: Part 1 - Southeastern and Southwestern United States. *Papers of the Peabody Museum of Archaeology and Ethnology,* 56(2).

Olson, D.E.
1963 Role of the White Sucker in Minnesota Waters. *Minnesota Academy of Science Proceedings*, 31:68-73

Pond, S.W.
1986 *The Dakota or Sioux in Minnesota as They Were in 1834*, [originally published in 1908]. Minnesota Historical Society Press, St. Paul.

Phillips, G.L., W.D. Schmid and J.C. Underhill
1982 *Fishes of the Minnesota Region.* University of Minnesota Press, Minneapolis.

Phillips, G.L. and J.C. Underhill
1971 *Distribution and Variation of the Catostomidae of Minnesota.* Bell Museum of Natural History Occasional Papers Number 10. University of Minnesota, Minneapolis.

Rapp, G., Jr., S.C. Mulholland, S.L. Mulholland, Z. Jing, D.E. Stoessel, C.L. Hill, O.C. Shane III, S.H. Valppu, J.K. Huber, J.B. Stoltman, and J.R. Shafer
1995 *Final Report: Hannaford Data Recovery Project, Koochiching County, Minnesota.* Ar-

chaeometry Laboratory Report Number 95-31. University of Minnesota, Duluth.

Rau, C.
1884 *Prehistoric Fishing in Europe and North America*. Smithsonian Contributions to Knowledge. Smithsonian Institution, Washington City.

Rojo, A.L.
1991 *Dictionary of Evolutionary Fish Osteology*. CRC Press, Boca Raton.

Rostlund, E.
1952 *Freshwater Fish and Fishing in Native North America*. University of California Publications in Geography, Volume 9. University of California Press, Berkeley.

Shane, O.C.
1996 Identification and Analysis of Fish Remains from the Horseshoe Bay Site: North and South Buildings. Report on file, Chippewa National Forest, Cass Lake. Science Museum of Minnesota. St.Paul.

Shay, C.T.
1985 Late Prehistoric Selection of Wild Ungulates in the Prairie-Forest Transition. In *Archaeology, Ecology and Ethnohistory of the Prairie-Forest Border Zone in Minnesota and Manitoba*, edited by J. Spector and E. Johnson, pp. 31-65. Reprints in Anthropology, Volume 31. J&L Reprint Company, Lincoln.

Stewart, H.
1977 *Indian Fishing: Early Methods on the Northwest Coast*. The University of Washington Press, Seattle.

Tomelleri, J.R. and M.E. Eberle
1990 *Fishes of the Central United States*. University Press of Kansas, Lawrence.

Tester, J.R.
1995 *Minnesota's Natural Heritage: An Ecological Perspective*. University of Minnesota Press, Minneapolis.

Weisel, G.F.
1960 The Osteocranium of the Catostomid Fish, Catostomus macrocheilus: A Study in Adaptation and Natural Relationship. *Journal of Morphology*, 106:109-129.

Whelan, M.K.
1987 *The Archaeological Analysis of a 19th Century Dakota Indian Economy*. Ph.D. Dissertation, University of Minnesota, Minneapolis.

1990 Late Woodland Subsistence Systems and Settlement Size in the Mille Lacs Area. In *The Woodland Tradition in the Western Great Lakes: Papers Presented to Elden Johnson*, edited by G. Gibbon, pp. 55-76. Publications in Anthropology Number 4. University of Minnesota, Minneapolis.

Minnesota Archaeological Society

Become an MAS Member Now for 2006

The Minnesota Archaeological Society invites you to share with us exciting discoveries from Minnesota's past. The Society, established in 1936, is a private, non-profit organization dedicated to the preservation and study of archaeological resources in the Upper Midwest. We meet at Fort Snelling for most lectures and activities and sometimes in the field for tours. In addition, we provide workshops and demonstrations at festivals and historical occasions all around the state. All persons with an interest in archaeology - those just beginning to explore the field as well as avocational archaeologists and professionals - are welcome.

In addition to receipt of Minnesota's only journal of archaeology, *The Minnesota Archaeologist*, published by MAS, and our quarterly newsletter, membership benefits include

- Slide lectures on current fieldwork and research in archaeology, anthropology and history. Past topics have included Minnesota's Old Copper Culture, ethnoarchaeology in East Africa, and local archaeoastronomy.
- Classes in fieldwork methods and artifact analysis, taught by professional archaeologists from government and private organizations.
- Opportunities to take part in field projects sponsored by MAS and other Minnesota organizations.
- Field trips to important archaeological sites, such as Jeffers Petroglyphs in western Minnesota and Effigy Mounds National Park in Iowa.
- Participation in special events like Minnesota Archaeology Week and the Fort Snelling Archaeology Fair.
- Social events - potluck dinners, brown-bag lunches, informal get-togethers - that allow you to share your experiences and insights with other members and working archaeologists.

Last Name: _____ **First Name and Middle Initial:** _____

Home Address: _____

City: _____ **State:** _____ **Zip:** _____

Telephone Number: _____ **Fax:** _____ **Email:** _____

Age: _____ **Gender:** _____ **Occupation:** _____

Send newsletters to my   **Home Address:** ✍   **Email Address:** ✍

Membership Categories (yearly):

Standard ($25): ✍	Student ($15): ✍	Canada Household (C$40): ✍
1 person	Institution ($40): ✍	2 or more persons
Household ($30) ✍	Canada Standard (C$35): ✍	Sustaining Member ($100) ✍
2 or more persons	1 person	Benefactor ($250) ✍
Senior ($15): ✍		

Sustaining Members will receive the official Minnesota Archaeological Society T-shirt; Benefactors will be seated as honored guests at the 2004 Annual Meeting to be held April 16.

Please make check or money order out to
Minnesota Archaeological Society, Fort Snelling History Center, St. Paul, MN 55111